Praise for *How We Go Home*

"This edited collection offers deep, experiential dives into law, policy, and life for contemporary Indigenous peoples in what is now the United States and Canada. These conversations and life histories, taken together, tell us a critical story of the effort it takes to live and transform structures that Indigenous peoples inherit and push against in bids for dignity, sovereignty, care, and justice in the twenty-first century."

—Audra Simpson (Kahnawà:ke Mohawk),
professor of anthropology, Columbia University

"This extraordinary book powerfully conveys both the cruel, ongoing dispossession of the Indigenous peoples of North America and their astounding spiritual wealth and resilience. *How We Go Home* introduces this complex history organically, through riveting and varied first-person stories skillfully woven into a larger tale. All those who seek to create a more just and sustainable way of living should be grateful for the essential wisdom shared in these oral histories."

—Amy Starecheski, director, Columbia University
Oral History MA Program

"Sara Sinclair's editorial vision in *How We Go Home: Voices from Indigenous North America* is both radically inclusive and extraordinarily caring. There are so many deep histories here that we need to talk about, that we haven't been talking enough about. *How We Go Home* requires us to genuinely hear and listen to the stories and the histories that have shaped Indigenous lives across North America. All of these stories resonated with me in an intimate and personal way—it's at times both comforting and alarming to read about so many diverging life experiences that so often strike parallels with my own. *How We Go Home: Voices from Indigenous North America* is an astounding achievement and a deeply necessary book that creates space for a multiplicity of Indigenous lived experiences."

—Jordan Abel, author of *Nishga*

"*How We Go Home* is a testament to modern-day I~~~
tion, often in the face of the direst of circ~~~
accounts on the frontlines of resistance and~~~

inspire and remind that Indigenous life is all about building a community through the gifts we offer and the stories we tell."

— Niigaan Sinclair, associate professor, Department of Native Studies at the University of Manitoba and columnist, *Winnipeg Free Press*

"The voices of *How We Go Home* are singing a chorus of love and belonging alongside the heat of resistance, and the sound of Indigenous life joyfully dances off these pages."

—Leanne Betasamosake Simpson, author of *As We Have Always Done*

"This book will inspire you, it'll piss you off; it'll take you on a journey of ugly things and beautiful things and back again. It's a hell of a read. Keep this one on your shelf and never let it go. Damn right."

—Simon Moya-Smith (Oglala Lakota and Chicano), writer, *NBC News THINK*

"*How We Go Home* confirms that we all have stories. These stories teach us history, morality, identity, connection, empathy, understanding, and self-awareness. We hear the stories of our ancestors and they tell us who we are. We hear the stories of our heroes and they tell us what we can be."

—Honourable Senator Murray Sinclair

"In this continent, oral history began with the creation and retelling of the rich, multilayered, and historical origin stories of Indigenous people whose lives were intricately bound to the land. The destruction and stealing of that land, and the systematic and highly personalized violence targeted against so many Indigenous communities, threatened the very act of storytelling itself. This book took my breath away, and then restored it. It refuses silence. It restores the word—and the field of oral history in unleashing the story of our origins."

—Mary Marshall Clark, director, Columbia Center for Oral History

"Heartfelt, stunning oratory and painfully revealing, Sinclair has gathered together a collection whose stories inform our history. A must-read."

—Lee Maracle, Sto:lo poet, novelist, storyteller, and activist

HOW WE GO HOME

Voices from Indigenous North America

EDITED BY SARA SINCLAIR

Haymarket Books
Chicago, Illinois

Published in 2020 by
Haymarket Books
P.O. Box 180165
Chicago, IL 60618
773-583-7884
www.haymarketbooks.org
info@haymarketbooks.org

ISBN: 978-1-64259-271-9

Distributed to the trade in the US through Consortium Book Sales and
Distribution (www.cbsd.com) and internationally through Ingram Publisher Services International (www.ingramcontent.com).

This book was published with the generous support of Lannan Foundation
and Wallace Action Fund.

Special discounts are available for bulk purchases by organizations and
institutions. Please call 773-583-7884 or email info@haymarketbooks.org
for more information.

Illustrations by Greg Ballenger.

Cover design by Michel Vrana. Cover image © Ryan Vizzions shows a
signpost pointing to home, erected in fall 2016 by those who came to camp
at Standing Rock.

Printed in Canada by union labor.

Library of Congress Cataloging-in-Publication data is available.

10 9 8 7 6 5 4 3 2

CONTENTS

Transcribers
Maryam Bledsoe, Charles Bowles, Rachel Carle, Julie Chintz, Basil Fraysse, Chris Hart, Molly Hawkins, Kaye Herranen, Mary Kearney-Brown, Ari Kim, Isabelle Lyndon, Josh Manson, Brenna Miller, Margaret O'Hare, Teresa Pangallozzi, Phillip Reid, Mai Serhan, Barbara Sheffels, Madison Wright, Marcella Villaça

Contextual Essay Research and Writing
Rozanne Gooding Silverwood

Additional Research
Carmen Bolt, Eliana Rose Swerdlow, Lael Tate

Curriculum Specialist
Suzanne Methot

Fact-Checking
Reading List Editorial, readinglisteditorial.com

Copyeditor
Brian Baughan

EDITOR'S NOTE

In the beginning of each narrative you will find key details about the interviews and the narrators, including the designations they prefer as Indigenous community members. Self-identity for an Indigenous person is a very personal choice: some narrators use their tribe names, others their nations or bands, and these are sometimes used interchangeably. In some cases, we use more than one entity.

INTRODUCTION

Stories of Return

When I was sixteen years old, I took what was essentially my first trip to Indian Country. I rode the train north across Ontario and on to Winnipeg. Crowds shuffled in and out at stops in small towns along the way. With each stop, more and more blue- and green-eyed passengers departed until almost all eyes remaining were dark brown. Skin became darker too. I looked around at the other Native passengers for signs of recognition. I remember thinking that they saw in my eyes what few people in Toronto ever did—that I was one of them.

Throughout much of North America, Indigenous peoples are so rarely considered, our existence so rarely remembered, that, outside Native circles, someone who looks like me is more likely assumed to be Latinx, or part Asian, or of some other not-immediately-identifiable heritage. This is true in Toronto where I grew up and in New York City where I currently live. But it is different in the prairies, and other places throughout the continent, where the mainstream population is aware that they live among Native people because we make up a larger proportion of residents there.

I realized this for the first time that day as my parents, sisters, and I headed west, on our way to a Sinclair family reunion. My paternal grandpa Elmer and five of his six surviving brothers and sisters were gathering on the grassy banks of Manitoba's Red River for a party. The day of the reunion was clear and sunny, and on a quiet walk with my grandpa, we visited the graves of his parents and ancestors, ending at the monumental grave of Chief Peguis. Peguis was a Saulteaux chief who arrived in what is now southern Manitoba in the early 1790s. When settlers first arrived at Red River in 1812, Peguis protected them and showed them how to subsist there, providing assistance on numerous occasions when they lacked either food or shelter. Peguis became famous for the care he provided, though he later became disillusioned by the settlers' trespasses on his reserve and other violations of the 1817 treaty he signed with Lord Selkirk.[1]

In October 2018, I traveled to another Canadian city, Montreal, where my mother grew up, to attend the Oral History Association's Annual Meeting. One evening, after I participated in a roundtable discussion on working with Indigenous narrators, I had dinner with my parents and a few of my mother's relatives who live in the city.

I don't remember how, but the conversation turned to the state of Canada's Indigenous peoples today. One relative, whom I have only met a handful of times and do not know well, was intent on driving this conversation. He seemed vaguely aware that my father is Indigenous (he's Cree-Ojibwe, Peguis Nation) and opened his line of questioning by asking my dad to quantify his Indigenous blood, unaware that blood quantum is a colonial construct used for the dispossession of title and land. And in this particular setting, it seemed, it was also behind his attempt to separate my dad from "real Indians." He said he didn't understand why First Nations people couldn't assimilate like the rest of Canada's "minorities." He didn't understand why they were not thriving like his wife's relations, my mom's family, Ashkenazi Jews whose ancestors landed in Canada after fleeing Nazi Germany. In his response, my dad referenced Canada's Truth and Reconciliation Commission (TRC), a component of the Indian Residential Schools

---

1. On July 18, 1817, a treaty was signed between Lord Selkirk and five chiefs in what is now called the Red River Valley of Manitoba. The Peguis Selkirk Treaty was the first signed in western Canada, preceding the formation of the Dominion of Canada by fifty years.

Settlement Agreement, whose mandate was to inform all Canadians about the physical, emotional, spiritual, and sexual abuse that happened to Indigenous children at the schools and the consequences of that abuse on succeeding generations.[2] The relative unashamedly acknowledged that he didn't know the TRC had been a national endeavor or much else about it, as he "hadn't really followed it." The evening was difficult mostly because he didn't actually want to learn or listen; he wanted to hear himself raise rhetorical questions, and he didn't intend to create the space for my father, or me, to answer.

To encounter this disinterest and apathy so directly over dinner with my own extended family was upsetting to say the least. And it was yet another reminder that history as it has been taught to most North Americans too often excludes Indigenous peoples, treating them as peripheral to the continent's story.

ORAL HISTORY WORKS

My own desire to make Indigenous history more widely accessible and my belief that *oral* history could provide a great tool toward this aim came about shortly after I moved to New York City to participate in Columbia University's Oral History Master of Arts Program. Shortly after arriving in the city, I went to my first Fry Bread Friday, a monthly gathering in the West Village apartment of Rick Chavolla (Kumeyaay) and his wife, Anna Ortega Chavolla. The couple has worked in educational and social justice circles for decades, and they are mentors and friends to a host of Native American students in the city. The first Fry Bread I attended brought members of the Cree, Crow, Navajo, Akwesasne Mohawk, and Oglala Lakota Nations together in our hosts' living room.[3] From reservations and cities across the continent, every-

---

2. The TRC hosted seven national events throughout the country to promote awareness and public education and received wide coverage by the mainstream press from its launch in 2008 to its official closure in 2015.

3. Navajo fry bread originated during the "Long Walk," when the US government forced Indians living in Arizona to relocate via a three-hundred-mile relocation

one had traveled a long way to achieve their positions as students and faculty at New York University and Columbia University.

The Native students at the Chavollas' get-together were attending university to support larger efforts to restore the self-sufficiency of their tribal communities. However, the historical practice of imposing Native assimilation through North America's settler educational systems made their relationship to schooling complex. Interested in how the legacy of assimilationist education continued to impact beliefs about the value of higher education in Native American communities, and more specifically how it was impacting the experiences of those who attended those institutions, I determined that my oral history thesis would explore the narratives of Native North Americans after they have finished their schooling and returned to their nations and reservation communities to work.

These narrators made modern American tribal history so compelling, so readable, so digestible that I very quickly envisioned editing a book compiled of their first-person narratives after finishing my program. I was familiar with the Voice of Witness series and was particularly interested in pursuing publication with them because of their education program, which brings their books' narratives and the issues portrayed within them into school and university curricula.

Narrator Ashley Hemmers had told me that before she was exposed to the resources that would help her to understand her own tribe's history and the history of colonialism in the United States, she was drawn to books about the Holocaust, available at her school library. The intergenerational trauma in those stories was something she recognized in her own community, and reading about other people's experience of it had helped her begin to understand the way it was playing out at home. Throughout my interviews for this book, that element of Ashley's story remained a central inspiration: I con-

---

to New Mexico. The government provided rations for the journey, including the ingredients of fry bread: white flour, sugar, and lard. Today the food plays a central role at powwows and other intertribal gatherings.

duct interviews so that I can share these stories, so that other readers might have that "aha" moment when they are able to more deeply understand the conditions of their own lives, and view the current moment in a larger historical framework.

With Voice of Witness, the project's mandate was expanded so that we might include narrators with a greater range of life experiences. We moved away from a specific focus on education and agreed that interviews would investigate the following questions: What is the living legacy of settlement, war, and treaties and of the resulting loss of Indian lands and life? How does this huge loss of land and life affect Indigenous people's efforts to, in Louise Erdrich's words, "protect and celebrate [the] core of [their] cultures"?[4] And finally, given that settler colonialism is ongoing, how does it affect Native lives today, as Indigenous peoples continue to fight with the US and Canadian governments for the resources needed to live?

Voice of Witness's mandate is "to advance human rights by amplifying the voices of people impacted by injustice." One important note: to best appreciate the issues underlying the narratives in this book, it is important to understand two things that make Indigenous rights distinct. One, those rights are inherently tied to land, because without access to their traditional territories and resources, Indigenous peoples' distinct cultures are threatened. And two, whereas most human rights treaties reflect an individualistic view of rights and are designed to guarantee individual rights, for many Indigenous peoples their individual identity is inseparable from the collective to which they belong, so they have an additional interest in the protection of their collective rights as a group.

Of course, in a book of twelve narratives, we knew we could not illuminate every kind of injustice experienced throughout Indigenous continental Canada and the United States. We have not included voices from Mexico in this collection. There are currently

---

4. Louise Erdrich, "Where I Ought to Be: A Writer's Sense of Place," *New York Times*, July 28, 1985.

634 legally recognized First Nations in Canada and 573 recognized tribes in the United States. And in both countries, there are tribes and communities that are not granted this status. The narratives we selected cannot represent the experience of all these individuals; however, we believe they do illuminate the most common themes.

Often, we pursued issues in the context of specific places. In Manitoba, Ervin Chartrand, James Favel, and Althea Guiboche spoke to the legacy of residential schools, intergenerational trauma, and its sometime corollaries poverty, homelessness, and incarceration. On Vancouver Island, British Columbia, interviews with narrators Blaine Wilson and Geraldine Manson about the Tsartlip and Snuneymuxw First Nations focused on the urban encroachment on traditional territories and the impact of environmental destruction on fishing, hunting, and traditional life. In Terrace, a small city in northern British Columbia located on Canada's Highway of Tears, narrator Gladys Radek centered the issue of missing and murdered Indigenous women and girls (the subject of a recent national inquiry). In the American Southwest—in Fort Mojave and Santa Clara Pueblo—Ashley Hemmers and Marian Naranjo spotlighted the struggles against environmental racism and for the provision of on-reserve services including health care, education, and language and cultural revitalization. In the Dakotas, with Wizipan Little Elk at Rosebud Indian Reservation and Jasilyn Charger at Cheyenne River Indian Reservation, a major thread emerged regarding treaty rights and natural resource extraction. At Six Nations reserve and in New York City, in interviews with Vera Styres and Robert Ornelas, the conversations covered issues including the disproportionate number of Native kids in Canada's foster care system and the emotional and spiritual consequences of being disconnected from one's Indigenous culture.

During the narrative collection process, the emergence and prevalence of two related issues was striking: the legacy of the residential and boarding school systems and the number of narrators, like Manson, Radek, and Charger, who had spent at least a part of their childhood in the foster care system. Many believe the foster care system has repeated the calamities of the residential schools, even after their closings. More First Nations children are in the care of Children's Aid Societies today than were forced to attend residential schools when enrollment was at its highest. More than half the kids in the Canadian foster care system are Indigenous and yet they make up only 7.7 percent of the general population.[5] In the United States, Native kids are placed in care at a rate 2.7 times higher than the rest of the population. This is a heartbreaking continuation of the legacy of removing Indigenous children from their community and culture.[6]

Collectively, the narratives in this book drive home how the long attack on and erasure of Indigenous land has simultaneously been an attack on Indigenous people, their families, and nations. This is the foundational context from which each of the following narratives should be read.

REVERSING INJUSTICE

My impression during each trip to meet with narrators, which intensified with each one, was a kind of awe at the vastness of this continent. The scope of the landscapes: British Columbia's tall dense forests and wide waterways, the flat forever of the Dakotas with its fields of wheat and sunflowers, the long drive through the high-desert Navajo Nation—all of this land I traversed made so plain the immensity of what has been taken from the continent's first people; and the urgency of the ongoing struggles to keep what remains. The land itself, and each nation's way of living with it, sustaining human life upon it, and future possibilities of these ways of being were all interrupted by

---

5. Cindy Blackstock, "First Nations Child and Family Services: Restoring Peace and Harmony in First Nations Communities" in *Child Welfare: Connecting Research, Policy and Practice*, ed. Kathleen Kufeldt and Brad McKenzie (Waterloo, ON: Wilfred Laurier University Press, 2003), 331.

6. National Indian Child Welfare Association, "Disproportionality," 2017, www.nicwa.org/wp-content/uploads/2017/09/Disproportionality-Table.pdf.

colonialism. The arrival of settlers in North America interrupted Indigenous peoples' many rich and mature cultures and societies, each with its own political, trade, and economic systems.

As this collection went to press, the COVID-19 global pandemic has upended lives around the world. Initially touted as a "great equalizer," affecting rich and poor alike, the pandemic instead exacerbated existing injustice and inequalities among the world's most vulnerable populations, including Indigenous North Americans. For historical perspective, during the H1N1 outbreak of 2009, Native Americans died at four times the rate of other populations in the US. In 2020, poverty, overcrowding, and a scarcity of running water on some reserves and reservations have resulted in high rates of infection for COVID-19 for several tribes. Lack of access to care and preexisting health conditions among these populations, including hypertension, lung disease, and diabetes, make those who do get the virus even more vulnerable to illness and death. As of April 23, the Navajo Nation was reporting 1,360 infections and 52 deaths among its population of 170,000 people, a mortality rate of 30 per 100,000. Meanwhile, emergency federal funding for tribal health organizations has been delayed by bureaucracy and an Indigenous community health center in Seattle that requested protective equipment was sent body bags instead. The COVID-19 pandemic reveals the structural inequities and colonial thinking that so often determines Indigenous life in the Americas. Instead of helping Indigenous peoples organize a response, or seeing Indigenous peoples as fellow citizens who deserve help, the government positions Indigenous peoples as expendable.

As with my trip "home" to Manitoba at sixteen, the following narratives are, in many ways, stories of return. Almost without exception, the people whose stories are shared in the following pages are working toward reversing a form of injustice and oppression that has directly impacted their own lives. Althea Guiboche, once homeless with her young children, is today a tireless advocate for Winnipeg's most vulnerable population. Gladys Radek, a survivor of sexual violence who lost her niece along Canada's Highway of Tears, became a family advocate for the National Inquiry into Missing and Murdered Indigenous Women and Girls. Marian Naranjo, herself the subject of a radiation test while in high school, went on to drive Santa Clara Pueblo toward compiling an environmental impact statement on the effects of living near Los Alamos National Laboratory. These are stories about returning to place, revitalizing culture and language, and re-forming traditional support systems.

These are also stories about what we all carry inside and the multiplicity of choices we can each make to recover what has been lost to us, to sustain what we have been given, to continue, to flourish. With patience, perseverance, and bravery, these narrators are working to continue their cultures and to rebuild their nations. Listening to their stories has helped me to recover pieces of mine.

For all my relations . . . *meegwetch*.

Sara Sinclair
May 2020
Brooklyn, New York, Lenape Traditional Land
and Huntsville, Ontario, Canada,
Anishinabewaki and Huron-Wendat Land

EXECUTIVE EDITOR'S NOTE

The twelve narratives in this book are the result of oral history interviews conducted over a three-year period between spring 2016 and fall 2019. With every Voice of Witness narrative, we aim for a novelistic level of detail and (whenever possible) a birth-to-now, chronologized scope in order to portray narrators as individuals in all their complexity, rather than as case studies. We do not set out to create comprehensive histories of human rights issues. Rather, our goal is to compile a collection of voices that (1) offers accessible, thought-provoking, and ultimately humanizing perspectives on what can often seem like impenetrable topics; and (2) can meaningfully contribute to the efforts of social justice and human rights movements.

In order to honor our narrators' experiences, Voice of Witness oral histories are crafted with the utmost care. Recorded interviews are transcribed and organized chronologically by our dedicated team of volunteers. Then, narrative drafts are typically subject to three to five rounds of editorial revision and follow-up interviews, to ensure depth and accuracy. The stories themselves remain faithful to the speakers' words (we seek final narrator approval before publishing their narratives) and have been edited for clarity, coherence, and length. In some cases, names and details have been changed to protect the identities of our narrators and the identities of family and acquaintances. All narratives have been carefully fact-checked and are supported by various appendixes and a glossary included in the back of the book that provide context for, and some explanation of, the history of Indigenous North America.

We thank all the individuals who courageously, generously, and patiently shared their experiences with us, including those whom we were unable to include in this book. We also thank all the frontline human rights and social justice advocates working to promote and protect the rights and dignity of all Indigenous peoples in North America.

Finally, we thank our national community of educators and students who inspire our education program. With each Voice of Witness book, we create a Common Core–aligned curriculum that connects high school students and educators with the stories and issues presented in the book, with particular emphasis on serving marginalized communities. As we continue to amplify a diversity of voices in our book series, we are also committed to developing a curriculum that directly supports students in English Language Learner (ELL) communities. At the time of writing, about one out of every ten public school students is learning to speak English. In California alone, ELLs account for 19.3 percent of the total public school student population, and this number continues to grow. In response to this need in our education networks and beyond, in 2018 we launched our first oral history resource for ELLs, and we continue to expand our offerings in this area.

Our education program also provides curriculum support, training in ethics-driven storytelling, and site visits to educators in schools and impacted communities. I invite you to visit the Voice of Witness website for free, downloadable educational resources, behind-the-scenes features on this book and other projects, and to find out how you can be part of our work: voiceofwitness.org.

In solidarity,
Mimi Lok
Cofounder, Executive Director, and Executive Editor
Voice of Witness

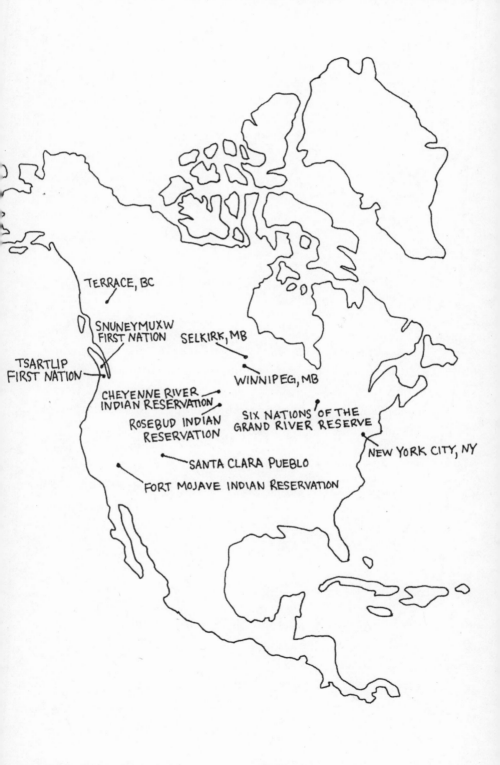

TERRACE, BC

SNUNEYMUXW
FIRST NATION

SELKIRK, MB

TSARTLIP
FIRST NATION

WINNIPEG, MB

CHEYENNE RIVER
INDIAN RESERVATION

ROSEBUD INDIAN
RESERVATION

SIX NATIONS OF THE
GRAND RIVER RESERVE

NEW YORK CITY, NY

SANTA CLARA PUEBLO

FORT MOJAVE INDIAN RESERVATION

GLADYS RADEK

GITXSAN / WET'SUWET'EN FIRST NATIONS[1]
FAMILY ADVOCATE
BORN IN: 1955, Moricetown, British Columbia
INTERVIEWED IN: Terrace, British Columbia

I picked up Gladys from her home on the outskirts of Terrace, British Columbia, and drove to our hotel where we spoke over coffee in the lobby. Save for a single smoke break and a moment when she paused to ask if I was okay after she shared a particularly harrowing memory, Gladys told her story in a low, gravelly voice with striking ease and strength.

Gladys is an active member of the First Nations community fighting for justice for the countless missing and murdered Indigenous women and girls in Canada, where Indigenous women are six times more likely to

---

1. See Editor's Note.

be victims of homicide than non-Indigenous women and girls.[2] *Gladys focuses especially on the dozens whose lives have ended in violence or who have simply disappeared along what has come to be called Canada's Highway of Tears, a stretch of Highway 16 between the cities of Prince George and Prince Rupert in British Columbia, where twenty-three First Nations border the road.*[3]

Terrace is also located on this stretch of highway. In September 2005, Gladys's niece, Tamara Lynn Chipman, went missing. For Gladys, Tamara's disappearance was the catalyst to start the Walk4Justice in Vancouver, which she organized with Bernie Williams, who lost her mother and three sisters to violence. This walk for awareness, and the work of others, helped bring the issue of missing and murdered Indigenous women and girls to the forefront of Canada's national conscience. Today, the scale and the severity of the violence faced by Indigenous women and girls is considered a national crisis. Growing up in the foster care system, Gladys's own life has also been dramatically shaped by this violence.

Research suggests that the heightened risk to Indigenous women and girls is yet another consequence of decades of government policy that have impoverished and fractured Indigenous families. According to Amnesty International, "Deep inequalities in living conditions and discrimination in the provision of government services have pushed many Indigenous women and girls into precarious situations where there is a heightened risk of violence. These same inequalities have also denied many Indigenous women access to services needed to escape violence."[4] *Along*

---

2. Human Rights Council, *Report of the Special Rapporteur on Violence against Women, Its Causes and Consequences*, 2019. For more on Indigenous missing and murdered women and girls in Canada, see appendix essay 2.

3. Prince Rupert is a port city of around twelve thousand in northern British Columbia. Prince George is northern British Columbia's largest city with a population of around eighty-six thousand. It is 571 kilometers east of Terrace.

4. Amnesty International, "Violence against Indigenous Women and Girls in Canada: A Summary of Amnesty International's Concerns and Call to Action," February 2014, www.amnesty.ca/sites/amnesty/files/iwfa_submission_amnesty_international _february_2014_-_final.pdf.

the Highway of Tears, poverty means low rates of car ownership and mobility, so people hitchhike long distances to visit family, or to go to work or school. This makes Indigenous women in the area especially vulnerable to predation. As a graphic reminder of this, a big sign above the highway near Kitsumkalum reserve just outside of Terrace reads: "Hitchhiking, is it worth the risk?"

HOSPITALS, INSTITUTIONS, AND FOSTER CARE

I grew up in hospitals, institutions, and foster care. I was born with tuberculosis, so I was placed in Miller Bay Hospital in Prince Rupert, British Columbia, at my birth in 1955, for three and a half years. My mother is originally from Moricetown. We're Wet'su-wet'en. My father is unknown. My mother met my stepfather and moved to Terrace for a short period of time, when I was one or two, and then they moved to Prince Rupert where my mom worked all her life, at the canneries. My stepfather was the natural father of my younger siblings. He was a hard worker and a hard player. He was very much a family man, and he was my mom's true love.

I got out of the hospital in 1958 and I lived with my mom for a year. My older sister Peggy and I were looking after our two younger siblings, and our baby brother died in our care. Because of that, I was placed in foster care in 1959.[5] I was put into a home in Kitimat, BC, with some white people who treated us very well.[6] It was me and my sister-cousin, Terry—she's my cousin, but we grew up as sisters because she was with us when we were apprehended.[7] They kept Terry and me together, but they split me up from my siblings at that time. My first foster parents tried to adopt us, but my mom wouldn't

---

5. Gladys was most likely placed in foster care because her parents had put her younger siblings in her care.

6. Kitimat is 205 kilometers away from Prince Rupert.

7. *Apprehension* is the official term used in Canada for the removal of children from their homes by child protection agencies.

sign the papers.[8] My surviving brother was raised in foster care in Kitimat, a block away from where we were. We didn't even know he was there. My sister Peggy went into very abusive foster care here in Terrace at the same time.

I was moved to another foster home in Terrace when I was eight because the authorities wanted to put me with a First Nations family. My foster brother, Glenn, who was eighteen, started raping me two weeks after we got into that home. I tried to report my abuse to teachers, Sunday school teachers, and even to government officials. I went down to the social work office when I was nine. What happened to me at that second home didn't have to happen. If somebody believed me, things would've been different.

Our foster mother was beaten by our foster dad once or twice a week. She was a good mom, but she was also a victim. She had a broken neck. She had scars on her face. She was hospitalized, and nobody did anything. The foster brother was raping me. The foster dad was raping his stepdaughter Diane, who was sixteen. Drove her crazy. She ended up getting sent to the mental institution because she kept screaming and trying to keep her stepdad away from her. And their answer to that was to send her to an institution for shock treatment. I'm glad that didn't happen to me.

Terry and I knew Diane was being raped because we were on the top bunk while the foster dad was raping her. And we tried to intervene as little girls, but it didn't work. We were too little, and if we said anything, we'd get beaten. On more than one occasion, we tried to jump on his back while he was raping her, and we'd just get a backhand from him, sometimes knocking us out cold. But we would try. And Diane's parents ended up sending her away on three different occasions that I can remember. The last time that they sent her, she had her shock treatment, but she was also screaming so much that she cracked her voice box. So doctors surgically removed

---

8. For more on the historical and contemporary prevalence of Native children in US and Canadian foster care, see appendix essay 2.

it. She ended up only able to whisper. She died a few years later in a car accident. She was with a drunk driver. She was labeled "crazy." But she wasn't crazy, she was abused. We remained in that home for five years.

ESCAPING VIOLENCE

I didn't meet my mother again until I was twelve years old. My foster mom told me that my birth mom was in the hospital in Terrace for a gall bladder operation. After school I walked to the hospital and visited her. That's the first time I'd laid eyes on her in years. At that time, I was pretty angry at the world, including my mom, because of the violence and sexual abuse in the foster home. We didn't make plans to see each other again.

When I was thirteen, I made plans to run away. Back then, there was one major hub that everybody escaped to, and that was Vancouver. Vancouver was calling me. I was going to hitchhike out of Terrace and fend for myself. And when my foster parents caught wind of that, they decided they didn't want me anymore. They didn't want me in the first place. They were in the business of foster care for money, and so they decided, *Well, if she's going to start running away, then we'll just send her back to Prince Rupert to her mom.* So the system ended up putting me back with my parents, but due to the anger that I was feeling, and the hurt and the pain I was going through at that time, there was nobody who could console me. I ended up staying with my parents for just a short period of time, two years off and on.

From there I was put into a group home, and then shipped off to Burnaby in 1971, to a reform school, the Willingdon School for Girls.[9] I was sixteen, and that was a real eye-opener for me. It was like a jail. Believe me, that's not the answer when you're dealing with kids who've been harmed. Jail just makes them angrier.

---

9. Burnaby is a city of around 232,000, thirteen kilometers east of Vancouver.

When I ran away after three months, I was introduced to the Downtown Eastside of Vancouver.[10] I learned how to play pool. I learned how to survive on the streets. I made friends quite easily because at that time there were a lot of us kids on the streets, escaping violence in our northern communities. I started bumping into my relatives, and everybody knew my last name because we had a huge family that had been migrating south to there since 1968.

A lot of my friends back then had turned to drugs, prostitution. Me, I hated men with a passion because of the abuse I'd experienced. I was a topless go-go dancer for a while, at seventeen. But I didn't like that, so I only did it for about three months. I had a friend from Kamloops who was also a dancer, and she and I got an apartment.[11] We had a roof over our heads. We had to do what we had to do to make money. I paid my rent. I had good food. I didn't have any real addictions other than drinking. I wasn't old enough to go into the bars, but I always found a way to drink. I could drink at the club I danced at.

Eventually I got caught and sent back to the reform school. This time I was seventeen. Again, I ran away after three months. I hitchhiked to Calgary, Alberta. I was dropped off in Alberta by the person I'd hitched a ride from at the Bragg Creek turnoff on the highway, west of Calgary. A cop picked me up. He said he stopped because it was pretty late at night, twelve-thirty or one in the morning, and I was not in a well-lit area. The first thing he told me was that he barely saw me there because I was so tiny. Then he raped me. After the rape, I couldn't say anything, I couldn't report it, because I was on the run. That left me vulnerable.

In Calgary, I started working at a pool hall because I loved to play. I found a big hall with a little café in it. It was called the

---

10. The Downtown Eastside is a neighborhood in Vancouver known for its high rates of poverty, homelessness, drug use, prostitution, and crime. The neighborhood has a large First Nations population.

11. Kamloops is a city in south-central British Columbia, Canada. It has a population of about ninety thousand and is about 350 kilometers northeast of Vancouver.

King of Fish, and since I was also worrying about getting food, I ended up being a waitress there. Paul and I met there in 1973. He pursued me. He knew I was young, but he didn't know how young because I told him I was of legal age, which in Alberta back then was eighteen.

The day before my eighteenth birthday, we got into a hit-and-run motorcycle accident on the highway. We were heading up to Sylvan Lake for my birthday party. Paul was a musician. He was going to play at a dance that night, and we'd just gotten our beautiful bike out of the shop that day. It was a 1200 Harley—twelve-inch forks, beautiful knucklehead motor, nice and shiny chrome—and we were heading over the last hill before Sylvan Lake. There was a driver who didn't like bikes, and when he came over the crest of the hill, he tried to wipe us out. My cousin, in front of us, was on a bike too. The driver just missed my cousin but hit Paul and me, and took off. Paul lost his right leg in the accident. He went flying one way, and his leg went flying the other. Our legs were caught between the motor of the bike and the motor of the car. The doctors tried to save mine. Four years later, after nine operations, I decided that I was tired of the operations and I asked them to amputate.

We got legally married on April 23, 1975, because I was pregnant. Back then, that was the thing you did. I had his son, Chris, in May 1975, and I left Paul on my birthday, June 9, 1975. We were married for a whole six weeks. It didn't work out because he kept on messing around. He had other women all over the place. And I raised Chris on my own. Paul didn't have anything to do with him.

MY SPIRIT WAS BROKEN

I had met Tom around the same time I met Paul, before I had Chris. When I went into the hospital, Paul left town because he had a gig in BC. He left me by myself in the hospital, and Tom came up to see how I was doing. He was actually the first one to provide for my son—a case of milk and a case of diapers. Tom picked me up from the hospital, and we ended up getting together.

Years later, I decided to go back to school. In 1984, I was at Alberta Vocational School in downtown Calgary for my high school upgrading and I hadn't quite finished grade twelve.[12] I started feeling nauseated in the morning, feeling really hungry, and I started craving grilled cheese sandwiches with ketchup. I went to the doctor, and sure enough, he told me I was pregnant. Tom told me when I met him that he'd had a vasectomy. And I thought I was scot-free with having just one child. And Tom, he doubted the baby was his, because he had had this vasectomy. I think he doubted me until our daughter was born, but she looked just like him so there was no denying that she was his. As someone from Germany, he was from the old school, and he wanted to be the breadwinner. I ended up having to quit school to stay at home with the kids.

Things were going well with Tom, but my spirit was broken. And in 1988 he convinced me to move back up to Terrace because he fell in love with the territory. We got married in 1992, when I was pregnant with my last one. I eventually had four more daughters with him. I had a beautiful house. I had everything I needed. I was a PTA mom, baking cakes for the whole community. My husband was a general contractor, so we had a business to run as well, plus fishing and hunting for the family. But anger was building up inside me. I couldn't deal with it because Glenn, my perpetrator, was still also living in Terrace. And the anger, the murderous thoughts that have always been with me, about what my perpetrator did to me, Tom didn't understand.

My spirit broke even further in Terrace, where I had to face not only my perpetrator but also his wife and kids. They found me. It's a pretty small town. His kids got attached to me, and they were crying to me about what their father was doing to them. Because he didn't stop with me, or just a few of us. He also abused his own children and

---

12. High school upgrading allows adult learners to complete the coursework necessary to achieve their high school diplomas.

his grandchildren. His kids call me "Auntie." They used to come to my house, and I sympathized with those kids. They had nobody else to talk to. The more I heard from my perpetrator's kids, the angrier I got.

In 1994, I'd bought Tom a rifle for Christmas. But I had an ulterior motive for buying it. I went out that winter and I got drunk one night. I drove to my perpetrator's trailer, and I had the rifle in my van, and I must have blacked out. I woke up just in time, when I was walking up the stairs of his trailer. It's a good thing I snapped out of it then, because if I hadn't, I would've shot him, and I'd be in jail right now.

That was when I decided that I had to leave. I couldn't face this guy every day. If I'd seen him on the street, I'd want to run him over with my kids in the car. There were so, so many murderous thoughts that I carried, and I just couldn't handle it anymore, so I left Tom and my children in Terrace and went to Vancouver.

I HAD TO DO SOMETHING TO SAVE MY OWN LIFE

I don't think it was the right thing to do, but I had to do something to save my own life. And that's where I really gained my voice. I started school again in 1996. And in 1999, I graduated. After graduating, I realized that I had to do something about the abuse, because it was going to eat me away. It was going to take my life. Two of Glenn's kids, two boys, had committed suicide, and I knew it was because he had sexually abused them. So in 2002, I went to the RCMP down in Vancouver, and I started the formal charging process against him.[13]

After pressing charges, one of the RCMP officers asked if he could meet me. I went to meet him, and as soon as he sat down, his tears broke freely. And I kind of thought, *What the hell? Why are you crying? This happened to me, not you.* He said, "It's nice to finally meet you. I'm the one who's been working on your case." I said, "What's up with the tears?"

---

13. RCMP is the Royal Canadian Mounted Police.

"This is one of the most difficult cases I've done."

"Why? You probably deal with sexual assault cases all the time."

"You know how many people I interviewed who might have been victims of this man?"

"No, how many? Ten? Twenty?"

"Probably a hundred and sixty."

A hundred and sixty probable victims of one man. The officer went to the reserve where these victims were from, and he found other people who were claiming abuse there. Glenn lived right across the street from another reserve in Terrace called Kitselas. And he was abusing some of the kids on that reserve too.

I had to move up to Terrace again in order to proceed with the charges. The most disturbing thing that happened during the court case was when the judge asked Glenn, "Sir, did you go to residential school?" He started bawling. And he said, "Yes, I did go to residential school." Oh, well, that exonerated him right away. So, he got two years' house arrest, two years' probation, and a hundred and fifty community hours. Two of us, myself and his stepdaughter, had come forward and pressed charges against him, and that's what he got in our judicial system for raping us for over five years apiece. I'm a product of the residential school too. I don't know who my father is, but that's not going to make me a rapist.

I learned after the trial that the court tried to put a publication ban on it.[14] I said, "Hey, wait a minute. I want this publication ban lifted." And I wrote a letter about why it should be lifted. I wanted everybody in Terrace to know that this man is a perpetrator. I tried to give the letter to victim services.[15] They treated me like garbage. They slammed the door in my face and said, "Okay, we're done. You're on your own now."

---

14. A publication ban is an order made by the court to prevent anyone from publishing or broadcasting information that might identify a participating victim or witness in criminal justice proceedings.

15. British Columbia's victim services programs are available to anyone who has been the victim of a crime.

I was driving around one night, and I thought, *Wait a minute, I know where the judge lives.* And I went and knocked on his door. He opened the door, and I said, "I want you to take this letter. I want you to read it right now." He read it. And I remember crying and telling him that we needed this publication ban lifted because Glenn wasn't the only perpetrator in our community. I said, "You are going to be protecting your community by doing this." And he lifted the publication ban that week. But there was only a tiny little write-up in the Terrace paper about Glenn being charged. That was it.

My brother's daughter, my niece, Tamara Lynn Chipman, spent a lot of time with me, and she supported me through the court case. She and her dog came over every day to make sure I was okay. Tamara spent a lot of time hugging me. She'd be waiting for me at my house after the court day was over. She was seventeen going on eighteen.

IT TOOK THE BREATH OUT OF ME

Throughout that time, I had a soulmate in Vancouver, Brent Houston. I was with him, and I promised him that I would be back. I gave myself one year to deal with all this, and then I went back down to Vancouver. But I came back to Terrace periodically because in 2005 Tamara disappeared from the Highway of Tears in Prince Rupert. And when she went missing, I got really angry. It took the breath out of me. It hit that close to home.

The reason that my sister-cousin, Terry, was in the same foster home as me when we were kids was because her mother was murdered in Vancouver, in 1959. I'd been hearing about it all my life. I knew a lot of people that had gone; a lot of my friends had been killed. And a lot of them were still missing. So there is a history. This is the history of our people.

I started meeting other family members who had loved ones who were missing or murdered, and I started compiling a database, and of course hearing the RCMP's bullshit, because they're in so much denial. I had absolutely no faith in the police in the first place because they've never respected our people in northern communities. I was raped by cops up here twice. I was beaten by cops up here. Nothing was ever done. I got a licking from them I don't know how many times. Why? Because I wouldn't take any crap from them. I wouldn't take crap from anybody.

In February 2006, my cousin Florence posted online that she was going to be organizing a walk from Prince Rupert to Terrace to honor Tamara and the other girls who were missing from our reserve, Moricetown. There are more women and girls in addition to Tamara, but only three of them were acknowledged by officials. When I heard about it, I was involved with the United Native Nations Society in Vancouver. I was just starting to get involved with the Union of BC Indian Chiefs. I started meeting other activists, strong activist women. So, when my cousin said that she was doing that walk, I approached the Union of BC Indian Chiefs and told them I wanted to go, and they paid my way up there and back.

On that visit to Prince Rupert, Florence and I were sitting in a parking lot outside a little church. I said, "Florence, did you know that they're having a symposium in Prince George at the end of March?" Her walk was to start on March 11. She looked at me and said, "No, I didn't know anything about it." I said, "Well, there's a symposium, the Highway of Tears Symposium, starting March 30. It's supposed to be for our families, for our missing and murdered women. How would you feel about instead of just walking to Terrace, we walk to Prince George?"

She went running inside the church. She was gone for two minutes. She came back and said, "Yup, you got walkers." Apparently, there were walkers already meeting inside.

In March, we all walked to Terrace. We walked through, and we kept walking. And in Smithers, we met Mattie Wilson, Ramona

Wilson's mother.[16] And we walked from Smithers to Prince George, 718 kilometers from Prince Rupert, where we met my brother and a whole bunch of other family members who were there.

That symposium was the best meeting that I've been to in all these years—the very best in terms of hearing the families' perspective, how the families feel. We had these breakout sessions where the families would talk, and it was the families that made recommendations to the government. The first thing that stuck out was racism. We talked a lot about police brutality. We were calling the police out, saying that we were being ignored. A lot of northern community families feel helpless because of the racism. If they don't like Indians, they don't like Indians. You can't change a cop's mind.

Research by Amnesty International suggests that police procedures for responding to missing person cases regularly fail to consider the pervasiveness and gravity of threats faced by Indigenous women and girls, which results in a failure to take timely and efficient action. In addition, police bias may contribute to a report of a missing person or a suspicious death being ignored, or an investigation receiving insufficient resources. According to Amnesty International, "The resulting impunity for violence against Indigenous women and girls contributes to an environment where such acts are seen as normal and inevitable rather than serious and criminal, and where women and girls do not seek justice because they know they will not get it."[17]

More than a year and a half after the symposium, in December 2007, the government was failing to implement the recommendations that

---

16. Ramona Wilson (Gitanmaax Band) went missing June 11, 1994, at sixteen years of age. She was last seen at her home in Smithers, British Columbia, and her body was found in a wooded area west of Smithers airport on April 9, 1995.

17. Amnesty International, "Violence against Indigenous Women and Girls in Canada."

we had pulled together.[18] I thought, *Well, they're not listening to us.* I went to my brother John's place in Barriere for Christmas that year.[19] John and I were driving to Kamloops one day. It was beautiful. Snow was out there on the highway, you got the river running through it, and I just had a feeling, and the words started coming out of me about this walk. I went back to Vancouver on January third, and I had this need to see my friend, Bernie Williams. I phoned her right away, and I said to her, "You know, people have been talking about how they feel it's necessary for a national public inquiry. How would you feel about walking across the country to advocate for that?" And she said, "Let's do it."

Neither of us even had a car. We didn't have anything. Me, I'm on public assistance. Bernie, she's a carver. She was making very little money with her art because she'd always end up giving it all away. She said, "Do it up. You need to write a mission statement." It took me just one day. I wrote down this mission statement, and I put it online, and I got a response seconds later from Ontario, from my friend Alfreda Trudeau in Sault Sainte–Marie.[20]

OVER TWELVE HUNDRED
MISSING WOMEN AND GIRLS

I put a letter out saying this was all going to be done by donation and volunteers. We started approaching family members and asking if they were interested in walking. I mapped it out from Vancouver to Ottawa; we'd all walk ten kilometers a stretch. We did it leapfrog fashion. The families started coming forward, saying: "Yes, we do

---

18. The *Highway of Tears Symposium Recommendations Report* can be viewed at www.highwayoftears.org/resources/documents-and-reports.

19. Barriere is a town of 1,700, sixty-six kilometers north of Kamloops, British Columbia.

20. Sault Ste. Marie is a city with a population of around seventy-three thousand people in northern Ontario.

need a national public inquiry. We need to address the police. We need to address the lack of resources for our organizations." I've never looked back.

The mission statement that I wrote for Walk4Justice 2008 had the word *genocide* in it.[21]

And the general public agreed with that mission statement, including its use of the word *genocide*. When you think about it, our girls who are disappearing—age fourteen to twenty-five is the average—those are their child-bearing years. So, if we have three thousand women who are missing or murdered, and we have an average of five children per First Nations woman—a national average—that's fifteen thousand children that we are missing for future generations. It's genocide.[22] Right now, the RCMP is saying there are over twelve hundred missing women and girls. We know there's more than that. But even one is too many. So how do we stop it? How do we stop the violence against our women? Where can our women live a sustainable life? Not on their reserves. Violence is happening there. And when we leave those reserves and go into the cities, well, we're targets there too.

All the walkers that we've had throughout the years have been volunteers. We haven't been paid for doing this work. These walkers took months and months of time away from their families to walk, to honor our women. And we provided everything for them, anything that they needed: clothes, running shoes. We looked after our walkers the best way we could with the donations we received. But our main point was to get this inquiry, and to get Canadian society to realize that this is an ongoing problem in BC, in Alberta, in Sas-

---

21. The Walk4Justice statement can be found at https://intercontinentalcry.org /the-walk4justice-needs-your-support.

22. The final report of the inquiry into Canada's Missing and Murdered Indigenous Women and Girls was released in June 2019. The report's commissioners also claim that Canada's Indigenous women and girls have experienced a genocide through "state actions and inactions rooted in colonialism." For more on these findings, see Niigaan Sinclair, "Genocide by Any Other Name," *Winnipeg Free Press*, June 3, 2019.

katchewan, in Canada. This is not an isolated problem. It's a problem nationwide.

The families' voices need to be heard. It needs to be a "families first" inquiry, because each of our family members know what the problems are in their communities, whether it be poverty, addiction, or the lack of social services. This national inquiry isn't *my* request for inquiry. It does no good for our family because Tamara is still missing. There's nothing this inquiry can do for us. But we can implement recommendations that are going to protect our women from having to hitchhike, or to help them gain access to treatment for addictions instead of chalking us off—each one just "another dead Indian."

We know the North West Mounted Police were formed to control the Indian "problem."[23] Well, they're doing it now: they're allowing the killing of our women to happen. So this inquiry is supposed to be a working tool, so that we can live in the environment that they've given us.

Tamara's son, Jaden, has run away now. And even though we reported him as missing, when the cops found him they just let him go. They said, "He's okay, he's staying with friends." So they don't give a shit either. He's fourteen. I can totally see a repeated pattern: the history of my childhood, what I went through with the police and with the Ministry of Children and Family Development. He's a good kid who needs a lot of love. He's very angry about things that have happened. The murder of his mother is affecting him very much.[24] And it's hard to know what to do with him because there are

---

23. Prime Minister John A. MacDonald established the force in 1873 as part of his efforts to secure Canadian sovereignty and increased settlement in a region populated by First Nations peoples. The region, then known as the North West Territories, included all of present-day Manitoba, and parts of Saskatchewan, Alberta, and Canada's northern territories. In its first decade and a half, the North West Mounted Police played a central role in convincing Indigenous leaders to sign treaties with the national government and to move their people onto reserves.

24. Tamara went missing from Prince Rupert in 2005. She is still missing today.

pretty much no resources for youths who've lost their mothers. He needs to have someone to talk to. He doesn't want to talk to his family about what's hurting him. He doesn't want to listen to anybody. I remember feeling that way.

JASILYN CHARGER

CHEYENNE RIVER SIOUX
ACTIVIST
BORN IN: 1996, Rapid City, South Dakota
INTERVIEWED IN: Cheyenne River Indian Reservation

I met Jasilyn at the Dairy Queen in Eagle Butte, the largest town on the Cheyenne River Indian Reservation. Cheyenne River's population of approximately twelve thousand live on 1.6 million acres of vast, rolling prairie, the fourth largest land area of Indian reservations in the United States, about the size of Connecticut.

The Cheyenne River Sioux were originally part of the Great Sioux Nation, whose boundaries at the time of their first treaty—the Fort Laramie Treaty of 1851—extended from the Big Horn Mountains in the west, Wisconsin in the east, Canada in the north, and Kansas's Republican River in the south. The Treaty of Fort Laramie significantly reduced those boundaries and in 1889, when the Sioux refused to sell an

additional 9 million acres, the government claimed the land through an
act of Congress and parceled what remained to create a group of Indian
reservations, including Cheyenne River.[1]

Jasilyn arrived at the DQ with her fiancé, Kalen, who spent the first
several minutes of our interview sitting close by. Jasilyn later shared that
she has become wary of the press since becoming something of a public
figure during the movement at Standing Rock.[2] *We spoke about a* New
York Times *article in particular, which was striking for the absence of*
Jasilyn's voice in a sketch of her life story. She told me it was written that
way because the journalist pieced it together by asking others in the com-
munity about her, instead of interviewing her directly.

In our conversation, Jasilyn spoke about her early life with her mom
and siblings, the years she spent in a series of foster care homes, and how
her life was interrupted when she was moved at the age of thirteen to a
mental health facility, where she lived until she was eighteen. Jasilyn was
released and returned home just as the local movement in opposition to
the Keystone XL pipeline was growing, in 2015. She landed on her feet
through organizing work in that fight and went on to become a founding
leader in the movement at Standing Rock.

WHEN WE WERE ALL DANCING

My very first memory is of being really tiny and dancing the Rabbit
Dance, named for what the dance was inspired by—the movements re-
semble those of rabbits. I'd always dance it with my twin sister. Mama
always told me to listen to the beat, move my feet with the beat. And
then, my older brother would join us, and he'd hold both of our hands
and dance with us. It was probably the last time all of my siblings, my
mother's children, were together, when we were all dancing. When I

---

1. To learn more about how treaties with Indian tribes have shaped North American history, see appendix essay 1.

2. See Saul Elbein, "The Youth Group That Launched a Movement at Standing
Rock," *New York Times Magazine*, January 31, 2017.

think about that, it makes me happy because we did it as a family. It gave us all joy, and it still does for me now. Sixty years ago, we would never have been able to dance.[3] Now we have that right, that freedom, to experience something that our elders would've been beaten for.

I'm from Cheyenne River Indian Reservation. My grandfather, Harry Charger, was chief of the Itazipco band. When he was younger, he was a pipe maker. He learned it from his grandfather at a very young age. And he couldn't tell anybody about it, he couldn't tell his friends or his family members. He had to keep it secret. He always told me he felt like he had to hide who he was.[4] He told me to go to powwows, go to Sun Dance, take advantage of those opportunities because there are so many who never got the chance to go. He told me, "You're never too young to learn, never too young to understand what your people have been through."

A lot of adults think that young people don't understand or don't listen. And we may not understand in that moment, but as we grow up, we carry that knowledge with us, and we begin to understand. And we won't have to go on living in ignorance. I think that's what I was spared. My grandfather talked to me like I was an adult, like I was old enough to hear these things.

I'M PRACTICALLY RELATED
TO THIS WHOLE RESERVATION

On my mother's side, I have five siblings, and on my father's, I have ten siblings, but I only have one full sister, and she is my twin, Jasilea.

---

3. Until 1935, Native American traditional religious practices were banned on reservations and people could be fined or imprisoned for practicing them. As a result, many spiritual practices were driven underground. The American Indian Religious Freedom Act of 1978 (AIRFA) was intended to affirm religious freedom. For more on AIRFA, see the timeline.

4. Pipe making is a sacred, often inherited tradition that was one of the banned religious practices noted above.

The siblings I have from my father, I've only met one. My mother's kids were split up among family members because my mother couldn't take care of us all. We got to play with each other, but we rotated through family members and foster homes until I was thirteen. I'm practically related to this whole reservation, so it's like everybody's my cousin. The community helped a lot. People would come by and say to my mom, "Hey, you need someone to watch your twins?" Or, "Do you want me to take them to the park?"

The foster homes were located on my reservation because the tribal court is really strict with trying to keep tribal members, children, on the reservation with Native American families, close to their parents. So I was placed in some rural communities, all within a sixty-five-mile radius of here. Some of them were my father's family. They'd tell me stories about my father, what he used to do when he was my age. And they'd have old pictures. Or some of his friends would come over and babysit us. They'd talk about our dad. We didn't get to know him because he died two months before we were born.

Oh, my mother! She's a very strong, independent, stubborn woman. She's like a bear. She takes care of her children with the sheer force of will, and she lays down the law. She and I didn't really see eye to eye as I was growing up, but as a young adult now, I try to be around her as much as I can, because I want to have her strength.

No matter what happened to her, she kept going, raising five kids. Their fathers weren't around to help, and she still did it. We could've gone to the adoption agency, or she could've aborted us, but she chose to keep us, and she toughed it out, and she raised us the best that she could. Someday I want to be half the woman that she is.

THEY SAID I WAS A DANGER TO MYSELF

When I was thirteen, my aunt died of diabetes in her sleep. And one of our traditions is bloodletting for healing. We cut ourselves and we let the blood return to the earth. It's a way for us to get all of our bad emotions, all of our bad thoughts, out. Staff at school saw my cuts. But they didn't understand them. They thought I was trying to kill myself. And so they called the Department of Social Services and got me taken away. Instead of trying to understand my tradition, they instantly thought there was something wrong with me. They said I was a danger to myself and other people.

Social Services took me to Regional Health Behavioral Health Center, the highest-security facility that you can go to that isn't correctional, and I was there for two weeks.[5] At Regional Health you don't get to have your shoes, no personal clothing, and you don't get to talk to people or go outside. There are no windows. Everything was controlled.

From there, I got sent off to Canyon Hills, a mental health facility for kids in Spearfish, and I didn't see my family again until I turned eighteen.[6] We went to school, ate, and slept in the same building. It was a Christian facility, so they took us to church every Sunday. But I appreciated that there was also a cultural adviser for Native American kids, and there was a sweat lodge nearby. So I still got to be connected with that.

I thought they were going to take just me away. But they took my sister too.[7] Separated at thirteen. That was our first time being away from each other. In our culture, you're not supposed to separate twins because they have a bond, a connection, and when they took us away from each other, we both got sick. She got walking pneumonia, and I was just really, really depressed. Like, it detached something. I felt a part of me was getting torn away. It physically

---

5. Regional Health, now called Monument Health, is in Rapid City, South Dakota, about 166 miles southwest of Cheyenne River.

6. Spearfish is 155 miles away from Cheyenne River. Many state and federal facilities are hundreds of miles from tribal communities. Lack of income and transportation pose major barriers for family members to visit.

7. The South Dakota Division of Child Protection Services took both girls, sending them to group homes on opposite sides of the state.

hurt me. Because I'd always had her there; I'd always had someone to talk to. And that traumatized me.

Low-income Native Americans receive the majority of their behavioral health care through the Indian Health Service, tribally operated programs, and off-reservation facilities, financed by a combination of local, federal, and tribal funds. In treating a "special minority population," these off-reservation institutions receive more federal funding to treat Native patients than they do for non-Native residents.

The facility wanted Native Americans to be admitted, to make money for the facility. That's what I felt I was to them: just more funding. They didn't care about my physical or spiritual needs. They didn't prepare me to be successful outside the facility. They don't prepare you for life; they can't teach you anything about life in there. But when you turn eighteen, the system just kind of loops you out.

My family didn't really know me. They knew me when I was a child, but they didn't know me as a young adult, and so they had a hard time trusting me or welcoming me back into their homes. When I came back, for example, I knew nothing about sex. There were sex-ed classes, but they didn't prepare you for what actually happens. I was trusting. I came back like, *Oh, I'm with my people. People who actually care about me. People just like me.* I was completely wrong. I trusted some people I knew when I was younger, and they got me drunk, and I ended up getting raped. It was on my eighteenth birthday. And that was my first harsh experience—that's what life really is. It's not what they teach you in sex-ed classes. It's not what they teach you in a textbook. I felt like I was robbed, that the system let me down.

"I KNOW WHO YOU ARE"

I wandered around the community for a while, homeless, couch-hopping with some friends. And then one day, my friend Kalen's cousin, Wotila Bald Eagle—we knew each other a little bit—he asked, "Do you have a place to stay tonight?" and I was like, "No, I don't." And he said, "Well, you can come home with me." It was kind of sketchy. I thought he lived in town, but he lived on the west end, which is sixty-five miles west of here.[8] He was driving me out, and I was just thinking, *Oh my God.* It freaked me out. *Where is he taking me? What's gonna happen to me?* And then I fell asleep. I woke up, and we're at his grandfather Dave Bald Eagle's ranch house. It was raining when we arrived, and Wotila brought me to his grandfather and he let me introduce myself, saying, "She needs a place to stay tonight." And without even really asking where I'd come from or what my situation was, his grandfather Dave said, "There's a room right there, there's clean towels for you to shower, there's food in the fridge. You can go take a rest." And that really caught me off guard, like, *Whoa, he wants to help me.*

I was only supposed to stay there for the night, but Dave was like, "You can stay 'til the end of the week." And I ended up staying there for four months. He didn't ask, "Where'd you come from? Where are your parents? How come they aren't helping you?" He let me tell him when I was ready. And he was really open. He said, "You could live here if you want to, my house is open to you."

Dave was in his late nineties, and he was the Mnicoujou chief in the west end.[9] The west and east ends each have two chiefs, and Dave was one of them. My grandfather was one of them. Dave told me once he'd heard my name, he knew he had to help me. He was like, "I know who you are, I know your family."

He always sat at the end of the dining room table. He just sat there and had his coffee. One day, I grabbed a cup of coffee too, and I sat right next to him. We were both just sitting there with our cups

---

8. Jasilyn is referring to the west end of the reservation, along Highway 212.

9. The Cheyenne River Indian Reservation is home to four bands: the Mnicoujou (Planters by the Water), Oohenumpa (Two Kettles), Itazipco (Without Bows), and Siha Sapa (Black Foot). Each band has its own chief.

of coffee for the longest moment. I just started talking, and he didn't say anything, he just glanced up at me. And when he looked at me, I felt calm. I didn't feel so nervous.

When I got to the points where I thought I'd cry, he'd just look at me, and I'd get my composure, and I would keep telling him who I am, where I came from, what I experienced. And he didn't judge. I told him I came from a psychiatric facility. He didn't think I was crazy; he didn't mistrust me; he didn't think I was going to steal anything. He just felt compassion for me. And that was the greatest feeling, not being judged.

Dave knew a lot of people who went through the boarding schools, a lot of people who went into insane asylums because they were spiritual people. Colonialists felt that people who "had medicine" were crazy, and they locked them up.[10] And he was telling me stories about some of his friends who went through that. He was like, "You're not crazy, they're just trying to silence you, doing the exact same thing to you that they did back then. Kill the Indian, save the man.[11] But you survived. And you found your way to me, and I was meant to help you." And when he told me that, it made a lot of sense to me.

Growing up, I felt like there was something wrong with me. The staff at the institution always told me, "If you were okay, you wouldn't need to be in here. If you were normal, you wouldn't be here, people wouldn't have sent you here." And hearing that from age thirteen to eighteen, all those adolescent years—they drilled it into my head that I have to take substances in order to be okay. For a long time, I felt that—I'm a danger. I needed alcohol, different kinds of pills for what they diagnosed me with. They brainwashed me to think, *I've got to take*

---

10. The Westernized term *medicine men* (or *medicine women*) is used to refer to traditional healers, communicators, educators, and mystics. They are believed to "have" or "possess" knowledge, gifts, or medicine.

11. "Kill the Indian, and Save the Man" was the famous mandate of Richard H. Pratt, founder of the Carlisle Indian Industrial School, for the education of Native Americans through the US boarding school system. For more on Indian boarding schools, see appendix essay 2.

this, I've got to not be me. And Dave told me, "You don't have to take those anymore. If you don't want to, I'm not going to make you." I threw them all away, and he helped me! He was just like, "Go outside." I finally had somebody in my life again to really support me, who had my back.

I HAD TO STAND UP FOR MYSELF

In the summer of 2015, when I was nineteen, one of my best friends killed herself. Her name was Candi. She was three years younger than me and really outgoing, spontaneous, always ready to have fun, laughing. I came back for her funeral and then a couple days later there was another funeral. We had a suicide epidemic here, and we had a couple murders, and it took a lot of my friends. A couple of our women went missing. We were losing our youth at a very alarming rate. I was worried about how many of us would be left and what would happen to the ones that were left bearing the tragedy of their classmates or their relatives not being here. It was heartbreaking, and it was suffocating. We felt like we were drowning in drug addiction, violence, murder.[12]

No one was listening to us, no one was teaching us. We didn't have a voice, so some of us decided to silence ourselves. And I got the feeling that I had to stand up for myself. A couple of my friends started One Mind Youth Movement. It started out with a couple kids meeting every Wednesday, talking about what happened that week.[13]

Our reservation looks at drug addicts as the enemy. If you get

12. See, for example, Eliza Racine, "Native Americans Facing Highest Suicide Rates," Lakota People's Law Project, May 12, 2016, and Jenni Monet, "A Native American Woman's Brutal Murder Could Lead to a Life-Saving Law," *Guardian*, May 2, 2019. And for more on the outcomes of intergenerational trauma in Native communities, see appendix essay 2.

13. One Mind Youth Movement (OMYM) is a group of youth leaders organizing out of the Cheyenne River Sioux Tribe in South Dakota. OMYM aspires to be "the change that we wish to see in the world, and the salvation that our ancestors fought for."

caught, it's like, "We don't want you here no more." We were like, "It's not their fault. They're sick, they need help." And we were devising ways to support them. If we can't make them stop, how can we support them so they don't endanger themselves, or overdose, or pass out somewhere, or get raped? We were trying to find the best ways to look out for one another. And we made an agreement that if we see a kid drunk or a little girl walking with five dudes, we would do something. We had each other's phone numbers; we knew where each other lived. And we had mentors who were willing to support us, open up their homes, who'd even come to pick us up at two o'clock in the morning. I was always worried about my friends because they'd get drunk and beat each other up. Or they wouldn't have anything to eat. Or their parents would kick them out. I always told them, "Hey, if you ever need a place to stay, or if you're in jail, or if there's something going on, call me. I'll help you."

WE JUST HELD THAT SPACE

That summer, I started seeing a lot of things in my community through a different lens. It was eye-opening to see what we were going through. And that's when the KXL protests started happening.

In July 2008, TransCanada Corp and ConocoPhillips, co-owners of the Keystone Pipeline (which runs through North Dakota, South Dakota, Nebraska, Kansas, Oklahoma, and Texas) proposed a major extension to the network. Dubbed "Keystone XL," the addition was designed to help the pipeline move hundreds of thousands of barrels of crude oil from Alberta to Texas. Because Keystone XL would cross the US border, the State Department was tasked with determining whether the development was in the country's best interest.

While TransCanada claimed that the Keystone XL pipeline wouldn't cross any reservation or tribal trust lands, the pipeline's proposed route did intersect original Lakota reservation territory established by the 1868

*Treaty of Fort Laramie. Cheyenne River Indian Reservation is just down-
stream from where the Keystone XL pipeline was set to cross the Cheyenne
River, and the tribe feared that a spill could contaminate its waters.*

My cousin, Joseph White Eyes, was at the Keystone XL pipeline
camp in Rosebud.[14] Joseph always asked me to come, though I was
still in that "I don't listen to nobody" phase. But I started getting
more involved. He wanted to teach us community organizing.

We did an Indigenous Rising march from this area. The march
was about uplifting the youth and giving them power to voice what
they had to say about KXL. We made banners, we got our own per-
mits, we organized with each other. We videotaped and document-
ed the whole thing. We held this on Highway 212. For about two
hours, we were singing songs, doing rain dances. And we just held
that space. No one bothered us or told us to move. They just waited,
took a different route. Some of them starting walking with us. Even
the homeless people stood with us. That was our first taste that we
can do things, that people will listen to us if we organize and communicate and work together. And it taught us unity, that if we put
aside our differences, we can come together for a common goal. It
was a small thing, but we got it done, and that really kicked us off.
And we celebrated when the KXL pipeline was denied.[15]

*Just a month after Obama rejected Keystone XL, the US Army Corps of
Engineers for the Omaha District published a draft of its plan to approve
the Dakota Access Pipeline (DAPL) route under the Missouri River, which
would travel nearly 1,200 miles from North Dakota's Bakken oil fields*

---

14. The Rosebud Lakota Tribe also had concerns about Keystone XL because part
of its designated path was set to cut through an area containing the tribe's historical
and cultural artifacts.

15. For more on President Obama's rejection of the Keystone XL pipeline, see
"President Rejects Keystone Pipeline, Invoking Climate," *New York Times*, November 7, 2015.

through South Dakota and Iowa to reach a terminal in Illinois. One sec-
tion of the pipeline, set to cross the river just north of the Standing Rock
Sioux Reservation, became the center of a fight over how the pipeline's
route was evaluated and approved by the federal government. Members
of the Standing Rock Sioux said that they were not adequately consulted
about the route and argued that the pipeline's proposed path, under a river
reservoir called Lake Oahe, would jeopardize their primary water source
and compromise tribal fishing and hunting rights. In addition, the tribe
argued that the pipeline construction would extend damage to their sacred
sites near the lake, further violating their tribal treaty rights.[16]

Just a few weeks after that march, there was a broadcast on multiple
radio stations here from Standing Rock.[17] It was like, "Hey, there's
a call out." The people at Standing Rock want people that fought
KXL to come and share their experiences. We were like, "Alright!"
We brought our youth movement. And, surprisingly, we were the
only ones there—the people who organized the call and a bunch
of kids from Cheyenne River Reservation. We sat there, and we
waited for a whole hour. Nobody else came. Not our chairmen, not
akichitas, who are the men we send to defend us, not medicine men,
just us. The organizers didn't take us seriously and said, "You're just
kids." But we showed them how to target youth to be more active,
because there's a lot more of them, they're more agile, they can do
a lot, they can get things done fast. They've got a fresh outlook on
things, are more creative, intuitive. We tried to tell them, "You need

---

16. The timeline of events at Standing Rock outlined in this narrative's interstitials draw
largely upon Rebecca Hersher, "Key Moments in the Dakota Access Pipeline Fight,"
NPR, February 22, 2017, www.npr.org/sections/thetwo-way/2017/02/22/514988040
/key-moments-in-the-dakota-access-pipeline-fight, and Carla Javier, "A Timeline
of the Year of Resistance at Standing Rock," *Splinter*, December 14, 2016, https://
splinternews.com/a-timeline-of-the-year-of-resistance-at-standing-rock-1794269727.

17. Like Cheyenne River, the Standing Rock Sioux Tribe was once a part of the Great
Sioux Nation. Standing Rock is about seventy-four miles north of Cheyenne River.

to get the youth here." And they're looking around, "Well, where are our youth? They didn't come to the meeting."

Chase Iron Eyes was there.[18] At the end of the meeting, Ladonna Brave-Bull Allard stood up and told her story.[19] Her son was buried on her land. A lot of her medicine was on her land. She just started crying and said, "I need help. My land is right next to the river, and my son is buried there. My land is open to you; you can come camp." So we helped create a plan. We shared how to better communicate with their youth. You know, not just to say, "You have to be here," but, "Can you help out? If you're an artist, can you make our banner? If you're a cook, can you do bake sales?" Older people, it's hard for them to really connect and talk with the younger generation. Because we're so tech savvy, we want to make memes, do Snapchat. Social media is one of the tools that we told them is most useful. We helped with different programs, different apps that work well for making posters, or doing podcasts, videos. Those are the things that we shared.

THE PEOPLE OF STANDING ROCK

On April 1, 2016, Standing Rock's first camp, the Sacred Stone Camp, was created to educate the world about the abuse of fossil fuels, the history of the cultural sites along the path of the pipeline, and to provide education on nonviolent direct action and civil disobedience against a billion-dollar oil company. Jasilyn, her mentor Joye Braun, of the Indigenous Environmental Network, her cousin Joseph White Eyes, and

---

18. Lawyer and activist Chase Iron Eyes is a member of the Standing Rock Sioux Tribe and the Lakota People's Law Project.

19. Ladonna Brave-Bull Allard is a Lakota historian and activist from Standing Rock who was a leader in the 2016 Dakota Access Pipeline protests. She founded the Sacred Stone Camp, the first camp of the #NoDAPL movement. In addition to raising her general concerns for the tribe's environment and water safety, she argued that an oil spill in the river would putrefy her son's burial site and that of many other ancestors.

friend Wiyaka Eagleman were the first people to camp on Brave-Bull's
allotment (piece of tribal land) to stand in prayer and ceremony.

The very first camp was called Sacred Stone Camp. All the chiefs, all the men, pipe-carriers, they came out and set up like twenty teepees. But nobody stayed. The only person who was up there camping was our mentor, Joye Braun. She has a lot of medical problems; she can hardly walk. And we were like, "She's up there by herself? What the hell?!" So we asked our chairman for some money for gas and food. We bought some cold cut meats, some sandwiches, chips, some Gatorade.

Our plan was just to stay up there for a couple days. But once we saw Joye up there alone, we ended up staying for a whole week. Nobody really believed in us. They were like, "The pipeline's still gonna go through, what are you five people gonna do? You can't stop it." But there were people who supported us. They'd bring us food, water. A couple of men broke apart their old corral and gave it to us for firewood.

We didn't have a GoFundMe, we didn't have anything like that.[20] The people who supported us, who came out to check on us—to make sure we had blankets, that we were okay, that we had water— were the people of Standing Rock. And I think that's really what motivated me to keep camping there. It was a calling. I thought, *No one else is going to do it, so we've got to.*

It was mentally challenging. We had no cell phone service, no TV, no YouTube, no nothing. We didn't know anybody there. We didn't know the community. But then we turned a spiritual corner. We thought, *We're here, this is like a prayer.* And it kind of reconnected all of us to our heritage because that's how we used to live. We were nomadic. We went without a lot of things—salt and sugar, Kool-Aid, pop. It taught us self-discipline, a lot of patience. We started gradually gaining people. Four months into it, we had twenty people living with

---

20. GoFundMe is an online fundraising and crowdfunding platform.

us, all from different places. But we had to learn how to work together, how to live with each other, how to listen to each other. Kalen, Joseph, and I, every night, would come together after a meal and discuss what happened that day. We would just be doing our chores—hauling wood, going to get groceries, helping trap fish, going swimming, taking care of the little babies—doing what the old people couldn't.

In July 2016, the Army Corps formally approved the pipeline plan, claiming its construction would create local jobs and cause only minimal environmental impact. On July 27, Standing Rock filed an injunction to stop the construction and sued the Army Corps of Engineers with the hope that the court would retract the Corps' permit. Two weeks later, Energy Transfer Partners, DAPL's parent company, countersued Standing Rock's chairman, David Archambault, and other tribal members for their attempts at blocking construction. Organized activity against the pipeline expanded after the tribe was sued; public knowledge and interest swelled, and by August, nearly three thousand people had joined the camp.

Eventually, we had a lot of non–Native American visitors. Some of the traditional camp leaders didn't want white people around at all. But we told them, "We need our non-Native allies." Because we can't just shut off the whole world. We need to show them that this affects all of us. We're here for the water. We're here to stop this pipeline. It always came back to that.

We also ran up against questions, like: How should the camp be run? What are the protocols? During ceremonies, the traditionalists would try to say women should always wear dresses in the camp and shouldn't talk to any of the men. Joseph and I were like, "So that means I can't talk to you. That's a barrier for communication." We're in the twenty-first century, and I'm two-spirited.[21] There's proof in

---

21. *Two-spirit* is a pan-Indian term used to refer to someone whose body houses both a masculine and a feminine spirit. It can also mean that they fulfill both gender roles.

our culture, pictures, stories about two-spirit women doing things that men did. Going to war and taking their place.

Today our culture is very masculine. We have a lot of male leaders. And I really wanted to encourage the younger women. You don't gotta sit in silence. You don't gotta hush when a man tells you to hush. You're an individual. And you can live your own life, because we have that freedom now. A lot of women fought for that freedom. And I wanted to honor that. Kalen had my back, Joseph had my back. They all supported me. We were like, "We're the young generation. We're going to lead ourselves." And we held fast to the Seventh Generation Prophecy that we are going to be our own leaders.[22] That we're going to break the chains of oppression, of racism, of the colonialism that has chained us to this reservation, and break the feeling we can't do anything, and we don't matter, and that no one's going to listen to us. I wanted to show the youth that they have a voice. *Use that voice, because you have a lot of power.* I tried to show them that by doing it myself.

THEY JUST ATTACKED
AND SURROUNDED THE WHOLE CAMP

On September 9, 2016, US District Court judge James Boasberg reversed a temporary stoppage in construction of a section of the pipeline that the Standing Rock tribe said intersected with a sacred burial ground. Boasberg ruled that "the tribe has not demonstrated an injunction was warranted here." The same day, the Department of Justice, the army, and the Department of the Interior issued a joint statement requesting that Energy Transfer Partners halt construction until a review of possible damage to tribal sites was completed. During this period, tensions between protesters and security workers had intensified and turned violent. Protesters reported that security workers had used dogs and pepper spray on them

---

22. The Seventh Generation Prophecy portended a time seven generations after first contact when Indigenous youth and allies would come together to give rise to an age of healing and rebirth for Native people and the continent.

during confrontations around the historical sites they were attempting to
protect. And on October 27, the Morton County Sheriff's Department
arrested dozens of protesters, deeming that they were "setting up illegal
roadblocks, trespassing onto private property, and establishing an en-
campment." Later reports claimed that some of the 141 activists arrested
that night had identification numbers written on their arms and were
detained in enclosures that resembled dog kennels. Tensions remained
high throughout November, during which police used water cannons and
tear gas on protesters in sub-zero temperatures.

I never got arrested up there because people saw me as a spokes-
person, someone to tell their stories. A lot of my friends, they put
themselves on the front line and got arrested. And they told me, "No
one's going to tell our story if we're all arrested. Get out there; get
invited to marches, protests in Washington, DC, New York." Tell
people what we do and what we did—that was my role. It was hard
to watch my friends go through that much suffering.

One of my friends, Trenton—he's like a brother to me, we started
on this road of protesting together. I watched him get dragged out of
Inipi, a sweat lodge, a sacred ceremony for us. Women go in with a
shirt and skirt, men just in trunks. And he didn't have trunks, so he
went in with just his boxers. The Morton County police and a private
security company called TigerSwan tore down the whole sweat lodge
and dragged him out, and they had him sit on the side of the road
wearing nothing but his boxers. And it was freezing cold that day. They
said that we were trespassing on government property. We told them,
"Just let us finish our ceremony, and we'll leave peacefully." But they
didn't wait for us to clear out. They just attacked and surrounded the
whole camp. The people who were on the outside made sure the wom-
en and children got out safely. And I watched them get taken down.

It was horrible. My sister-friend Malia—she's Hawaiian, a protector of Molokai—Lauren, who's Jicarilla Apache, a protector of Bears
Ears and their sacred mountains, Tashina, three other women, and I

were standing in front of the agitators who were throwing rocks at the police.[23] We were worried people around them might get hurt, so we took it upon ourselves to make a barrier between the cops and the agitators and everybody else. We mentally prepared ourselves. They're gonna throw racial slurs. They're gonna beat us. They're gonna yell. They're gonna mace us. We chose to put women on the front line, saying, "Are you going to beat women? I'm probably the same age as your daughter. Would you do this to your daughter? Would you let somebody do this to your daughter?" We'd shout at them, "You're supposed to protect us, you're the police! Why are you doing this?" And a lot of them would stop; a lot of them would have to switch out with other cops. They couldn't do it. But there were those who had no remorse. They would shoot rubber bullets at us. One woman, three down from me, got shot in the face with a rubber bullet. We were all women, mothers, daughters.

Seeing all that happen and seeing men doing it to us? It was hard to put myself in that position of abuse and take it with no retaliation. It was very degrading. I always tell younger women, "Never let a man lay hands on you." But we were there in prayer and we just took the hits, we took the beatings, we took the mace. We held together. I got maced like five times. My face was burning. And later that day all that mace ate at my skin and there were just big old red rashes all over my face. Kalen got shot with rubber bullets twice in the back. We had no weapons.

At the end of November, the Army Corps of Engineers declared that protesters who had not moved out of the camps by December 5 would risk arrest. And on November 29, North Dakota governor Jack Dalrymple issued a mandatory evacuation order of the camps.

---

23. Molokai is the fifth largest of Hawaii's eight major islands. Bears Ears is a US national monument established by President Obama to protect public lands containing historic and cultural resources of five local tribes: the Navajo Nation, Hopi, Ute Mountain Ute, Ute Indian, and Zuni Pueblo.

On the last day of the camp, Kalen, I, and another one of our friends stayed—we wanted to get arrested. But our friend's mom and some of the elders we hung out with were like, "No. If you want to stay, just witness what's happening to people. Videotape it. Remember it. And go home and tell people what happened." I was like, "I don't want to do that, I want to go with you guys. Let's go down with it." But they said, "No, no, no. We're old. This is our moment. We'll go down for you, but you need to go home and tell them what happened here."

We saw the last fire keepers get arrested.[24] And our friend's mom got arrested. None of us had weapons. But Morton County and other county police, border patrol were there too, and they were coming up on us like we were armed. They came up with full body armor, with SWAT gear and a bunch of guns. I felt like they were going to literally kill us all. They had helicopters with the guns on the side. We were like, "Why do you need those?" I was really scared, thinking, *What are they going to do to us?*

A lot of people were trying to get their stuff and go. And we tried to help as many as we could and observe as much as we could. Then, the police finally pushed us all to the river. We were all on the frozen river—it was basically a peninsula off the Missouri River that ran next to the camp. We had this rope stretched across it for people to hold onto in case the ice broke. And the police were cutting that rope. It was heartbreaking, that moment of getting pushed away from our home, where we'd lived for almost a year. We worked hard to make it a home. We gave up everything to be there. And then we got pushed out. It felt like I was being robbed.

The night before, a lot of people burned their camps because they would rather have seen them burn than be taken by the ranchers.[25] When the police cleared everybody out, they let all the ranch-

---

24. A sacred fire, first lit when the camp was established in April 2016, was kept burning by fire keepers who tended to it day and night until the camp was evacuated.

25. Ranchers and farmers in Morton and Sioux Counties own much of the land in rural areas surrounding the protest site.

ers come in and take whatever they wanted. We had sheep and pigs there; they just took them. We were like, "We worked hard for this. We aren't gonna let anybody just take it." So a lot of people just burned their camps, burned the kitchens. Everything was on fire and the snow was coming down. Some of the snow was actually ash. It was like Armageddon, like the world had ended, and everything was in chaos.

"I FOUGHT HARD FOR YOU"

Today, when I hear airplanes, I get flashbacks. Or when I hear shouting or police sirens—I know I'm not doing anything wrong, but I still get scared. Like someone's going to shoot me or something. It's hard to trust these people with badges. You come home, and you see the police. And it's just like, *How can I trust them to protect me?* I can't say I've come out of it perfect, but I have come out of it stronger. What worse could I go through?

We spent so much time birthing the movement, seeing it grow into something that impacted millions of people, that echoed across the world.[26] And to see it taken away, with just one swipe of a pen. When Donald Trump came into office, he signed the bill for KXL and DAPL access.[27] How can we be dismissed so easily? To be swept aside like we mean nothing, when we worked so hard to be heard. How could they do that to us?

After camp at Standing Rock, we came back here, to Cheyenne River. I found out I was two months pregnant. I was just . . . mind blown. And I didn't have that much support. The baby's dad left

---

26. For more on the global impact of the movement at Standing Rock, see Chief Arvol Looking Horse, "Standing Rock Is Everywhere: One Year Later," *Guardian*, February 22, 2018.

27. On January 24, 2017, President Trump signed executive memos to facilitate the construction of the Keystone XL pipeline and the completion of the Dakota Access Pipeline.

me for some other woman. He didn't want anything to do with me. And dealing with the fact that we lost the camp was heartbreaking for me. It was a lot to deal with. I fell into a depression. I didn't want to go anywhere. I just stayed in my room for like two months. I wasn't happy—at all.

I didn't really know much about being pregnant then. I didn't know that your emotions affect your child, and I ended up losing my son. The miscarriage was probably worse than getting maced, the pain that I went through. It was really hard. I buried him at his dad's grandfather's place out in the west end, right next to the creek. When I lost him, it kind of snapped me out of my depression. He became my motivation. I have something to protect. Now *my* son's buried by the river. Now it's my turn to fight for him. I attended ceremonies and I laid him to rest. I vowed to him that he's going to be safe, that no oil was going to touch him. He's in the ground now, so it's my duty to protect the earth.

I know I'll see him again. When I went to ceremony, he said he'll come back to me when I'm ready and when it's safe for him, when his future is secure. I don't want to have a kid knowing I can't give him fresh water. I want to make sure that my children have a good future. And when they do get here, I want to be able to tell them, "I fought hard for you. I fought for your water. I fought to make sure you have a good life." I want them to be proud of their mom. So that's something that really got me out of blaming myself for the miscarriage. I didn't get over it. But the pain I still feel from it fuels my passion to keep going. He has become my inspiration. Sometimes I wonder what life would be like if he was still here. He would've been one year old.

It's still hard for me to adjust. I never asked to be a leader, or to be a mentor. But I've come to understand that even if I don't want to be, I can't walk away from it. While I was going into a depression when I came back from Standing Rock, Joye Brown sat me down. She was like, "A lot of young women, a lot of young men saw you speak. What would they do if they'd got inspired by you and then one day looked on Facebook, or on the news, and they see that you're gone, that you killed yourself? You're just giving that choice more power, telling them that suicide is okay. That person who did that amazing thing gave up, so I can give up." She said it would plant a seed of hopelessness inside of them. I heard that, and I was like, *Dang. That's kind of right.* When you're in grief, you don't think about who it's going to affect. But it has a domino effect. Your grief doesn't go away when you die. It just transfers into someone else, someone else carries it. I didn't want to do that. So I started trying to help my friends with suicide prevention. I'd say, "Whenever you feel sad, come talk to me. Talk to someone. Go for a walk. Ask me to go for a walk. I'll listen to you."

We met a lot of people at Standing Rock who became family. And when we call upon them, they're going to come. They're just waiting. I hope it doesn't come to that, but I fear it will because we now have anti-protesting laws in South Dakota. You can't wear masks. No more than twenty people can gather at a federal property at once. And if you do, you'll go in for a felony.[28] That's because South Dakota doesn't want what happened at Standing Rock to happen here. KXL keeps sending letters to our tribal chairman, Harold Frazier, like, "What can we do to make sure that this doesn't turn hostile?" I loved what our tribal chairman said: "Just don't build it. It won't get hostile as long as you don't build it." And then they sent him another letter: "This is when we're going to start construction." He sent them a letter back saying, "We'll be waiting." To have a chairman who supports the youth, I just love it. It gives me hope that we can become the bridge that links the young and old, the past and the future, because both are essential for us to live.

---

28. For more on these new laws, see Zoë Carpenter and Tracie Williams, "Since Standing Rock, 56 Bills Have Been Introduced in 30 States to Restrict Protests," *Nation*, February 16, 2018.

WIZIPAN LITTLE ELK

ROSEBUD LAKOTA
EXECUTIVE DIRECTOR
BORN IN: 1980, Rosebud Indian Reservation, South Dakota
INTERVIEWED IN: Rosebud Indian Reservation, South Dakota

*I arrived in Pierre, South Dakota, in a twelve-seat Beechcraft turbo-
prop plane. It was 8 p.m., and the sun was still setting in the wide-open
sky. The next morning, I drove south one hundred miles over plains and
through cornfields to reach the city of Mission on the Rosebud Indian
Reservation. Established in 1889 by the United States' illegal partition of
the Great Sioux Reservation, Rosebud's million acres today are home to
twenty-one thousand of its thirty-four thousand enrolled tribal members.[1]*

---

1. This partition was in violation of the Fort Laramie Treaty of 1868. For more on
the Fort Laramie Treaty, see the timeline. And for more on historical treaties, see
appendix essay 1.

Wizipan stood tall outside the building that houses his office at the Rosebud Economic Development Corporation (REDCO). He was squinting through his glasses into the sun, smoking, his braided hair long on his back. It had been a busy morning. Anticipating my arrival, he was taking a moment to clear his mind.

Wizipan is executive director of REDCO and manages development projects on the reservation. He tells me that Rosebud contains the nation's fifth-poorest county, with an unemployment rate of 80 percent on the reservation. In addition to creating jobs, he hopes that REDCO's businesses will soon act as a revenue source for tribal social services, including education and health care. The United States is legally obliged to provide these services, mandated by its federal Indian trust responsibility. In exchange for the land gained through treaties, the United States promised to protect treaty rights, lands, assets, and resources and the general welfare of tribal members. But in practice, these agreements are unfulfilled: on-reservation education and the Indian Health Service are chronically underfunded by the federal government, despite its obligations.

So for Wizipan, his work is about sovereignty, or strengthening the authority of his nation to govern itself. As he puts it, "Maybe the federal government doesn't like that we're doing something. They're going to use the carrot and stick and say, 'We're going to pull your federal funding.' Sovereignty is being able to say, 'That's fine. Go ahead and pull your funding. We're going to do things our way.'"

After our first meeting I joined Wizi, his wife, Donna, and their eighteen-month-old son, Kheya, for dinner. In the late afternoon sun, Wizi chased Kheya around the yard while Donna grilled chicken and corn on a hibachi. The next morning, a Saturday, I returned to Wizi's home to find the family eating breakfast. Kheya sat in his high chair watching The Berenstain Bears, *in Lakota.*[2]

---

2. To learn more about the Lakota *Berenstain Bears* Project, see www.lakotabears.com.

"WE'RE TIRED OF BEING POOR"

It was foretold. There's a well-known prophecy. Everyone talks about the seventh generation and what that means. For us, there was a man who went up into the Black Hills and had this vision of hieroglyphs of seven elk. The first elk is big and then they start to get smaller until the sixth elk is really, really small, and then the seventh elk is big again. And what that means is there's going to be a period of time when we lose our ways. But that seventh generation, everything is going to come back, and it's going to come back strong. That is what we are in the midst of.

Why is it coming back? One, it's destiny. Two, you're starting to have people ask, "What does it mean to be Indian?" People are having an awakening and realizing, "Hey, we just want our lives to be better. We're tired of struggling every day. We're tired of being poor. We want to change things, and we want to be who we are."

THE ONLY SURVIVING CHILD

My great-grandmother's life predated the reservation. Her English name was Nettie Four Horns, and her Indian name means "Stands Four Times." She survived the Wounded Knee Massacre.[3] She was ten years old in 1890. She was the only survivor from her family. She had five children; my grandmother, Edna Little Elk, was one of them. And her Indian name means "Brings Her Horses Home." She was born in 1918 and was raised by her grandmothers in a very traditional way. Her mother died when she was young and her father remarried, but his parents lived with the family, so she spent a whole lot of time with both grandmothers. They were her primary caregivers.

---

3. The Wounded Knee Massacre, a conflict between the US Seventh Cavalry Regiment and the Lakota peoples on the Lakota Pine Ridge Indian Reservation, resulted in the massacre of up to three hundred Lakota individuals and twenty-five US soldiers.

When she was four or five years old, she was forcibly removed from her home and put into the St. Francis Indian School, a boarding school run by Jesuits.[4] Her experience there was very traumatic. She was locked in closets. Starved. Beaten a lot. She was singled out because she was a troublemaker, because she wouldn't stop speaking Lakota. The "incorrigible" kids, the kids who just wouldn't come into line, would be stripped naked and tied up spread eagle, and they would be beaten with a horsewhip.

There was a Jesuit who was the head of everything named Father Hartman. One day my grandmother was being taken by Father Hartman to be beaten just as her father was arriving to visit her. Her father beat up the priest and took her away, and then she was enrolled in the day school.[5] From there she went to eighth grade and that was as far as her schooling went. She was married three times and had three children. My mother, Elizabeth, is the only surviving child.

Despite my grandmother's very negative experience with education, she felt that it was extremely valuable. My mother said that there may not have been any food in the house, but there were always books. My mother went to Flandreau Indian Boarding School, and from there she went on to Augustana University where she met my father, who's non-Indian and from Kansas.[6] She went on to Howard University and then to Cornell to get her master's degree, and in 1979 they moved home to the reservation.

---

4. Jesuits are a Roman Catholic order of priests founded in 1534 to do missionary work. For more on boarding schools, see the glossary and appendix essay 2.

5. In addition to Indian boarding schools, the US operated some on-reservation day schools.

6. Flandreau Indian School is an off-reservation boarding school operated by the Bureau of Indian Education in Flandreau, South Dakota. Even today, for many tribal communities, whose populations are spread across large territories, boarding schools remain the best and sometimes the only opportunity for access to a high school education.

A CODE THAT YOU LIVE BY

I was born in 1980. We lived in Grass Mountain, which is a small community around here.[7] It was my grandmother's land, her father's land. The first years of my life we grew up in a small trailer house. In the beginning, we didn't have running water. We had an outhouse. It was really cold. In the wintertime, there would be frost on the walls. I absolutely hated our trailer house. Everyone lived like that. That was the normal world around us, but it felt wrong.

My mother started the tribe's social work office and my father worked for the Sinte Gleska University at the time.[8] It was just me and my grandma at home. We had a routine. I'd get up, and she'd braid my hair and cook me breakfast, and she'd talk to me. She told me, "You have to have a code that you live by: everything that you do, you don't do it for yourself, you have an obligation to your tribe." In Lakota thought and philosophy, one of our purposes on earth is to be a good relative. The word *Lakota* means to be an ally. That's what it means: a friend. And so everything you do is to be a good relative and not just to your blood relations but to everyone and all of creation.

I spent a lot of time riding horses. Around age five or six, I got my first horse and all day, all summer, all the time I was on a horse. My sister, Tate, wasn't born until I was six, so I spent a lot of time alone in the early years.

My father quit his job to homeschool me. It was very much about trying to utilize cutting-edge, alternative methods of education. He was a hippie, very into sustainability and growing your own food. We had big gardens. He was very into Waldorf.[9] He told traditional

---

7. Grass Mountain is a community located along the Little White River and BIA Highway 5, between Rosebud and Spring Creek, in Todd County, South Dakota.

8. Sinte Gleska University is a four-year private tribal college located in Mission, South Dakota, on the Rosebud Indian Reservation.

9. Waldorf education is a humanistic approach to teaching based on the educational philosophy of the Austrian philosopher Rudolf Steiner.

stories. All coupled with this whole thing around work. He was always working on stuff. There was a master carpenter who came and lived on the reservation for a while and I got to learn about woodworking from him. We ended up building our own house. I remember being around seven years old and working on our house. That was actually part of my homeschooling, learning about measuring and math.

I was somewhat isolated and protected, and I wanted to go to school because I wanted to have friends, people my own age. I started regular school in sixth grade, and I didn't start to learn anything new until about ninth grade because my dad had taught me so much. The only thing that I didn't know how to do was write cursive.

What I did learn about was social interaction. I learned how to survive in some respects. Of course, I had friends and relatives that I'd hung out with as a little kid, but I went from spending a lot of time by myself to every day being in the classroom. I was exposed to a different kind of environment that was informed by poverty. You know, on the reservation, you have the beauty of the culture and our traditional knowledge contrasted with the reality of poverty. We have the worst socioeconomic statistics in the country—us, Pine Ridge, and other reservations.[10] Eighty percent unemployment; one of three women raped—it's probably higher than that.[11] Sexual abuse is a reality, so is overcrowding, malnutrition, drug use. People bring that stuff to school. How do you survive in a culture like that? It's a

---

10. Pine Ridge Indian Reservation is an Oglala Lakota reservation in southwest South Dakota. Like Rosebud, Pine Ridge was originally included within the territory of the Great Sioux Reservation. According to 2010 census data, Shannon County, which is entirely encompassed within the reservation, is the second poorest county in the United States.

11. Native Americans constitute 10 percent of South Dakota's population, yet they represent 40 percent of its victims of sexual assault. According to a National Institute of Justice Research Report from 2016, 56.1 percent of Native American women have experienced sexual violence in their lifetime and 14.4 percent have experienced it in the last year. Of these women, 96 percent experienced sexual violence by a perpetrator of another race or ethnicity.

dysfunctional environment. It can be very abusive. How can you be a healthy individual when everyone around you is unhappy? That can be incredibly difficult. I had to figure out what my niche was going to be. Very quickly I learned about sports.

I remember playing high school basketball—one side of the gym would be Indian and the other side would be white. One of these towns, they still had the "No Dogs or Indians" signs up. And everyone's yelling racial stuff back and forth. The other side is white supremacist in army fatigues. This is cowboys and Indians. And you're a seventeen-year-old kid trying to process that.

But I was really, really lucky in high school because with my mom and dad and my grandma there was an expectation that I would go to college. That I would go off, do something, and come back. That's what I wanted to do. My original intent was to go to school to become an architect, and I wanted to do that here on the reservation. My parents had been involved in a community development project, and they brought in some architects who do alternative construction using local materials. All that good green stuff that people talk about now. And I got this idea: *That's what I want to do with my life.* My high school counselor told me, "I think you should find a junior college." I remember that very distinctly. Going to a four-year college just wasn't the expectation at the school.

"FIND YOUR OWN WAY"

I didn't even know what Yale was. A friend of the family had gone to school with a professor at Yale, and they came out to visit. They met me and said, "You're the kind of person that Yale recruits. You should apply." So okay, I said, "I'll apply." Mostly because my parents said, "Apply." I didn't think anything of it. I didn't know what it meant. I didn't know what it was. Just no clue whatsoever.

I got in. They have a big orientation weekend, so I went and I met some of the other students. I remember having a very distinct feeling that I didn't belong. I remember leaving that visit with the clear impression that everyone expected me to fail. I thought, *You know, fuck you. I'm going to go and I'm going to make it.* At the same time, I was also like, *Holy smokes, I don't think I can make it.*

At the orientation I said, "I need to get more experience." Rick Chavolla, assistant dean and director of the Native American Cultural Center, and Richard Shaw, the dean of undergraduate admissions, said, "Just so happens there's this new school, Native American Preparatory School in New Mexico.[12] A lot of our students do what's called a post-grad year after high school. We'll help you contact them."

At NAPS, the expectations were way higher. I actually had to work. It was awesome to be expected to perform at a high level, because people cared.

I'd grown up learning about treaties and our Indian history. But at NAPS I was given books about it. I remember being introduced to Vine Deloria and to a new intellectual tradition.[13] I remember I was reading Plato and *God Is Red*.[14] So I wrote this essay, "Plato Was an Indian."

The next year, 1999, I went to Yale's pre-orientation program for minority students. It was the week before everyone else arrived for freshman year. I remember my mother said, "You're going into the belly of the beast. How you come out is really up to you. You can go and become like everyone else, or you can find your own way."

I remember getting there and being around all these new minority students and I'm like, *Wow, everyone is just so smart.* They had

---

12. Native American Preparatory School began in 1988 as a summer academic program founded by Richard Ettinger. The program expanded in 1995, to establish a full-time residential school. The school's mission was to increase the number of Native Americans attending Ivy League colleges. Because of financial difficulties, the school closed in 2002.

13. Vine Deloria Jr. (1933–2005) was a Standing Rock Sioux who wrote more than twenty books about the Native American experience.

14. *God Is Red: A Native View of Religion* is a work of nonfiction by Vine Deloria Jr. The book explores Native American religious views and practices.

these talent contests and shows. Everyone is doing all this stuff, and it was just like, *Wow, I have no talent.* I'm just a kid from Grass Mountain! I remember thinking, *Okay. My talent is I can survive. That's my talent. I can survive anything.*

This is the Ivy League, where people of power go, where their kids and their grandkids are going to go. It's more than money. It's wealth. These are the grandkids of the people that the buildings are named after. You can drink the Kool-Aid and do what's best for you as an individual based on your desire for wealth and power.

And how are you going to stay true to yourself and to the original reason you go to a place like that? What are you going to do with that privilege that you've been given? Are you going to use it for personal gain or are you going to take everything you get there and go full bore? I was always told, "You go out, learn everything you can, and come home." That's the charge I was given.

I had to learn to think a little bit differently. I remember freshman year we were taking this class on climate change, population growth, and infectious diseases, these big-picture global issues. I was doing research for a paper and was using winter count as a source.[15] The teaching assistant looked at it and said, "This is an invalid source. Winter count is not a valid source. It's not written."

You have to be able to think and process information in two ways. Writing a paper on buffalo, for example, on what buffalo means from an Indigenous traditional perspective versus what it means from a Western perspective. You can't bring any of your traditional knowledge into this paper because "it's not valid," it's not going to be accepted. So you're constantly doing this translation back and forth. You're thinking about a concept in Lakota and saying, *It doesn't translate, but I've got to make it fit.*

---

15. Winter counts are histories or calendars in which events are recorded by pictures, with each year represented by one image. Each year is named for an event and they are organized in chronological order to give the tribe's oral historian an outline of the community's history.

One of the most difficult things that I always felt was guilt. Here I am, I'm given this incredible opportunity. I'm having fun. I'm enjoying myself. I have all this privilege and my friends are at home, what are they doing? I don't deserve this. Because in reality, the guys that I went to high school with, they're smarter than me, they're more talented than me. I just had a few small advantages that they didn't have. That's why I'm here. That weighs on you, and you hear of bad things happening to classmates back home and you feel guilty for having those privileges.

During Thanksgiving break my freshman year, I was home on the rez, cruising around late at night, and I had this moment, kind of an epiphany: *Things are not right here. The level of poverty and dysfunction is not right.* Some of that big feeling I had when I was young but couldn't articulate, I finally had the vocabulary and the experience to articulate it.[16] I knew right then and there that I couldn't be an architect, because what I wanted to do was not possible. No one on the reservation was going to come to me and say, "I want you to design a culturally appropriate green home that incorporates who we are as Lakota people." People are concerned about where they are going to get their next paycheck. People are concerned about having gas in their car. People are concerned about not having enough diapers for their baby. So I knew that my purpose had to be in helping raise the overall standard of living for people in the community. That became my goal. And that took me on a journey that I'm still on now.

"LEARN THE US SYSTEM"

I have an auntie who I can blame for my career path. Her name is Rosalee, and she did some work for a private foundation. We started talking, and she said, "Well, why don't you do an internship for me?" She had me do this study on traditional leadership and what

16. For more on the effects of intergenerational trauma in Native communities, see appendix essay 2.

that means today. How do traditional Lakota values and character-istics translate in a modern-day society? For example, how is Lakota generosity displayed and how does it relate to leadership? Sitting Bull and Crazy Horse were known for going out and hunting and bringing back food for people, especially those who couldn't hunt for themselves.[17] Well, what does that mean today—when there's not a system or mechanism where our leadership is held to that kind of standard?

My auntie said, "You need to learn the US system. The best way to learn is to go to Congress. You should go work for Tom Daschle.[18] He's a good guy." So I did that the next summer. DC was awesome. Another place where I learned so much. I remember thinking, *I'm Indian, and I've got to work twice as hard to be considered half as good.* I met new tribal leaders from across the country. I learned about tribal issues, treaty rights, and funding. I was immersed in it.

In February 2007, I had just read Barack Obama's book, and I was thinking, *Hey, I like this guy.* I was getting ready to graduate from law school and didn't know what I wanted to do.[19] I set up a meeting with Pete Rouse, Daschle's chief of staff. He said, "Well, what do you want to do?" I said, "I want to work on economic development and Indian issues." Pete asked, "Who are you sup-porting for president?" I said, "Obama." He said, "Well, good. Tom

---

17. Crazy Horse (ca. 1840–1877) is recognized as a visionary leader, celebrated for his fierce commitment to maintaining the Lakota way of life. He fought against US encroachment on Lakota land after the Treaty of Fort Laramie, and when the War Department ordered all Lakota onto reservations, he became a leader of the resistance. In 1876, Crazy Horse joined forces with Sitting Bull in the attack that destroyed Custer's Seventh Cavalry. For more on this attack, the Battle of Little Bighorn, see the timeline.

18. Tom Daschle, born 1947, is a member of the Democratic Party. He is a former US senator (South Dakota) and former US Senate majority leader.

19. Wizipan graduated from Yale in 2003 with an undergraduate degree in American Studies, with an emphasis in American Indian Studies, and from James E. Rogers College of Law–University of Arizona in 2007.

is going to support him in the *Washington Post* next week. Do you want in on the campaign?"

I started working on the Indian vote strategy in 2007. We created a comprehensive presidential platform. The campaign was creating all these "czar" positions, specific policy people at the White House level, to tackle all the issues. So we said, "Let's create an Indian position." And that's how the Indian Affairs position in the White House Domestic Policy Council was created.[20]

Obama won, and I got asked to be part of the transition team. I went to DC.

THE ONLY INDIAN IN THE ROOM

I was a political appointee to the Department of the Interior. The first day I get there, I go to my first meeting, and there are no other Indians in the room. And I don't mean at the political appointee level—I mean at the staff level. I remember thinking, *I'm the only Indian in the room. What's going on here?*

It was a tremendous experience to work on some really great issues, but you never accomplish a fraction of what you hope, of what you believe needs to happen. And you're stuck working in a bureaucracy that's 150 years old, with its roots in *eradicating* Indians. Indian Affairs was moved from the Department of War to the Department of the Interior. We were stuck in with the rocks and bears, you know? What does that tell you?

It reminded me of Yale again: great individuals there, but institutionally extremely racist. Not because anyone there hates Indians, but because of the way the structures are set up. The Indian programs are not built around the idea of nation-building. They're set up to hold us

---

20. In 2009, Barack Obama appointed Kimberly Teehee (Cherokee) to the newly established position of senior policy adviser for Native American Affairs. As a member of the Domestic Policy Council, the person holding the position was given a direct advisory role to the president on issues affecting Indian country.

down, to hold us back, and to keep us out. I got my nation-building theory from the University of Arizona law school, but my belief goes back to my uncle Sam. He's always said that the money should just flow. We signed treaties; we gave up land. But we never gave up any of our mineral resources.[21]

We sealed these treaties with our pipe.[22] We have a treaty with the US government. We call it the Nation of the Long Swords. We gave up our right to certain portions of land and said, "You guys can live here in exchange for recognizing that this area is ours and will always be ours and that we have a fundamental right to live here."[23] But sometimes your relatives don't act as they should. Your brother might be mean to you. Your uncle might yell at you. Sometimes you have relatives that abuse each other. What you have to do is hold them accountable. Part of holding the US government accountable is saying, "Hey, we became relatives when we smoked the pipe and made this treaty. We need you to act in a good way. We need you to be a good brother." We need to hold each other accountable. That's what being human is.

You can't make up for past injustices, but you can make up for current injustices that are rooted in past injury. A contract still exists between our nation, the Great Sioux Nation, and the United States.[24]

---

21. Many tribes have collective ownership of the mineral resources located subsurface within their territories. For some tribes this ownership has been explicitly gained, through modern sovereignty acts. For others, like the Lakota, this ownership has been a constant because their subsurface materials were never ceded through treaties, or these materials exist on unceded lands, or both.

22. For many Indigenous people, the sacred pipe plays an important role in traditional ceremonies. The tobacco smoke carries prayers to the ancestors and creates a link between the living and spirit worlds. The pipe was shared to seal peace agreements with the colonists.

23. For more on historical treaties, see appendix essay 1.

24. Signed on April 29, 1868, the Treaty of Fort Laramie, also known as the Sioux Treaty of 1868, is an agreement between the United States and the Oglala, Mnicoujou, Brulé Lakota, Yanktonai Dakota, and Arapaho Nations. For more on the Treaty of Fort Laramie of 1868 and the Black Hills War, see the timeline.

In order for the treaty not to exist, we have to vote it down. We'll never vote that down. It's law.

THE DOCTOR KEPT SENDING HER HOME

Established by Article VI of the Constitution as the "supreme law of the land," the treaties signed between sovereign American Indian nations and the United States, by virtue of being agreements with the US, distinguish Native Americans from other marginalized groups in the country. Native Americans' civil rights, including access to quality housing, education, and health care, were secured by the treaties, in which Native Americans ceded millions of acres to the US. The duty of the US to provide health care in particular was articulated in the language of the Treaty of Fort Laramie of 1868: "The United States hereby agrees to furnish annually to the Indians the physician . . . and that such appropriations shall be made from time to time, on the estimate of the Secretary of the Interior, as will be sufficient to employ such persons."

Later, this idea was generalized and mandated by federal law: the US government became responsible for all Native Americans' health care, "to ensure the highest possible health status for Indians and urban Indians and to provide all resources necessary to effect that policy." The Indian Health Service (IHS) was established in 1955 to fulfill that commitment. Today the IHS operates 46 hospitals and 230 clinics, for which it hires medical personnel and determines what health services to provide its clientele: the 2.6 million Native Americans who live on or close to reservations.[25]

A few months before my sister, Tate, gave birth in 2009, she started having breathing problems and chest pain. It escalated after she gave birth. About five months afterwards, it really got to her. She had been consistently going to the Indian Health Service and complaining of

---

25. David Montgomery, "What Do Native Americans Want from a President?," *Washington Post Magazine*, May 13, 2019. The interstitials in this narrative on the Indian Health Service are based on information from this article.

chest pain and trouble breathing and fatigue. The doctor kept sending her home saying, "You're experiencing the stress of being a new mother." One morning she woke up and she could barely walk. She was coughing up blood. She went to IHS and saw the doctor, and the doctor said, "I'm going to send you home."

It just so happened that there was another doctor there that day on detail from the National Guard who said, "Well, let's take X-rays to see what's going on." No X-rays on my sister had ever been taken before.

The IHS suffers from a chronic clinician shortage, which has serious consequences for its patients: their access to care may be limited and continuity of care compromised. The IHS struggles to meet local market salaries and find adequate housing for its staff. In addition, many IHS facilities are located in extremely rural regions (some are so isolated they are deemed "hardship posts"), which also contributes to low employee-retention rates. Many clinics try to fill vacancies with contractors or other part-time employees like those provided by the National Guard, whose physicians work one weekend a month and two weeks a year. This patchwork assembly of staff results in a highly inconsistent quality of care.

The new doctor took one look at the X-rays and said, "Your lungs are completely full of fluid and your heart is twice the size of a normal person's heart. We need to fly you out immediately." She was flown from Rosebud Hospital to Sioux Falls.[26] In Sioux Falls, her heart rate jumped up to 160 and it just would not come down. So then she was flown to the medical center at the University of Minneapolis, where they got her stabilized and she was diagnosed with postpartum cardiomyopathy, which is heart failure associated with childbirth, and was told that she needed a heart transplant. If she didn't want a heart transplant, because she was young, there was a chance her heart would slowly start to reduce in size and that she

---

26. Sioux Falls is about 220 miles east of Rosebud.

would heal herself, but there was a 30 percent chance that she would die. She decided not to have the transplant. For two years she tried to control her diet, her lifestyle habits.

The morning my sister died it was just her and her son, Pajuta Ska, who was two at the time, at home, and she was racing to try to get to the hospital. She was found facedown in our driveway. She was just twenty-four.

Despite its mandate to provide "all resources necessary" to ensure good health care to Native Americans, the United States spends only a third of the money on Native Americans that is spent per capita on health care nationwide. The IHS received $5.5 billion in 2018, plus $1.2 billion through Medicaid and other program reimbursements. To fully meet the needs of the IHS and the population it serves, the National Congress of American Indians is calling for an increase of six times its annual budget, with a call to achieve a budget of $36 billion over the next twelve years.

One obstacle to meeting the pledge of "all resources necessary" is that most of the IHS's physicians are primary care or family practice doctors, so the service contracts out almost all of its specialty care. However, Congress doesn't provide enough money to the IHS to cover these referrals (in 2018 just two-thirds were covered). As a result, the IHS has to ration care for what it deems the most critical or life-threatening needs. In 2018, this resulted in the denial of about eighty thousand service requests for procedures considered less urgent.[27] This kind of dilemma for physicians means that conditions like Tate's are more likely to go undetected, become more acute, and result in lasting injury, or as in Tate's case, early death.

The big talking point at the time was, "Federal prisoners get more in health care than American Indians do." The average American is going to spend around $10,000 on health care a year, and it's $4,000 or

---

27. See "The Never-Ending Crisis at the Indian Health Service," *Roll Call*, March 5, 2018, www.rollcall.com/news/policy/never-ending-crisis-indian-health-service.

$5,000 per Indian. So why isn't the discussion, "We need to raise the Indian Health Service budget from $4.5 billion to $12 billion"? No one talks about that at that level. No one makes it an issue. You can pick any issue and everyone is stuck advocating and arguing over who gets a bigger slice of the pie, when the real discussion should be, "We need a bigger pie." We have to fundamentally change the discussion.

Rosebud has a thirty-five-bed IHS hospital; its emergency room was closed for seven months in 2015–16 after federal inspectors learned of broken sterilization equipment, a baby born on its bathroom floor, and a heart-attack patient whose treatment was severely delayed. Nine members of the tribe died during the ER's closure and five babies were born in ambulances en route to clinics fifty miles away. The shuttered emergency room led the tribe to file a federal court lawsuit based on its 1868 treaty rights. The tribe wasn't asking for money; it wanted a "judicial declaration that the federal government is violating the treaty and for an order that the IHS should raise the health of tribal members to the 'highest possible' level."[28]

GOD, FAMILY, WORK

Donna and I met at my uncle Sam's in 2010. It was right before a sweat lodge that we were having. I'd never really believed in love at first sight and soulmates or anything like that, but when I saw her it felt like someone punched me in the chest, right in the heart area. I'd never felt anything like that before.

Two weeks after my sister passed away, Donna moved out to DC with me. We debated whether or not to move my mother and Pajuta out to DC with us or if we should move home. I'd committed to serve one term with the Obama administration. But my priorities

---

28. Montgomery, "What Do Native Americans Want from a President?"

have always been God, family, work, and in that order. The people
that I go to for spiritual guidance told me that it was time to come
home. That I'd done what I needed to in the outside world. So we
moved home, but we had no idea what we were going to do.

It was very difficult for me and Donna being newly married and
going through all of this. We really had to put a lot of faith and trust
in each other to make it. We took the summer to try to deal with
everything, to help my mom and my stepdad and to try to help with
the baby. We were living at my mother's house. There's just nowhere
to live on the reservation. There are very few houses and the market is
extremely tight because of the scarcity and the high demand. There's
an apartment complex here—they have a small number of apart-
ments that go for $800 a month and are non–income restricted—
and there's a waiting list five hundred people deep. Todd County is
one of the poorest counties in the entire United States.[29] I didn't even
pay $800 a month when I had prime real estate in Tucson, Arizona,
and I could walk two blocks to the law school. We ended up living
with my mother for five months.

I'd always made it a point to come back as often as I possibly
could, to keep in contact with people and to make sure I maintained
my connections here. I made sure that people saw my face here. I think
that's why the tribe brought me in right away when I asked if I could
work for the community—there was really no question. I put together
a nation-building proposal that we could work on as a tribe. Some
people gave me a hard time, but that's part of the initiation of coming
back. You have to prove yourself a little bit. No one's going to give you
anything simply because you have a fancy degree or title. You've still
got to earn it. I'm okay with proving myself no matter what, and if I

---

29. According to the 2010 census, western South Dakota is home to the three
poorest counties in the United States and four of its top ten. Ziebach County, with
the highest poverty rate, at 50.1 percent, lies within Cheyenne River Indian Reservation and Standing Rock Indian Reservation. Todd County, which lies entirely
within the Rosebud Indian Reservation, had a poverty rate of 49.1 percent.

can't prove myself, then I probably shouldn't be in any kind of leadership position at all. To me, that's having that pre-reservation Lakota attitude. Crazy Horse didn't say he was a great leader and then sit in the back and direct people. He was at the front line when they went into battle.

Our culture has always been fluid and dynamic, but our values and our spiritual beliefs are set in stone. They're written in the stars. But the everyday culture has to change. One of the things that a young man would traditionally do is *zuya omani*. *Zuya* is a journey. It's going out and doing something. *Omani* means to walk. So *zuya omani* means to go out and walk and do something. For a young man, that was typically going and stealing horses from a rival tribe or proving oneself in battle. It was also just walking and traveling and seeing what was in the universe.

We have stories of people who traveled until they came to water, and they couldn't go anymore. So they went to the ocean. Our trading networks went to the ocean. One of our ceremonies requires a shell that you can only get from the West Coast. There's another story of a group of young men who said they were going to go south. They woke up one morning and looked up into the trees and saw *sunka wicasa*—"dog men" in the trees, monkeys. So they went down to probably the jungles of Mexico.

I viewed going off to college as my zuya omani. I can't prove myself by going and stealing horses from the Crows, but I can go out and do the same thing in college. You're not fighting with bows and arrows and guns, but you're going out and learning and fighting against poverty, fighting against social injustice. You're fighting for the rights of Indian people. You're fighting so that children can have a good life. That's how you embrace a modern context.

WHAT WAS WORKING WITH TRIBES

My next move was to REDCO, the Rosebud Economic Development Corporation, in 2012. It was founded in 1999 and modeled after very successful organizations like Ho-Chunk Inc., run by the Winnebagos in Nebraska and Chickasaw Nation Industries in Oklahoma.[30] Ho-Chunk Inc. is a quarter-of-a-billion-dollar company. CNI is a billion-dollar company. REDCO had fired the previous executive director. He was the third person to have that position and no one wanted the job. They brought me on board and handed me an organization that was $4 million in debt with three failing businesses and said, "Go for it."

There are some other individuals out there, tribal members with great educational and professional backgrounds, and part of my goal is to create a place to help them contribute. I've told them, "Hey, I'm warming up the seat for you." And their response is, "It's not the right time for me to come home." Or, "I don't want to deal with the politics." Or, "You can't pay me enough." So we need to create a situation where we can make it worth their while to come home.

One of the greatest things in DC was I got to see what was not working with tribes, but I also got to see what was working with tribes. Who were the successful tribes? And how were they doing it? And how can we take what they are doing and make it work for us? We know the federal government owes us full funding for health care. That right stems from treaties.[31] It's also a human right. Howev-

---

30. Ho-Chunk Inc. is the economic development corporation owned by the Winnebago Tribe of Nebraska. Established in 1994 with a single employee, Ho-Chunk now employs over a thousand people, 57 percent of whom are members of the Winnebago Nation. Ho-Chunk's mission is to "use the Tribe's various economic and legal advantages to develop and operate successful business enterprises and provide job opportunities for Tribal members." See https://hochunkinc.com /annual_report_2018/Ho-Chunk_Inc_-_2018_Annual_Report.pdf.

31. Treaties between the US government and Indian tribes often include calls for providing medical services, including physicians' services and the presence of

er, we're not going to get full funding for Indian health care anytime soon. Well, the successful tribes that have the best health care systems take federal money and supplement that with other money. So we need to create business to generate revenue that we can apply to government services like health care and education.

PATIENCE, PERSEVERENCE, AND BRAVERY

A big change in my everyday life was when my first baby was born in 2013. His name is Kheya, which means "turtle." I asked my uncle Sam to name him. Turtles represent patience, perseverance, and bravery, and they're also the symbol for North America. So if my son is a patient, perseverant, and courageous man and is connected to North America, I'll be proud. We had my second son, Tokala, in 2015 and my third, Wase, in 2018.

I've often asked myself why I've had a pretty good career and done some cool stuff and other people haven't. It's something I continue to think about. Well, there's this whole body of research on resilience. On why some people can survive huge, traumatic life experiences and come through it, and why others can't.

First and foremost, you have to have someone in your life who shows you unconditional love; somebody who shows you that love no matter what you do or how badly you mess up. My grandmother was the epitome of this; I was immersed in the depths of unconditional love.

Two, you've got to have a purpose. The people who have a purpose in their life, that purpose helps drive them through adversity. My purpose comes from my grandmother. She always told me that I needed to go and learn about the outside world and come back and help our people; to improve people's quality of life.

Three, you've got to have grounding. You've got to know where

---

hospitals for the care of Indian people. For more on the treaties between the US government and Indian tribes, see appendix essay 1.

you come from. If you know where you come from, that's going to
help you to know where you're going. I'm Lakota. *Ma Lakota*. We are
a part of the Oceti Sakowin, the "Seven Council Fires," what we call
the alliance between the Lakota, Dakota, and Nakota. And within
that I am Sicangu Band, "Burned Thighs," and within that I have a
sub-band.[32] In Lakota society, that's really where your identification
comes from. Your heritage, that's who you are. And I have a history
that our family has to live up to.

Four, you have to have a mentor, somebody who takes you under their wing, whom you can bounce ideas off, and who is going
to help you. I've been so lucky to have different mentors in different areas and stages of life: the spiritual side, in college, professional
mentors, in law school. If you can maximize those four factors, your
statistical chance of success, however you want to define it—having a
good life, a good job, pay—all that stuff is going to be exponentially
greater than the people who don't.

So I can point to instances where I've had those things. Do I
represent the best and brightest of Lakota people? Not even close. I
just had a few advantages. There are tons of other people who with
few advantages can do great things. And that has to be a big part
of my life, our life—to give people those same advantages and to
support them and watch them grow and see what they become, see
what they do.

But if all you're doing is leaving, going off and getting educated
and spending the rest of your career and life in the outside world,
that's not going to help us. You have to instill the values of the Lakota
identity in people. That's actually going to give them the resilience
and the drive to perform at a high level and the drive to come back.
Then we have to create opportunities for them to come home and to
welcome them with open arms.

---

32. The Oceti Sakowin is composed of seven bands, which are further organized
into sub-bands and extended family clusters.

GERALDINE MANSON

SNUNEYMUXW FIRST NATION
ELDER IN RESIDENCE
BORN IN: 1952, Campbell River, British Columbia
INTERVIEWED IN: Snuneymuxw First Nation

Geraldine is elder in residence at the Nanaimo campus of Vancouver Island University (VIU), a position now common at postsecondary schools in Canada and some colleges in the United States. In this role, she promotes Indigenous ethics, values, and knowledge at VIU, and helps to support and retain Native students by offering them traditional knowledge and spiritual guidance. I had planned to meet Geraldine at VIU, but she had been in and out of the hospital twice over the preceding two weeks with kidney and lung infections. She was kind enough to meet with me anyway, at her home on Nanaimo Reserve 1. The reserve consists of a handful of city blocks between the river, the railroad tracks, and

the main highway that intersects Nanaimo. Geraldine's house, built in
1965, sits between the train tracks and the river.

The Snuneymuxw are Coast Salish people, with territory on Vancou-
ver Island's East Coast, the Gulf Islands, and the Fraser River in British
Columbia, Canada. The Snuneymuxw currently live on the smallest re-
serve land base per capita of any First Nation in the province. The lack
of land is a result of violations of the Douglas Treaty of 1854, which the
British colony of Vancouver Island entered into to access the rich coal de-
posits in Snuneymuxw territory.[1] This has created intense economic and
social burdens on the nation, in addition to a chronic housing shortage.
About two-thirds of its population of close to 1,700 live away from home
because it is impossible to make a livelihood on such a small reserve.

We sat in Geraldine's living room, where she occupied a blue recliner
chair with a fleece blanket tucked around her legs. She summoned a lot of
energy and sipped coffee as she told her story. Geraldine was forced to be
at residential schools from age six through twelve and was placed in the
foster care system afterwards. Geraldine told me how she met her husband
on visits home to see her sister, and said she found strength and healing by
sharing her story with her mother-in-law, who created community around
her. Geraldine also credits her mother-in-law with making her a "student
of learning how to love again," something she recognized had been lost to
her in residential school. Today Geraldine keeps her loved ones close. As
she spoke, she referred to the large photographs of her friends and family
hanging on the room's walls. Geraldine opened our conversation with her
traditional greeting:

Au si:em s'ulxwe:n, si:em siyeyu; si:em mustimuxw
E:nthe pe C'tasi:a, Snuneymuxw
Uy' kwunus si lumtula
Hay ce:p qa kwuns ulup skaqip tu Snuneymuxw tumuxw a nu
kweyul

---

1. Sir James Douglas, the Hudson's Bay Company's chief factor, negotiated fourteen treaties with Vancouver Island First Nations from 1850 to 1854. For more on
the Douglas Treaties, see the essays and timeline in the appendix.

My name is C'tasi:a from Snuneymuxw
I am happy to see you
Thank you for gathering here today on traditional lands of
Snuneymuxw

C'tasi:a, my traditional name, was given to me in 1990, and it belongs to my great-grandmother, Jenny Wyse of Snuneymuxw. It means one who holds knowledge, one who holds the wisdom. I've been given the opportunity to share the knowledge I hold, as it's not for me to keep; it's for those who are interested in understanding who we are as people. This knowledge I have was given to me by my dear elders who have mentored me over the years.

There is a quote that I hold dear to my heart: "From the mountains, to the rivers, to the oceans, and back to the land." All the resources that each component holds are so important to understand. The name of each area of our traditional land has meaning. Mount Benson, which we call "Te'tuxwtun," means "grandmother" of all mountains. To the north of us, Neck Point, Ska'lum to Departure Bay, is known as "Stililup," meaning "deep water." Another place where we hold traditional land, where we once lived, is Gabriola Island. At Boat Harbor, the land tells a story through the archaeological sites that lay beneath the grounds where our ancestors once lived and left evidence of those lives. Every area has meaning. *From the mountains, to the rivers, to the oceans, and back to the land.*

INDIAN AGENTS CAME AND TOOK US AWAY

I don't really know too much about my parents because I was at residential school from age six to twelve, first at Alberni Indian Residential School, then at St. Michael's in Alert Bay.[2] Some of my first

2. Alberni Indian Residential School was opened by the Presbyterian Church in 1890. In 1995, one-time supervisor Arthur Henry Plint was sentenced to eleven years in jail following charges of abuse by thirty former students. St. Michael's Indian Residential School, also known as Alert Bay Indian Residential School, was

memories are of being strapped, being abused. Other things I remember: being in a lineup, looking at other girls and seeing that we all had the same beautiful locks, looking up at a black-and-white TV, eating hard biscuits that we got as a snack, getting our hair cut so short. I remember sitting on the steps crying when my mother first left.

One day, after I'd moved to St. Michael's, we got to go on a picnic on the beach nearby. I was ten. I heard my name being called, and I saw that it was my younger sister, Florence. I didn't even know I had siblings in Alert Bay.[3] Florence was seven, and she was crying. She told me her story of being abused in foster care and we planned to run away. So we hid. Once it got dark, we planned to swim from Alert Bay to an island where we'd seen lights. After realizing it was too far, we hid again, but we saw flashlights coming; we got caught by the supervisors of my dorm. We didn't see each other again until we were allowed to come home, when I was twelve, a year and a half later. But from that moment on we got badly punished. Those were not good days.

I was allowed to come home to Nanaimo in 1965, right after I got out of St. Michael's residential school, when I was twelve. I think they were transitioning all of us out since St. Michael's was closing down.

We came home on a weekend—we got to see our mother for probably two days. My mother only had a two-bedroom house. Four of us had returned—Vera, Sonny, me, and Henry—and she already had my younger brother and sister with her. So there would have been seven of us living in a two-bedroom house, and that wasn't ac-

the largest of those operated by the Anglican Church of Canada from 1929 to 1975. See the glossary and appendix essay 2 for more on residential schools and their intergenerational impact on Native family systems.

3. Geraldine has seven living siblings: Teresa, Marge, Wayne, Orville, Sonny, Florence, and Gloria. Six others, Tessie, Vera, Henry, Gary, Darrel, and Ronnie, are deceased.

ceptable. Our parents had separated. And then that Monday, Indian agents came and took us away, put us into foster homes.[4] They didn't say why we were being placed in homes. I guess my mom was being monitored by the welfare people and they felt she wasn't capable of looking after us yet.

Non-Indigenous child welfare authorities began removing Indigenous children from their homes and communities long before the 1960s, but a planned, systemic effort to apprehend Indigenous kids, now known as the Sixties Scoop, was officially enacted in 1965.[5] The practice was maintained through the 1970s and into the '80s. Families that were judged "insufficient" in some way by white social workers lost their children to the system instead of receiving support to care for them. These alleged insufficiencies included homes in which children shared beds and those in which families lived on a traditional diet of dried meat and berries and had no refrigerator.

I remember very clearly the day we got put into the station wagon. The Indian agents pulled into a Dairy Queen to get us ice cream. That's how they had gotten us into the vehicle, because they were going to buy us ice cream. And I told my siblings, "Let's run, I'm gonna run. I'm not going to a foster home, I'm running away." No one would run with me. But I ran. Eventually they caught up to me. They put me somewhere—I don't remember where—into another foster home. And again, that evening I climbed out the window, ran again. This time they put me in jail overnight. And

---

4. Throughout the nineteenth and much of the twentieth century, the Indian Act mandated that decision-making rights and obligations of First Nations people be removed and placed with the federal government minister responsible for them, and Indian agents were tasked with implementing this policy on reserves. For more on the foster care system as a continuation of historical trauma, see appendix essay 2.

5. *Apprehension* is the official term used in Canada for the removal of children from their homes by child protection agencies.

from jail they sent me all the way over to a foster home in Chilliwack, on a farm.[6]

My brother Ronnie was two years older than me and he would write to me, but I stopped getting any mail from him shortly after I moved to that home. I kept asking the foster parents why I wasn't getting his letters. And finally, after church one Sunday, they told me to sit down, and I found out that he'd passed away. I ran into the bathroom and locked the doors. They asked what I was doing in there, and I don't know why, but I plugged all the windows and everything. I turned the electric heat on. I turned the hot water on. Everything that was hot I turned on. Heat was going to help me die. When I was a little girl—one of my brothers, Gary, at age two, fell asleep by the wood stove and died. I thought he'd been killed by heat. So that's what I was trying to do. And the foster parents got upset with me. Sent me to my room. And that was the end of that.

I told the foster mom I was going to run. So I guess she got a hold of the Indian agent and got me moved, from Chilliwack to Abbotsford, to another foster home.[7] It was even worse. I got placed in a foster home that was very religious. Before I ate anything, I had to pray. They gave me a little Bible to pray all the time. It was a very racist town. I was always bullied. I'd had enough, so one day, when the older daughter and I got into an argument, I pulled the phone out of the wall and the police ended up there. I told them, "I just want to go home, back to the island." They said, "We can work at it, to get you back home, but you have to settle down."

The Ministry of Children and Family Development did find a foster home for me on the island, with the McNeils. That was the kindest foster home I was ever in. They put me in John Barsby

---

6. Chilliwack is 182 kilometers east of Nanaimo, on mainland British Columbia.

7. The two towns are about thirty-four kilometers apart.

School.[8] I was thirteen. Again, I was always defending myself at school, getting into fights with white girls. They were just bullies, and me, being angry, I wouldn't allow anybody to bully me or the other girls that were picked on. I found myself stepping in and protecting them. I felt that everybody was against me.

A year later, after I finished grade eight, I got expelled. So the foster parents started to homeschool me. They never punished me or lectured me. One day, I got caught smoking, and they didn't punish me. They just explained why I wasn't supposed to be smoking. They went out of their way to include me in their space. Then one day, Mr. McNeil told me they were leaving for Gold River, but I didn't want to go, I couldn't go, it was just too far. Nanaimo was where I wanted to be. So I had to move to another foster home. And that seemed to be okay for a while. But the next foster father was trying to touch me, to do things. I found him not to be trusted.

THE APPLE OF MY EYE

While I was in foster care, there were a couple of times that I was able to come home in the summer. I'd stay with my oldest sister, Vera. She lived in Cedar, on a farm.[9] This was when I met Butch Manson from Snuneymuxw First Nation. I was thirteen, and he was a year older. At the time, Butch was going out with my cousin, Gloria, who lived on the reserve. He had a best friend, Carl. Gloria asked me to go on a double date with them one weekend. She said, "You need to come and go out with Carl." So that's what I did. Butch's house was next door to my cousin's—it was an old house. That's where we partied, had good old music. Carl was too short, and I wasn't into dating him. But that weekend, I guess Butch and I caught each other's eye. And after a while, I went to his home. It

---

8. John Barsby Community School, in the city of Nanaimo, serves students grades eight through twelve.

9. Cedar is about 8.5 kilometers southeast of Snuneymuxw.

was so warm and family oriented. That's when he said, "I want to ask you seven words."

I said, "You do? Yeah, okay."

"Will you be my girlfriend?"

"Oh. 'Will, you, be, my, girlfriend'—that's not seven words."

"Well, okay. But will you?"

"Okay."

So I went running over to Gloria's house. "Guess what? Butch asked me to be his girlfriend." She started crying right away, and I just looked at her. I said, "I'll see you later." Well, golly gee, I was only thirteen. And that night, Elvis's song, "One Night," was playing. That song became my song forever and ever. Butch and I started as just a summer thing; I had to go back into foster care. But we've been together ever since. I call him the apple of my eye.

I met his mother that year too. I told her my story of being in residential school and foster care, all the things that I've been through. If it wasn't for her, listening to the journey that I'd been through—right from residential school, the troubles, the abuse, the sexual abuse, to my foster home, and to the loss—I don't know where I would be.

"SIGN THIS PAPER TO PUT HIM UP FOR ADOPTION"

When I was only about fifteen and a half, I got sick. I was throwing up, nauseous. So I told Butch's mother, "I'm not feeling well." She brought me to the doctor. I found out I was pregnant. And I said, "I can't be. I don't know how that would happen." The doctor asked, "You have a boyfriend?" I said, "Yeah." He asked, "Do you have sex?" I said, "What's that? I thought you get pregnant by French kissing, not that way!" That's how naïve I was.

So I went back into the waiting room, and I told Butch's mother what happened. I said, "I didn't know you got pregnant that way." She just started laughing and said, "Oh, you've got lots to learn." She didn't get mad or anything. She added, "And we have lots to teach." So I stayed at the foster home till it was time to have the baby.

During this period, many Indigenous women reported pressure by nurses, doctors, and social workers to give up custody of their children at birth. Some of these officials thought that if the children were apprehended early enough, they wouldn't be marked as Indigenous people. Like the residential school system that preceded it, the Sixties Scoop was part of a wide-ranging plan to disrupt Indigenous lifeways on traditional territories and to assimilate Indigenous people into the Canadian mainstream.

Going into labor, I remember the pain, I remember screaming. And then when it was over, they put me into the room and the nurse came in and she said, "You need to sign these papers to verify you're the mother of your son. And I would encourage you to sign this paper to put him up for adoption."

I said, "I'm not putting him up for adoption."

"Well, I encourage you to."

"No, I want to see my son. I want my son. I need to learn how to breastfeed him."

"I talked to the doctor about it."

"No. I want to talk to the doctor, not you. I'm not giving my son up for adoption."

I got to see Derrick for a little while. But I couldn't take him home with me. The ministry put him into another home. I cried and I cried. And I said, "Why can't I take him home, to my foster home? He's my son." Oh, I fought and cried.

They put me into another foster home, and this got me even angrier, more upset. I ran away to Butch's home. Our son was living in a foster home uptown. We got to go and see him every two weeks for about an hour. That was ridiculous. An hour wasn't enough. Eventually, Butch's parents got custody of me, and then it took another year for my mother-in-law to get Derrick back. And because they got custody of me, we could stay with them. That's how I got out of foster care.

Derrick's aunts, my sisters-in-law, stepped in to help, and they are the ones who really nurtured him. In the old days, the grand-mother and the aunties would take over and show a new mother the teachings related to raising a child. And they really did that for me. They nurtured my son and at the same time, I learned how to be a mother. A year later, in November, we had our daughter, Tina Marie. My third child, Darren, came two years later.

They taught me how to be with my babies. You know, it's twenty-four-seven being a parent. You've got to be patient with them. You've got to learn about the different types of whining. The food that you give them is different from what we eat. And because I was a residential-school survivor, I didn't know how to bond, so I had to learn bonding all over again, being loving and nurturing. I had to be a student of learning how to love. My mother-in-law would talk to me about when she was in residential school—about not being loved, and not being hugged, and not having birthday parties and all of that. We didn't have that in our days when we were in residen-tial school. And not having those opportunities, not being hugged and loved, I had to learn to be patient with my children. I couldn't be stern with them like, "Get up, make your bed. Do this." I was told, "Get up, make your bed. Make it perfect." If it wasn't perfect, my bed was stripped. I had to learn it was okay for them not to make their beds. It's validating, the love, saying, "I love you. Have a good day." Forgiving them when they did wrong and not being harsh with them. I never spanked my children once when they were growing up, not once. All the things that I was told when I was in residential school, I had to erase all that, decolonize my mind and nurture the loving mother.

I remember, once, Butch and I were arguing. I ran over and told my mother-in-law, "He's at it again!" She said, "You get over there and fill that tub up and you guys go back to back! And don't you get out of that tub until you settle it!" I'd come home and fill up the tub and say to Butch, "Mom says we gotta get into the tub back to back and settle it!" Back to back so he wouldn't be able to dominate the conversation and I wouldn't be able to cry to get out of it. So we had to talk through it. Where did the argument begin? And why? We did that. Never again did we argue like that. We were blessed to have her.

IN MY HEART

When I was seventeen, Butch's mother introduced me to the elder's circle. With the support of my mother-in-law and the elders, I was also going to Malaspina College, to get the other education I needed. They said you need to walk in both worlds so it's time to go back and get that *qwalnitum* education.[10] I did my upgrading. I did courses as a clerk-typist, in medical office assisting, hairdressing, and long-term care—everything I could get into my pockets.

I went to school during the day and in the evening I went to the elder circle. I started getting the traditional knowledge, learning about how the elders got their teachings: how they lived; how they grew up; all about the land. I learned everything about our traditional territory: what was in it, the place names, the language, the songs they instilled in here, in my heart.

One evening I went to them and said, "Guess what? I got accepted to a practical nursing program." My mother-in-law got up, and she said, "No. No more courses. We need you here to continue learning from us. To continue learning the language. To be our eyes and voice and legs when we are no longer. Be with us."

So I told my husband what had happened, and he said, "It's up to you what to do." I thought about all the things my mother-in-law did for me, and for us, how she got me out of foster care and every-

---

10. *Qwalnitum* means "white."

thing that she taught us, and the next evening I went back. I said, "I'm here." And that's how my journey began.

There were six elders who were a part of that journey. I was mentored by them. One day, one of the old men, Anderson Tommy, Situxwuluq, turned to me. "Time for you to sober up now," he said. I just nodded because I didn't know what he meant. In my mind I'm thinking, *How did they know I was out last night?* So Situxwuluq kind of smiles at me. And Auntie Ellen White says, "You know what he means, honey? He means for your mind to sober up. He means that your mind needs to remember everything we're telling you because you're the only one here. Everything that you learn from us today, you have to keep it in here, in your mind." I said, "Oh gosh! I can do that." And old man Situxwuluq says, "I bet I know what you were thinking. We were young once too, you know. We wouldn't tell you to stop that." And they all start laughing.

I learned how everything evolved. We'd go learn about the plants, going back to where they were growing. We'd learn about all the place names, how every place name is attached to meaning; how the old ancestors gave a name to a certain place for a reason. There are over sixty place names here within our traditional territory. And all communities use their place names to mark the invisible boundaries within their community, to show where they hunted and fished and where their spiritual sites are.

When we went to Gabriola, to the petroglyph sites, they would tell me the meaning of those images, the meaning pertaining to our longhouse culture.[11] Some are meant to act as a compass. The image could be of the river, or it could be of the mountain. On a journey, it tells you where to go. And some of the images tell you a story of

---

11. There are more than seventy known petroglyphs on Gabriola and neighboring islands. The petroglyphs are sacred carvings on large sandstone bedrock or boulders that record the history of the Snuneymuxw people. The longhouse is a long and comparatively narrow traditional dwelling; various types were built by different peoples throughout Indigenous North America.

hunting or fishing. There are so many petroglyphs within our traditional territory, and some of the images are the same in other communities, so that shows us that those peoples traveled.

And they taught me stories, like about Haals, who was a creator, a powerful individual back in his time. He had an argument with Thuxwum, who had the power of the wind, and Haals turned Thuxwum into stone. People say, "Oh, here comes Haals, better not get him angry because he's gonna turn you to stone." But if you know how to awaken Thuxwum, you can make the wind come or calm down. These stories are what the old people wanted to teach me. They said, "You have to know what we give you and have it in your heart." To give to those who are struggling. To keep telling them there is light.

We don't have our old people to embrace this need. I see us as the young elders who have witnessed the old people. We are the ones who have to step up to the plate. I was their shadow. And each one of them said, "We see something in you. The passion, the light. You may have been damaged. But there was also something in you that we're going to give you back."

My mother had moved from Nanaimo to Vancouver to Pigeon Park, into a one-bedroom house. My husband and I went over to visit her when I was nineteen. She had a hot plate in there and she boiled us each a hotdog. We went to a store and I remember my mother looking at a dress. And I was looking at something else. I should've bought her the dress, but I bought something for myself instead. I regretted that. She went out of her way, helped me, boiled us her last wieners.

We didn't keep in touch with each other much because she didn't have a way to contact us. And she didn't come over to Nanaimo often. She was going to come home for Christmas the year my daughter was born, but she passed away the evening of December 23. She fell and had an aneurysm.

IT'S LIKE BEGGING FOR FUNDING, FOR LANGUAGE, FOR A CULTURE

I started working for the band back in the early seventies as a home-maker. We had elders in the community and homemakers would go in and take care of them. We had housekeeping duties, cooking or cleaning their homes. And then when I got more training, I became the coordinator; I oversaw the homemaking program. From there, I went on to become the coordinator of the elders' program as a whole. When the comprehensive treaty process got up and running in 2000, I became the cultural coordinator of the treaty program.[12] My responsibilities were to liaise with the elders and do the cultural history component: bringing the elders together and hearing the history of the traditional territories from them, getting their input.

In 2008, Auntie Ellen, who worked as the elder in residence at Vancouver Island University, and who was still mentoring me, was ready to retire. She said, "You need to come up here. Take my place." I said, "Oh, Auntie, I work for the band."[13] Auntie said, "Well, you could work there part time and come up here part time." My boss said, "Yeah, you can do that." And then in 2012, I got an offer to work at VIU full time. The elders laughed and said, "Well, it's time for you to move up there. Start helping the students. We think you're ready to go." To say goodbye they hosted a huge luncheon for me, and I became elder in residence to take care of our students at VIU.

---

12. Historic treaties address only some Aboriginal rights to land throughout Canada. Land and resource-related negotiations are ongoing in parts of Canada where treaties were never signed. Since 1975, Indigenous groups have signed twenty-five new treaties with Canada, called "modern treaties" or "comprehensive land claim agreements."

13. In Canada, an Indian band, or First Nations band, is the unit of government for peoples subject to the Indian Act. Each First Nation is represented by a band council. For more on bands, see the glossary.

The needs of the students range from general support to wanting to learn about their own identity, their customs, or culture, to connect with it. There are over sixteen hundred First Nation students at the three different university campuses: Powell River, Cowichan, and Nanaimo. We have Inuit, Métis, and other First Nation students attending our school.

Today, five days a week, I co-teach the Pathways program, which includes all First Nations students from the Adult Basic Education program. I go into their classes and teach history and talk about who we are as First Nations people. We take them on field trips. I go into the nursing program and to the classes on early childhood education, child and youth care, home care aid. If they're going to work within our community, how should they prepare for it? If they're going to go into a facility or into the hospital, they need to know the importance of protocol when working with a First Nations individual, whether that's a young mom or an elder.

I get invited to speak to white neighbors who want to find out how they can help our community. I say, "You can help by just being here, understanding who we are, and understanding our history, where our land base is." Before the Europeans arrived, we had ninety-eight thousand hectares of land. We survived by using the resources of the land and waters. Back in the 1850s, one of our members went to Victoria to a blacksmith shop and saw this blacksmith working over a fire of black rock. And he said, "Oh, I have a lot of that rock. We have that in our villages," which caught this man's attention immediately. "Where's your village?" he asked. So he told him where his village was, and this blacksmith went and told James Douglas. Douglas came to our community and, lo and behold, the Hudson's Bay Company started exploring, looking for coal here. Over thirty sites were marked for coal within our traditional territory.

Today we have probably 266 hectares of land within the four reserves that we live on. We're a Douglas Treaty Nation. So we have a right to go after the Canadian government for not protecting our land, for not protecting our rights. Our nation still has, I think, eight more claims under the Douglas Treaty. Because we are urban and the land base that's available around here is very minimal, we're after the land instead of compensation in dollars. We can use the land for economic development and housing. We're slowly being squished, because the land around us is now owned by other people. What you see on the shoreline, on Eaton Street, and on Center Street, that's all we have. If you ride along Center Street, you can see the poverty in some of the yards. A high percentage of our people are on social assistance.

My house is old. It was built in 1965, I think. We've been waiting to build a new house for ten years now. We can't get our house built because the infrastructure needs updating. The federal government has to upgrade the sewer along the shore. And they can't upgrade the sewer because the Department of Indian Affairs hasn't given the funding to do so yet. It's all got to do with funding. Just look how long it took Number Two Reserve to get water hooked up.[14] It took years.

Our Snuneymuxw population is around two thousand. And with Canada being the larger nation, it's frustrating, because we're governed through funding that is necessary for our nation to survive. It's like begging for funding, for language, for a culture. We wouldn't have lost our culture, especially our language, if it wasn't for the residential school system. We wouldn't be losing our members to addictions if it wasn't for Canada, if it wasn't for the Europeans coming and taking our land, if we weren't stuck on reserves, and if we'd been left alone to do what we wanted to do in the beginning. I recall a royal statement that said, *You will be taken care of. You won't be starving.*

---

14. In 1992, groundwater contamination was found on No. 2 Reserve, its wells were closed, and for twenty years the community was reliant upon water trucks to meet its daily needs. In 2010, a deal was made in which the city of Nanaimo would provide water to the reserve as long as the Snuneymuxw paid the $500,000 (Canadian) cost of building the water infrastructure necessary to return potable water to the community.

We will look after you.[15] Wow, for gosh sakes, is this what it means to be taken care of? Mothers and grandparents burying their young because of addiction? We've lost how many now through suicide?

About a month ago, I received papers from my lawyer from the Sixties Scoop Network.[16]

I believe now the reason I was asked to put my first son up for adoption was because they thought that my foster father might have caused that pregnancy. And that's why they moved me to a new home after Derrick's birth. I also learned more about my parents from this paperwork. My dad was twenty-six years old when I was born, and my mother was only twenty-four. We ended up in residential school because the Indian agent felt that with my father away fishing a lot, my mother couldn't care for all of us, didn't have enough money for all of us.

After going through these papers, I reflected on my mother's life. She went backwards, stayed in that one room. The Canadian government took her life away from her, took her spirit when they could have helped her, gotten her a bigger house, and given us all back to her.

And the Canadian government is still dictating to us! Our leadership, they're still being dictated to. I get so frustrated because the Canadian government is racist. Our Indian Act, it's racist.[17] Our leaders had no input into it. That's racist. "Truth and reconciliation,"

---

15. Geraldine is referring to the Royal Proclamation of 1763. In that document, King George III recognized that Indigenous peoples had rights to the lands they occupied and promised to protect them.

16. The Sixties Scoop Network, or National Indigenous Survivors of Child Welfare Network, is a national not-for-profit organization that provides information and support to survivors of the Sixties Scoop. The "Sixties Scoop" refers to the decades-long practice of adopting First Nations / Métis children out of their communities without the consent of their families or bands. For more on the Sixties Scoop, see the timeline.

17. Since Canada was founded in 1867, its federal government has been responsible for Aboriginal affairs. The Indian Act, enacted in 1876, gives the government

they say. I say, "They know where they can shove that." I don't dwell on how I was harmed, but I reflect on it.

I think about my mother, and I think about my life as a child, the role I play now today and the teachings up here, what I do, all the projects I've done. What the elders have given me—the traditional knowledge, the language, the songs they instilled in my heart—are now being spread across campus to the sixteen hundred First Nations students at our school.

---

jurisdiction over many aspects of Aboriginal life including Indian status, land, resources, education, and band administration.

ROBERT ORNELAS

LIPAN APACHE / YSLETA DEL SUR PUEBLO
RETIRED SUBSTANCE ABUSE COUNSELOR
BORN IN: 1951, Long Beach, California
INTERVIEWED IN: New York, New York

Robert lives on the Upper West Side of Manhattan, in a small apartment a few blocks west of Central Park, where he has lived for forty years. He grew up in California, and his work with the ballet brought him to New York City. I met Robert several times, and each time, he occupied a chair by the windows at the front of his home. A small television mounted on the wall opposite him broadcast twenty-four-hour news and his Pomeranian, Baba, sat at his feet or on his lap.

As a child, Robert says, he didn't really know what Indians were. He describes the shame he felt about being an Indian as a kid, how he believes that shame shaped his early life's trajectory, and how he sought out healing through knowledge—about North America's settler-colonial

95

practices and legacies—and community. He especially found community in the Sun Dance, a healing ceremony primarily practiced by Indigenous people of the Plains cultures, and in the recovery movement, with Alcoholics Anonymous and Native sobriety groups.

On each of my visits, Robert sat surrounded by plastic tackle boxes full of beads. Robert started beading when he was in the hospital recovering from back surgery in 2014. He said, "Every year I make maybe fifty to a hundred strands of beads for the Sun Dance ceremony. It's a kind of a meditation for me, to make everything with intent. And a lot of that comes from getting sober too—beading is like practicing making choices."

NEVER ANY TALK ABOUT BEING NATIVE

Ornelas is a Spanish surname. My great-grandfather adopted that name because at that time, people understood that you would be treated better as a Mexican, with a Spanish name, than you would as an Indian. The Texas Rangers killed Natives of my great-grandfather's generation for a bounty as part of state law enforcement.[1] What they subjected Native people to was tantamount to terrorism; they were really brutal to Indians.

My father is from El Paso, by way of San Antonio. He's Lipan.[2] My dad was in denial about his Native-ness. He never talked about it. He was so paranoid. My mother was also from El Paso, and her parents were Mission Indians.[3] There's a mission in El Paso, in Ysleta. During the Pueblo revolt, the Pueblo kicked the Spanish out, and

---

1. The Texas Rangers were a law enforcement agency founded in 1823. During the Texas Revolution, they established themselves as the guardians of the Texas frontier, principally against Native Americans.

2. Lipan Apache are Southern Athabaskan people who live mostly throughout the US Southwest today.

3. Mission Indians were Indians of the Southern and Central California coast whom Spanish Franciscans and soldiers forcibly removed from their traditional homelands to live and work at twenty-one missions established between 1769 and 1823.

then the Spanish kidnapped a bunch of Indians and built a mission there. My mom's upbringing was sort of Catholic, but no Indian completely submits to a religion, so her foundation was a combination of Catholic belief and Indian storytelling.

My grandfather on my mother's side was one of my favorite people when I was a kid. He spoke Spanish mostly. When my mom was sort of sick of us, she'd send me over to stay with him overnight. And he'd watch basketball with me, even though he didn't understand it. He'd sit up with me until eleven at night, and he'd give me coffee with a little bit of milk in it. I felt really safe being around him. My father's parents had more armor. The suffering that they'd survived made them kind of afraid. In that part of the family, colonialism had made them believe that they weren't good enough.[4]

My mother was beautiful, petite. She looked like a movie star with dark hair. My parents used to dance. She was a good dancer. Men were attracted to her, and my father was very afraid of losing her. I think my father was kind of clingy, so that was difficult. He couldn't keep up with her; I know he tried to as much as he could.

My older sister, Gloria, my younger brother, Richard, the baby, Arthur, and I lived with my parents in Watts, in South-Central LA. And I was a mama's boy. When my mother would make tortillas, I remember hanging onto her dress or apron. My dad was a longshoreman. My mother worked all day trying to keep the household running. We didn't have the best clothing, but we didn't go to bed hungry. We didn't know that we were poor until kids started teasing us at school.

When we'd come home from school and had been mistreated—a teacher had called us stupid—our parents told us not to engage. "Don't get involved in that; you can't do anything about that." We learned not to call attention to ourselves. In our neighborhood, Chicano studies was kind of a big deal and Black people were being beaten down and we were just hiding. This was in 1960. There was never any talk about

---

4. For more on Indigenous perspectives of historical trauma, see appendix essay 2.

being Native. One of the things I was told was, "You can make yourself invisible." That was my major practice. That's what my grandmother would tell us, in a story of shapeshifting, and I took it as a literal thing.

The result of our family being hated was that we learned to hate ourselves. The biggest lie is that one person matters more than another. That lie is so deeply, deeply ingrained. And that's affected our people. It affected my particular family in the belief that they don't matter.

I'D FOUND THE PERFECT REMEDY
FOR ALL MY FEELINGS

My siblings and I found out about my parents divorcing when I was eight years old. My mother hadn't been at the house for weeks. My parents took us to my paternal grandparents' house. Once we got there, my dad broke down in tears and begged my mom not to leave. My sister and I were sitting there. When they got divorced, that really splintered the family completely. It was devastating. My mom couldn't take all of us, so she took the two younger ones, and Gloria and I stayed with my dad.

That same year, I found alcohol. The first time, I was with the sixteen-year-old kids down the block, and I drank four quarts of beer. I wound up going home in my underwear, just my underwear, because I had thrown up on myself, so the teenagers had to water me down. I remember having this incredibly bad hangover, and my dad gave me orange juice, Alka-Seltzer, and 7Up. He knew what to do for a hangover. The next day he didn't yell at me; he wasn't mean about it or anything. I'd found the perfect remedy for all my feelings.

Growing up in Watts, we felt unsafe because everywhere we went, we were either being looked down upon or being told what to do. The gangs were very severe. The police were very hostile to brown people, and we felt that hostility. We didn't think that we could succeed. We were considered non-persons. In order to survive,

I had to join a gang—the Little Sinners—when I was about ten. The Little Sinners were just a group of brown kids. One of them had gotten beaten up, and so they started gathering friends as protection. It became obvious to me that it was necessary to do. The gangs that we chose to be in were the brown gangs of course. There weren't enough Indigenous kids for us to have our own gang.

I was willing to be the first one in for a fight. And as the first one in, people notice you, so I was made president and I could relax after that. I didn't have to prove myself over and over and over. It made me somewhat respected and I didn't get tested as much.

GOING FROM BOYS TO MEN

The Little Sinners were just neighborhood kids who got together on a regular basis. We all aspired to be in the Big Sinners. They were sixteen-year-old kids, so they were like adults to us. The Big Sinners lived ten doors down from me, so I'd skip school to go over there and drink wine and watch them make out and stuff. I started hanging out with the Big Sinners when I was twelve. They wanted me to be their lookout. They knew that at lunchtime, the guy at the neighborhood hardware store counter where the guns were stored would leave. The Big Sinners snuck in and picked the lock, and they stole about sixteen guns. I got caught by the police. I didn't say anything. I didn't snitch. They sent me to YA, the California Youth Authority, which was for sixteen-year-old kids.[5] They sent me there on a short "scare him straight" program. It's against the law to send someone so young, but they would experiment with brown people. When you're twelve and you're in with sixteen-year-olds, that's like going from boys to men.

I was there for two weeks. The guards don't keep watch, and I got jumped every day and beaten up. I got beaten up until the guys

---

5. The California Youth Authority is now called the Division of Juvenile Justice.

beating me up got tired. That really scared me; they beat the fight out of me basically. I realized that I couldn't use my fists to get out of situations. That was also the time the Crips came to the neighborhood. They came six thousand strong, and with guns, because it became about drugs. And from that experience of being in YA, I decided that I was a coward. The next time I was cornered, I was going to get a gun. If I shot that person, and went back to jail, I was going to stick the knife up somebody when they tried to make me do something, and then I was going to be in it for life.

So when I got out of YA, I did what I'd never imagined—I didn't even know it was possible to do. I really didn't. I decided to leave the gangs. At that time, it wasn't blood in, blood out. They were allowed to jump you out for a year.[6] Every time they see you, they can jump you, your own guys. They jumped me three times in one month and that was it. After that they left me alone.

Because I still had this sort of soul sickness, this sadness in me, I'd drink every weekend. Me and my friend Jimmy, another Indian guy, would steal so much alcohol from this store that the owner said, "Listen, if you come to the back of the store at midnight, I'll sell it to you." I'd drink in an area with just Jimmy and a couple of friends. I'd make a big splash, and then I'd go and drink by myself. I was very good at hiding it. I got caught stealing something at a store when I was about twelve, and my father was so upset with me that he punched me, as if I was an adult. The next day I had a black eye. When I saw him, I saw how brokenhearted he was. I decided, *I'm not going to mess up*. Later, when I was drinking, I'd call him up and say, "I'm spending the night with the neighbors." He didn't want to know what I was doing, he just wanted to know I was okay. I came and went as I chose. I'd hitchhike to Northern California and be gone for three or four days. I didn't really hear from my mom during that time.

---

6. "Blood in, blood out" refers to a common gang initiation ritual of having to kill someone to join and not being able to leave unless by death. To "jump in or out" is to withstand a beating in order to join or leave.

A part of the soul sickness for me was being ashamed of who I was. The cousins I met on my father's side were also very unaware of our culture. They never talked about being Native either. At the time, during the seventies, what we were being taught about Indians was so minimal and so negative. In school, they weren't teaching us anything about Indigenous people or history. We were taught Indians were savages, that we were wiped out. When I was growing up, Native people were really sort of hidden. We had no collective voice so there was no reason to say you were Native; there was no sense of pride. We didn't want to be César Chávez. We didn't have any allegiance to the Black movement. And we were way behind on creating any kind of civil rights movement for our people. So I didn't have any connection with Indian people who accepted being Indian and lived their lives as Indians. I knew that I'd been taught not to talk about it, not to explore it, and not to even acknowledge it. I knew that something was missing.

The summer when I was thirteen, my aunt came to visit and she took me to Arizona for a month. They lived on a Navajo ranch—her husband was Navajo—and I started to learn more about Native people from them. When I left my environment and there wasn't that pressure of surviving the violence in my neighborhood, the impact of my family history became noticeable to me. With those cousins in Arizona, I started to become curious about where I really belonged and who my people were.

I WAS IN HIDING

When I was about fifteen, I got recruited to a school that had a very good high school football team. My father moved us to that neighborhood, Carson, so that I could attend.[7] But by my senior year of high school, I stopped playing football. My thing was to hang out at Denny's and write really bad poetry. I was in hiding, trying not to

---

7. Carson is a city in Los Angeles County, about ten miles south of Watts.

have interactions, trying to be self-reflective. But I went to a perfor-
mance of Patty McBride and Edward Villella, and I thought it was
the most incredible thing I'd ever seen.[8] He was incredibly athletic,
and she was incredibly beautiful. It was like a dream world, and I
was like, *Wow!* I'd never seen anything like that before. The beauty
really struck me. It was so satisfying to be engrossed in something
beautiful. And I started to wonder, what other kinds of beauty am
I missing?

I went to Europe for a year right after high school when I was
seventeen and a half. I went with a one-way ticket and eighty dollars. I was trying to find my way. I wanted to be a citizen of the
world. I hadn't reckoned with my own culture or found any pride
in it yet. When I got to Europe I bought a bottle of that Johnnie
Walker Black Label and drank it that night. And then I drank my
way through the year as I followed the gringo trail: England, Ireland,
Amsterdam, France, Spain, and Italy.

I got a ticket back to New York City. After a few months, I
hitchhiked to Northern California to attend junior college. It was
very easy to get into and it cost like $160 for the year. I saw that there
were dance classes there, so I started to take them, and I got involved
with a company called Dance LA while still in college. Then I started
taking ballet classes with the Los Angeles Ballet Company. I knew
the technical director and he asked me to come work with him there.
Ultimately, I became stage manager.

The level of ballet, in terms of the artistry, in terms of what I
was being exposed to, was high. There were guest stars from the New
York City Ballet, people who just were phenomenal. I decided that
I wanted to come to New York because Mr. George Balanchine, the
director of the New York City Ballet, was probably only going to live
about five years more, and I wanted to be around him. I was enamored with the process of how ballet was created. I was a good dancer,

8. Patricia McBride and Edward Villella are legendary New York City Ballet stars.

but I had horrible feet for professional ballet. I had done everything as a dancer that I was capable of doing, but I was still in love with it. The stage manager for New York City Ballet had also come to LA a couple of times and he'd asked me to help stage manage for him while he did these little concerts. So when I was around twenty-four, I moved to New York, and I got introduced to the ballet company. I knew four people in New York City when I moved here. And that was it. All four were bartenders. They'd been dancers in LA and had moved here. At that age, that was the life for me. We were the greatest partiers on the face of the earth.

My wish was to be a stage manager here, and Ronald Bates, the NYCB stage manager, had introduced me to the head carpenter, who took my number. He said he would call me if someone didn't show up for work and that's how I got the regular job. There was a period where I worked eighty hours a week, which is really a silly competitive thing. And that particular boss was the best teacher I'd ever had, but he had very strict rules about how you can't miss work. So I had to work when he asked me to. When I was about thirty, I started to experience a lot of back pain from injuries I experienced on the job—lifting things improperly, working sixteen-hour days through light injuries, which turned into big injuries. I tried to manage it with painkillers, but I needed surgery.

THIRTY-SIX PERCOCETS A DAY

In 1995, at forty-three, I had that surgery. They had to take a bone out of my hip and put it in my back. They sent me home with two hundred long-acting morphine capsules, and that was a really bad idea because I became addicted.

I was a voracious drinker. I loved tequila. I had those four friends—they were magnificent friends, the best partiers, really the most fun you can have—and so we'd go out, but there was always a point when I wanted to go home and just drink quietly by myself.

And that was starting to happen more and more. Drinking would work for a little bit; it would quiet that soul sickness. I knew though that it wasn't working when somehow, after being out drinking in public, I would wind up in brawls. So I thought, *I'm not going to drink in public anymore.* I thought that was the answer. I'd go to work, buy two six-packs of beer, and then a bottle of tequila on my way home. And then I'd drink until I passed out and get up and go to work the next day. I did that for fifteen years. That's just really sad and brutal. Vacations? I never took them, I'd just drink.

But I hit bottom because of the pills. After the surgery, I did things that were really dangerous. I knew how to write prescriptions. I stole the scripts pad from my very good dentist friend. We had done drugs together when we were younger. He didn't turn me in even though I'd put his license in jeopardy. I was living here in this apartment, and had a hospital bed since the surgery. There were no lights in the apartment that worked except for the bathroom light. The paint on the walls was peeling because the radiator leaked, and it would fill the apartment up with smoke. There was no place to walk. The area around the bed was covered in old pizza boxes. Around the bed were also tequila bottles that, if I couldn't make it to the bathroom, I'd urinate in.

This went on for about four years. I had a moment of clarity in 1998, when I was forty-seven. I was just lying on the bed. There was stuff all over it. I pushed myself up to the coffee table, where I had an answering machine. And it had a red zero on the message indicator. I realized that no one had called me for two months. I had very good friends who—after years—I'd finally got to leave me alone. When they'd call, they didn't know I was drinking, they just thought I was okay. And I realized that I could die. I wasn't scared of dying—the idea of dying wasn't the most horrible thing, because I was slowly killing myself and I think I knew it. I thought to myself, *Okay, so you die.* But then I thought, *Well, it will take them a month or two to figure out that I'm dead. They'll have to break in because the apartment smells so bad.* I was worried about being embarrassed by the apartment and the smell rather than dying.

I was also in this situation where if I didn't take six Percocet every four hours, I would have a seizure. I was taking thirty-six Percocets a day. I said, "God, please help me." I hadn't said "God" in twenty years. I was embarrassed at the idea that God would do anything for me, because of who I was. I mean, I didn't go out and hurt other people a lot. I wasn't that kind of drunk. Most of the pain that I caused people was in not showing up, as a brother, a friend, a son. And that's a lot of pain. When you're drinking, you think, *That doesn't mean anything, because I'm not hurting them. I'm not stealing their money.* But people care about you, and they'll always care about you, whether you think they do or not. I didn't quite understand that. I was so isolated and withdrawn.

When I was a kid, I'd made statements to friends, "Man, I want to get a job where I don't have to talk to anybody or work with anybody." And I'd finally achieved that perfect isolation. There were people out there who still cared about me, but you know, they weren't reaching out anymore. They weren't expecting to hear from me or to see me. If somebody called me and wanted to have dinner, I'd say, "Oh, I'm having dinner with somebody else." Whatever. I had the ability to pull it together for twenty words, twenty-five words. Over and over and over. So when I said, "God, please help me," I put my head down and was able to sleep for more than six hours. And it was a restful sleep.

I DECIDED I DIDN'T WANT TO DIE

Before I went to sleep, I called my doctor. And I said, "Could you please put me in detox?" And he called up Beth Israel, which was at Fourteenth and First. When I woke up, like any good alcoholic or drug addict, my first thought was, *Well, maybe you overreacted.* But the physical symptoms of the detox had started—the sickness and all the sweating, it sort of got moving.

When I got to the hospital, I immediately collapsed, and they put me on an IV. It was like, that was it. All the will I had got me to that point. I became much weaker once I was in there. I couldn't lift my head up. I was just completely drained of energy. Very slowly, I started to come around. In some ways, it was enjoyable, because the fight was over. The war was over. I decided I didn't want to die.

At the time, you were allowed to stay in the detox six days, and I was only in for three or four. When I left, a counselor told me that I should go to AA meetings and gave me a meeting book.[9] I came home and I slept for twenty-four hours, and when I woke up, I had this incredible fear that had plagued me before. I didn't want to leave my house. I thought people were after me. The mental detox actually looks like a mental illness: there's paranoia, anxiety, it's hard to finish a thought. Especially when you're detoxing from opiates, the physical effects last seventy-two hours; mental lasts two weeks. At one time, there was such a thing as a thirty-day detox program; now it's just the 1 percent that gets to go to those.

I had seventy-five bottles of tequila in the apartment, and I poured them all out in the sink. That's an insane thing to do, because that would normally trigger someone to drink. I also had pills and I flushed them down the toilet. But I couldn't leave the house, so I called the counselor—she'd been in recovery for twenty years—and asked her if I could come and see her because I wanted to be committed to something. I went and she said to me, "Two blocks from here, there's a meeting. And this place has fifty-four meetings a week. So you can go there anytime you want."

I was the kind of guy who would cry through a whole meeting because I would over-identify. It was such a release for me, and when I left, I didn't know if I was going to come back—because I still had the fear. But when I did go back, the guy who was at the door, who was severely mentally ill, said, "Oh, day two!" This guy had been

---

9. Alcoholics Anonymous (AA) is an international fellowship of men and women who have had a problem with alcohol.

there for years and years and years. He talked to himself, he talked to the walls, and he was probably one of the most beloved people at this meeting. He'd keep track of five, ten people's day count; he was so helpful to so many people as they walked in the door. I sat in the second row for four years. You see the same people, and you don't know anything about them, but all you want to hear is a message of how they stay sober. I was fighting just for the next day. You know, you hear people wax eloquent and just say some of the most incredible things in Alcoholics Anonymous. And for me, it was just that realization that I didn't want to die. That was pretty much what I would say in meetings: "I don't want to die." And people would cheer because, you know, it was the truth.

Martitia and I met at an AA meeting and we got sober together. She went to all the same meetings I did and once in a while we'd talk about movies and stuff like that. We didn't have long conversations. One time I asked her if she wanted to go to a movie. She said yes.

I WAS AFRAID OF EVERYTHING

I didn't want to go back to work at the ballet because I was afraid that it was too much of a trigger, that it would bring up feelings that I couldn't control. I was one of these guys who'd cross the street if there was a liquor store. Not to mention when I first got sober, I couldn't walk the streets. I was afraid of everything. Oddly enough, those were really special days. Guys from AA would take me out to coffee, and I'd be in the corner, afraid to leave. I'd sit in the corner for three hours. Slowly, slowly, slowly, I was able to figure things out. And it's really just like learning basic skills over again. You know, "I'm out of toothpaste, what do I do?" Go buy some toothpaste. Things like that.

The way I became a counselor, at Alcoholism Council of New York, was kind of weird. They ask people who are newly sober to come to this program. And newly sober people are incredibly defiant. I was one of those. I didn't know I was defiant, I didn't know I was non-compliant. But I'd argue with the teacher about *everything*. I was like a little misbehaving twelve-year-old student. Somehow, the career aptitude tests I took in this program kept leading back to how I'm good with people, how I would be a great counselor, and my thinking was, *No! I don't want to work with people who are as big a pain in the ass as I am.* That would be karma. Somehow, I got offered a scholarship, a stipend, everything, to go to school to become a certified substance abuse counselor.

When I was in school, one of the instructors recognized that I was Native, and she said, "There's this guy, Don Coyhis, who does Native recovery," and she gave me the website address. Coyhis was having an event in Colorado, and he gave me a scholarship to go and funds for a hotel room. So I went and met him. I met magnificent people and elders, and I was just astounded at how long they could stand up and talk, the serenity and the calmness that they displayed, and how nobody ever interrupted them. And that became really attractive to me. He introduced me to other people who taught me a whole different model for how to work in recovery based on healing.

THE LOVE OF MY LIFE

I didn't really think that people could stay married and stay in love. I needed some sort of an absolute, so my belief then became that people *don't* stay in love and *don't* stay married. That's how I lived my life. Once I started drinking really heavily, I started not having relationships with women, not even friendships that were sort of sexual. So when I got sober, it was like I had to relearn how to live. I really didn't know how to function. And I didn't know how to interact. I didn't know how to have any kind of interpersonal relationships when I got sober.

But during this time Martitia and I went to the movies once a week. And we didn't really talk a lot. We didn't go out for coffee afterwards. I just sort of walked her to the bus stop or something. And I'd always make sure that there was a seat between us. I told her that I had really bad knees, because I didn't want to go beyond that. I didn't want it to be a physical relationship until I knew that it was something I could handle, or that it was something that was right. We went to sixteen movies before she kissed me. So it was very odd, and I liked that. I wasn't really smart or thoughtful, but at least I was doing the right thing in terms of my behavior.

It took five years, but I overcame the paranoia and anxiety, and Martitia and I got married in 2006. The unfair part for her is that I started having health problems right after. I had a hernia surgery; I had a knee replacement. And then I had a quadruple bypass. I had a second spinal fusion in 2014, which really took it out of me. There was no way to predict that that was going to happen. But I think she's kind of like me in her stubbornness. If you make a commitment, you don't break it, even if you're denying yourself certain pleasures.

She really is the love of my life. I mean, we're completely opposite in terms of temperament. We laugh and joke about it because people think that I'm the spiritual one. They see us together, and they always look at me with some sort of strange reverence. They think I look like some wise Indian, but she's more about spiritual action. She meditates every night. She'll say prayers in the morning when we wake up.

I went to Sun Dance for the first time when I was forty-eight. Sun Dance is a ceremony that the Lakota people practice for the people who suffer. You suffer so that the people around you don't have to suffer. It's not a prideful thing. In actuality, we should be praying that we don't have to Sun Dance anymore, praying that our people stop suffering. As a Sun Dancer, you dedicate your life to other people. You live your life with integrity. You live your life with honesty. You live your life with courage, bravery, humility. An important part of humility is recognizing the things that you're good at and not putting yourself down. And giving those things as offerings to other people.

When you go to Sun Dance, you have to make prayer ties. To make each tie, you put a little tobacco in a little piece of cloth. All the ties are attached to one string, and you can't break the string. If the string breaks, you have to start over. It takes a lot of dexterity, and when you start, it's really difficult. And you have to do four hundred and five of these ties. My first year, I dropped the bundle. And they got tangled up. I worked on them for sixteen hours straight, to try to untangle them, and I couldn't. And in that process, I thought, *How stupid are you? How dumb are you? How unorganized you are. You've been making messes all your life.* People were walking by, laughing. Some people would stop and try to help me for a while. They'd get frustrated and say, "You've got to figure this out." And I'm thinking, *I'm not going to dance. I don't deserve to dance. This is an honor that gets bestowed.* So I expected I wouldn't go to dance. I went over to the intercessor, and I said, "Look what I did." And he asked a guy who just was sitting there—this guy had severe mental issues—he said, "Take him to the tree." And the guy took me to the tree. He was very kind, very gentle, and he found a way to wrap the strings around the tree. He was just supportive and said, "You'll be all right."

When I go to Sun Dance, all the physical ailments that I've kind of suppressed come to the surface. I don't usually walk into camp. I can't lift my head because my back hurts so much. So that first day, that's how I danced. And, you know, you pray and dance, and as the day goes on, it gets hotter and hotter. Your legs are burning, and you're dancing beyond the physical point that you thought you could. You're praying and saying, "Creator, help me, please, help me. I'll do anything if you just help me get through this." And then at the end of the day, you feel kind of good about yourself because you think, *Man, I really prayed hard. I got through the day. I'm pretty good.*

The next day when I went in to dance, I was able to stand straight up. When I looked around—we had a big Sun Dance—I saw maybe forty people. And they'd been praying for me. You could see it.

They'd acknowledge me. They'd smile. And so it makes you think, *Oh my God, I'm so arrogant.* I think that my prayers are powerful. But it's really other people's prayers. Because in reality it helps them to pray for me.

ASHLEY HEMMERS

FORT MOJAVE INDIAN TRIBE
TRIBAL ADMINISTRATOR
BORN IN: 1985, Fort Mojave
INTERVIEWED IN: New York, Las Vegas, and Fort Mojave,
California, Arizona, and Nevada

In 2013 Ashley Hemmers was on the East Coast to attend the opening of the Native American Cultural Center at Yale. We met up in New York City, where our mutual friend Rick Chavolla connected us. I asked Ashley about her early life and childhood and we spoke for the next two hours. She suggested we meet again, at her home in Fort Mojave, so that she could share the rest of her story.

Four months later, I flew into Vegas and the following morning began the drive to Fort Mojave.[1] Our day began at Avi Kwa Ame, the crowning peak of the Newberry Mountains, from which the Mojave believe they were created. We ended our journey at the southernmost tip of the valley, the Needles Peaks, at the end of the Colorado River. The

1. Fort Mojave Indian Tribe is a sovereign tribal nation located at the intersection of California, Arizona, and Nevada.

Mojave believe that when they pass on, after they are cremated and tradi-
tional rites are performed, the spirit rises from the body and, over a series
of days, it travels to the peaks to meet the medicine man who resides there
and who can see whether someone has lived in a good way.

There, on the Mojave reservation, in the space between creation and
death, Ashley took me to visit where her people live today. The reserva-
tion is composed of forty-two thousand acres in Arizona, California, and
Nevada. Economic institutions—including two casinos, a golf course,
and alfalfa and cotton farms—generate resources that have dramatically
improved conditions from the years when Ashley was a child. At the time
of our conversations, Ashley was working as a grant writer to support
the Mojave government's funds for the programs, operations, and capital
projects that serve its roughly one thousand members.

THE STORY OF THE BUZZARD
AND HOW HE BECAME BALD

My great-aunt, Gertrude, told me one of my favorite stories when I
was a little kid—the story of the hummingbird traveling from Needles to Yuma. One day, my aunt goes, "Osha!"—that's what everyone
calls me because I was born a preemie; *osh'cha'nuu* means "tiny," like
"tiny baby."

"Have you ever heard the story of the buzzard and how he became bald?" she asked.

"You know how the buzzard has a huge wingspan, and he can fly
so fast—faster than the eagle? Well, one day, the hummingbird said,
'You know what, buzzard? I'm tiny, but I can beat you.'

"And the buzzard said, 'No way! I'll give you a day to fly ahead,
and then I'll catch up and beat you to Cocopah.'[2]

"The hummingbird said, 'I'll take that advantage.'

---

2. The Cocopah Indian Tribe's traditional territories included parts of present-day
Arizona, California, and Baja California. Today their reservation is in Yuma County, Arizona.

"And so the hummingbird, he's trying to go really hard with his little wings. The buzzard started out the next day, and he just took big flaps of his wings, but right around the midpoint, that buzzard wanted to rest. But the little hummingbird, he had heart, he kept going, and when he was almost to Yuma, the buzzard caught up and pushed the hummingbird out of the way and injured him. The hummingbird was mad—he'd almost beaten the buzzard!

"At Yuma, everyone was clapping for the hummingbird. And the little hummingbird's friend, the fox, was there. So you know what the tricky fox did? He went and cut the buzzard's hair. And you know what Mastamho, our Creator, did? He never let it grow back, to show how the buzzard was such a cheater."

After hearing that story, I kept wondering why the buzzard's hair never grew back. And my grandma told me, "There's a saying in Mojave and it means, 'Watch what you say, and watch what you do,' because you may hurt someone's family, someone's friend, along the way. The fox was the hummingbird's friend. The buzzard cheated to beat the hummingbird. And now look at his descendants, they're bald everywhere!"

WHEN WE HAD OUR LIVES

In our tribe, many of my grandma's generation were shipped to Phoenix Indian School and Sherman Indian School.[3] My grandma was placed in Poston War Camp #2 and later sent to Phoenix Indian Boarding School. She still sleeps with the light on because of

---

3. The Phoenix Indian School was operated by the Bureau of Indian Affairs from 1935 until 1990. The Perris Indian School in Perris, California, was an off-reservation high school that opened in 1892. Renamed Sherman Indian High School in 1971, and still in operation today, Sherman's students are drawn from over seventy-six tribes from across the United States. Almost 70 percent of the students are from reservation communities. For more on the intergenerational impact of Indian boarding schools on Native families, see appendix essay 2.

the things that happened there.[4] But when my grandma was at the school, she saw that people who read were smart and were in positions of power. My grandma lived with us when we were kids, and when my brother and I got home from school, she'd make us read for an hour. It could be the *New York Times* that she got from the library or the *Needles Desert Star* or books that she found because we didn't have money to buy them.

My grandma had gone to college late, become a certified nurse's assistant, and worked at an old folks' home in Bullhead City.[5] My mom worked as a manager at the casino. She was worried about me because I was a girl. So on my first day of elementary school, my grandma and mom dropped me off on their way to work at four in the morning with my aunt Iser. Iser was seventy, an old Mojave woman, and she had a cousin Audrey, who loved to sing songs, and who was jolly but always drunk. I remember the first day walking to the bus. I had really long, braided hair. Iser made breakfast for me—a tortilla—and I took that with me, and Audrey walked me to the school bus, all drunk and singing songs and telling me stories.

I got on the bus, and I went to school. It was bad between whites and Indians. I come from a very culturally traditional family—and we were poor. Other kids pulled my hair. I remember getting off the bus at the end of the day and being upset. My aunt Audrey held up my chin, and asked, "What's wrong with you, Osha?" I said, "Nothing." Audrey said, "Tell me what's wrong or I'm going to get mad."

---

4. During World War II, the Poston War Relocation Center, or Poston Internment Camp, was the largest of the War Relocation Authority's American concentration camps for Japanese Americans. Poston was built on the Colorado River Indian Reservation, over the objections of the tribal council. For a brief period after the war, the US government brought Native Americans to Poston, where they were promised land for farming and a house. For more on this history, see "Japanese Americans Weren't the Only US Citizens Housed in Camps," Public Radio International, October 18, 2017, www.pri.org/stories/2017-10-18/japanese-americans-werent-only-us-citizens-kept-camps.

5. Bullhead City has a population of around thirty-nine thousand and is located along the Colorado River in Mohave County, Arizona.

So I told her, "Well, so-and-so pulled my hair." And I remember Audrey hitting the side of the bus with her hand and the kids looking out, and her saying, "You mess with my niece again and you're going to get one of these," gesturing with her fist. All the kids kind of turned around, and she started laughing. I was shocked. She said, "Don't let anyone bother you, you are the person you are. They're just mad because no matter how good they are, no matter how much money they have, they can never be you."

After that, no one really bothered me. I was a quiet child and just did my own thing. I think it helped me accept early on that I could be an individual. I just went to school like it was a job. When I came home, that's when we had our lives with all my cousins and my family.

WHAT I WAS WORTH

I always had this idea that I wasn't worth anything. When I was smart, people would say, "Oh! She's trying to be a smarty." Other times, it was, "Oh, she's just an Indian." And if I was misbehaving, they'd say, "Oh, that's so-and-so's daughter. She's his *other* child."

My dad wasn't a good guy. I never met him, but I heard he did a lot of bad things to a lot of bad people and it got him. He served time and when he got out of jail someone shot him, execution style, and that was that. I don't know my dad's name. He loved my mom and she loved him, but we were not his family. We were something else.

When I was twelve, my mom and I had this fistfight. I'd been hanging out with *cholitas*, hanging out with people who were gangster, getting into bad stuff early.[6] We'd given it to each other pretty hard, we'd ruined the room, both of us resting on the floor. Right then, I saw how hard she'd fought and what I was worth to her. But my mom wanted something more for me and she loved me enough to fight me for it.

---

6. *Cholita* is slang for tough girl.

People might look down on her. They might think that you shouldn't get in a fight with your twelve-year-old child. But we were living in some pretty hard times and for me that fight was a sign of parenting. That she did that, that she was able to pull that out without having been parented herself, I was amazed. And sitting there on the floor that day, looking at the room we'd just destroyed, I realized how much she loved me. As we sat there exhausted next to each other, I remembered her saying, "Don't you want more than this? You can be better than me." I was like, *Shit yeah, I don't want this. If I can be really good at being bad, I can be really good at being good too.*

WARD VALLEY

My grandma and my great-aunt, Gertrude, in their older years were big on culture, on protecting our rights, on being Indian. So my brother and I got to know what they thought was important about being Mojave. We were their second chance. Part of this was going to various cultural events. They taught us tribal song and dance. We were able to build the relationship with them that they had wanted to have with their children.

When I was in middle school, between 1995 and 1999, the US Department of the Interior and US Ecology had plans to dig trenches to dispose of nuclear waste at Ward Valley, about twenty miles outside of Needles.[7] The tribe took this very seriously because water is important. I mean, it's a given; we live in a desert. But also for cultural reasons—we believe that the Colorado River is our life source and it's the life source for all our animals, for all our children, and our children's children.

My grandma and my aunt took us to some events the tribe had

---

7. US Ecology is a hazardous waste compliance and disposal company with headquarters in Boise, Indiana. Needles, California, is a city of close to five thousand people that lies on the western banks of the Colorado River in the Mojave Valley.

at Ward Valley.[8] There were protests on the road that led to the site. Every day when I came home from school, we'd go to Ward Valley. We'd go home to shower, go to school, then go to Ward Valley. Sometimes people would sing. There were elders from all over. People from the American Indian Movement came out and helped build the sacred fire.[9] Our grandmas would be socializing with different people, laughing and joking around.

We didn't have a permit or legal standing to be there. The state declared they were going to work with various agencies to remove us. The day of the standoff there were hundreds of people there. There were police cars on the freeway.[10] I remember one of our guys, Stephen, saying, "We're going to go down fighting."

It clicked again that I was different. You know, I'm Indian. You hear these stories when you're a kid of the Longest Walk or Sitting Bull, of all these big phantom Indians, and here we were, a group of Indians—*our* leaders, *our* chairman, people we knew—standing up for something that we believed in and our elders showing us that it was important to fight.[11] I'd never seen that in my own community.

---

8. Ward Valley is sacred land of the five lower Colorado River Indian Tribes, about a hundred miles southwest of the Mojave reservation.

9. A sacred fire is believed to open a doorway allowing people to communicate to the spirit world and is often lit to start a ceremony or sacred event.

10. In February 1998, the US government ordered the evacuation of the protest camp, which protesters had occupied since October 1995. The alliance and its supporters, including the American Indian Movement, maintained a nonviolent occupation of the camp. They kept seven fires aflame to create the space for people to gather and sing. For more on this, see Phil Klasky, "Ward Valley: An Extreme and Solemn Relationship," The Mojave Project, http://mojaveproject.org/dispatches-item/ward-valley.

11. Organized by the American Indian Movement in 1978, the Longest Walk was a cross-country trek of 3,200 miles intended to represent American Indians' forced removal from their homelands and raise awareness about the US government's ongoing infringement upon tribal sovereignty. The leading figure of Plains Indian resistance in what is now known as the United States, Sitting Bull (1831–1890)

I'd never seen my tribe come together in the way that it came to-gether during that protest. It really showed me that even though we were in the modern era, we were still having the same fight. Someone wanted to come on this land and put crap on it, and we were telling them no.

The tribal vice chairman called all the children to come stand in front. The adults said, "It's going to be really scary. We're going to go down there. People are going to yell at you. Don't worry. There's a law that says we as Indians can pray and not be bothered, so we're going to fight them with their own laws this time." The plan was that Preston, an elder from Fort Yuma, was going to sing, and us kids would be in front. Under the Religious Freedom Act, we could sit in prayer.[12] When we do ceremonies and when we dance and sing, that's group prayer to us. Preston started singing, and we started dancing in front of the entrance to the dirt road. The police were there and they had a SWAT team, they had mace, they had rifles.[13] They came in with these big police vehicles and bullhorns saying, "Please step aside."

The one thing I remember so clearly about that night was that as soon as Preston started singing, it all became very real. Not just for us, but for everyone. You could feel the nontribal police were not used to this; they didn't want to touch these children. The people who live in Needles, some of the police, they were concerned too because it wasn't just about us using the water. It was about them

---

was a spiritual and military leader of the Hunkpapa Lakota during critical years of resistance to US government policies.

12. The American Indian Religious Freedom Act (AIRFA) of 1978 is a federal law that was enacted "to protect and preserve for American Indians their inherent right of freedom to believe, express, and exercise the traditional religions of the American Indian, Eskimo, Aleut, and Native Hawaiians, including but not limited to access to sites, use and possession of sacred objects, and the freedom to worship through ceremonials and traditional rites." US Government Printing Office, 1978.

13. SWAT is an acronym for Special Weapons and Tactics.

and their families. Their families were pioneers, their families were railroaders, their families have lived along this river, and we may not have cohabitated peacefully all the time, but there was a sense of them belonging. The people from farther away, FBI agents and the other state police, they were ready to go in. But when we started singing, there was this hesitation, and then all of a sudden, I started seeing the vehicles move away.

I heard this huge war cry from one of our guys. It's something that we don't hear often. But I heard it, and I saw my great-auntie hear it, and a peace came over me. I could see in her face that she was proud. She looked like a statue that night. She started crying. After that first cry, we heard all the guys cry out. Then we heard the women cry too. We sang and danced all night.

ANOTHER PART OF AMERICA

Something cool happened in my sophomore year of high school. In 2009, Palo Verde College, based in Blythe, California, had started a hub in Needles so people could earn their associate's degree or learn a skill. But because they were using Needles High School for classroom space, high school students could go to the college for free. My math teacher, Mr. McDonald, told me that I should go. I'd go to high school from seven to three, have an hour break, and from four to six I'd go to a college class.

Once I'd enrolled, the admissions office sent me these camp flyers. In my junior year, I got one from the Ivy something or other. I never knew anything about the Ivy League. I thought it was the same as a community college. And so I applied and I was accepted to the summer program for Ivies. The program picks where you go, and I got sent to Yale. I thought, *Oh! This is fun.* I worked with my tribal education department director, Christina Cameron-Otero. We wrote a fundraising letter and we went to all the businesses in my area, hustling this letter. And my grandma helped. She'd sell breakfast burritos. We ended up raising the $3,000, plus enough for the plane ticket, which was good because this was really the first time an Indian student from the village was asking for something from the tribe for education.

I was in New Haven for three weeks that summer. I didn't have any money to do all the fun stuff with the other kids, so I stayed in the library and pretended that I was working on research. But then, at Ivy institutions, there are academics who give talks, and they have food at those talks! One day I heard some guy giving a talk about maps, and I thought, *Wow! People can talk about maps and make a living.* So I asked all kinds of questions like, "What do you do when you're done with the maps?" And he goes, "You can never really be done with the maps, because there are other new maps." I remember thinking, *There is more! Outside of my community, there are other communities where people communicate in a different way and it's not about daily survival. There's another part of America that I don't know about.* When I went back home, I talked to the professor at the community college. I said, "I really want to go to school."

My mom worked, and we saved. I read a lot of the stuff explaining higher education for immigrant families because it gave an overview for people to understand what the system was. No one in my tribe before me has ever been to an Ivy institution as far as I know. And hardly any—five or six—have graduated from a college, in my generation or before.

I ended up doing really well on my SAT. Mr. McDonald and I looked at where I could go with my scores, and the Ivies were possible. I looked at Yale, and said, "I really want to go back there." I wrote this whole narrative of my story, where I was from and what I wanted to learn. That spring I got a phone call. A man said, "May I please speak with Ashley Hemmers?" I said, "Who?" Because everyone calls me Osha. But I go, "Yeah, this is her." He says, "We'd like to welcome you to New Haven." I thought, *Stop playing around, it's not very nice.* At that time, a lot of people were joking with me,

"Oh, you're waiting for your acceptance letter," so I thought it was a prank. I hung up the phone. And he called back and said, "I think the connection got messed up." I was like, "What? Oh my God! I'm so sorry." He said, "We're inviting you to Yale."

GO FORWARD

The day I left Fort Mojave, in 2003, my mom, my grandma, and I piled into our shitty little red Chevy. It was kind of gray that day. In the summertime, in Needles, if it's gray, it means a monsoon. It's a bad sign. Monsoons are bad for us Mojave. Where I live, there are flash floods. When it rains, it comes down all at once.

But we got in the car, and soon the rain was coming down in sheets. We're driving through, and we didn't have a heater, and we didn't have a way to get rid of the fog on the windows. My mom was like, "Let's turn back. It doesn't have to be today." And I was talking myself out of going. But my grandma said, "No. You're going. It'll be fine, and we'll get you through this." So we keep going, and the rain gets harder, and then there's a big wash, and my mom slows a bit, but my grandma is like, "Just go through it!" So we drive into it, and then we're sitting in the middle of it. I'm like, "Let's just turn around!" My grandma says, "You've come too far. If we turn around, then all the water is going to turn around too, and it's going to be an even bigger problem. We're going to go forward like you're supposed to."

We got out of that scary wash, and it started drizzling a little bit, and it started getting lighter, and then it got sunny. My grandma said, "See, this is just like everything else. People don't want you to succeed. They don't want you to do what's important for your life and they're going to put everything in your way so that you psyche yourself out and give up. Osha—you don't give into it."

We had breakfast at the airport. I gave my mom a hug. I gave my grandma a hug. I had a hundred dollars in my pocket. My mom was like, "You'll make it work until next month when we have some more money." I said, "I'll be fine. There's free food there so don't worry," and I got on the plane to Bradley International Airport.

I arrived in the afternoon and I caught a shuttle service to New Haven, and then I had forty dollars in my pocket. I checked into the hotel that had been booked for me for the night, and I went to find something to eat, so then I had thirty dollars in my pocket. I didn't know how close Yale was to the hotel, and I was scared to talk to people who looked important. I didn't want to bother someone in a suit and I didn't want anyone to think that I didn't belong. So I took a cab to Yale, and then I had twenty dollars in my pocket. And when I got there, I told the cab driver I'd give him ten more bucks if he'd help me with my luggage because my room was on the fifth floor. And so the taxi driver helped me up to the fifth floor. I didn't feel like I fit in. At all. I was a different color. I was just different in general. But somehow, I made it through a dinner with some other students that night. And that was my first day at Yale.

It was true about the free food. Every day that fall when I walked into the cafeteria, I was overcome with guilt. My home had been a two-income household—not because I had a mom and a dad, but because I had a mom and me. My suitemates had come to Yale to find themselves, to become adults. I knew what it was to be an adult. I'd been an adult for years. I'd seen what adulthood looked like. This was the first time I could be a kid, and by that, I mean I could study. I could study everything I wanted to, and it was free. In that way, I was fortunate to have come from where I had because I loved being in class. I worked really hard, and that helped me to feel less guilty that I wasn't at home helping out. I knew the struggle that my mom was having because I'd left. I was on a full scholarship at Yale, but I knew there was less food on the table at home, that there were more beans on the stove and less meat.

PROBLEMS WITH INDIANS

All of a sudden it was October and it was Indigenous People's Day—Columbus Day.[14] At home we'd never really pay attention to it, but out here some people celebrated Indigenous People's Day, and there were also people who had problems with Indians. It was during the time of those Mastercard commercials, where they'd say something like: "Dinner and a movie: $35. Something else: $50. Talking with someone you love: priceless." And some students had chalked on the streets of New Haven: "A thousand squaws murdered: so many castellanos. An Indian assimilation: this many castellanos. Opening up a new land of freedom and democracy: priceless."[15] What really got me was that they had used the term for the actual coin from Columbus's time. I thought, *Only at Yale would someone know the name of the coin.* There was also a lot of graffiti around campus like, "Squaws are sluts and whores." They made little poems about Indian women. I come from a place where people who didn't like Indians just called you a savage to your face. I remember being seven years old and having a redneck who worked for the railroad tell me, "You're a fuckin' savage no-good-piece-of-nothing and you'll never amount to shit." I can still see the hate in his eyes. So it was almost like, *Is that it?* And then it hit me—*What am I doing here, with people who don't understand?* They know nothing about my tribe. They know nothing about my history. They also know nothing about the history of Indians in the Northeast.

I remember calling my mom and saying, "This is bullshit. I didn't work my ass off to get to a place where I can be called a squaw." She was like, "What?" She started laughing. I said, "I'm being serious

14. Indigenous People's Day is a reimagining of Columbus Day, converting the celebration of colonialism into an opportunity to reflect upon the historical truth of the genocide and present-day oppression of Indigenous peoples in the Americas.

15. *Castellanos* are a Spanish coin. King Ferdinand (1452–1516) and Queen Isabella (1451–1504) of Spain funded Christopher Columbus's voyage to the Americas, and the Spanish currency was the first European one used in the Americas.

mom; I'm being called a squaw." She said, "Don't even worry about it. Just get that good *Nyamasav* education and come back.[16] So what if they have a problem with you."

I talked to other Native students, and we decided that we should do something about this. I made an appointment with the dean of student affairs. I went in there and I brought the pictures we'd taken of the graffiti. I said, "This is unacceptable. I'm here at this school, and you guys said you wanted diversity, and I'm about as diverse as they come. There's only one Mojave girl here, and I don't appreciate being called a squaw-slut." I was just really upfront with the dean. She was Italian from New York, and when I first talked to her, she said that when she was younger in New York, everyone used to mistake her for being Native American because she had long braided hair. One time her husband told her, "You look too Native American." She said, "I know how it feels to be objectified."

I asked her, "Do you have a Federal Enrollment Number that lets you know that the government is keeping track of you?"[17]

"No, I don't."

"Then don't talk to me about being Native. Because until you have a number assigned to you—I'm 0-8-2-6—then you don't know what it feels like to be a ward of something. That's what being Native feels like." From that point we built a strong relationship. I think she appreciated the fact that I wasn't kissing up to her and that I wanted to have a conversation with her without all the bureaucratic nonsense. I found that I had a voice.

---

16. Mojave word for "white."

17. 0826 is Ashley's Fort Mojave enrollment number. Although tribal membership was traditionally determined through kinship and clan systems, the federal enrollment system began as a result of the Indian Reorganization Act (1934). Tribal enrollment has a troubled history, as it originated as part of a strategy for solving the American Indian "problem." See glossary for more.

NATIVE STUDIES EXISTED

Because of the number of veterans in my area, the library at home had a lot of stuff on World War II and on the Holocaust. I was really into learning about the Holocaust when I was younger because of the intergenerational trauma and the assimilation issues it raised. I could find similarities between how I was growing up and what was happening during that time period to a certain group of people.

I didn't know that Native studies existed. I had no clue. But I went into Yale thinking, *Man, I really want to know more about the Holocaust.* And then I found out through the history department that there was more. I was seeing these broader themes that happen in communities that are impoverished, or communities that have had certain policies imposed on them. That's when I really got into studying government. I ended up studying the history of Native sovereign development from 1940 to 1965. It covered the Indian Reorganization Act, how tribes became constituted as they exist today, and how different governments structured themselves and prepared the way for the self-determination of the seventies.[18]

BEADED GRADUATION STOLES

I started applying to law school in 2006. I'd always wanted to study law, and as an undergraduate history major, a lot of seminars about the federal framework of Indigenous communities included Indian law. I thought this would be a good next step to explore—to understand systems, not so much that I wanted to be an actual lawyer.

Around April of that year, my senior year, I got a call from my grandma. She said, "You need to talk to your mom."

---

18. The Indian Reorganization Act (IRA) was a piece of federal legislation passed to grant certain rights to Native Americans. The IRA included a reversal of the Dawes Act, which had privatized commonly held Indian land, a return to self-government on a tribal basis, and a restoration of tribes' rights to manage their own assets. For more on the IRA, see the timeline.

"Why? What's going on?"

"You just need to talk to your mom."

"Okay, put her on the phone."

"What's going on, Mom?"

"I'm sick."

"What do you mean?"

"The doctor said I have stage four lymphoma. It doesn't look very good."

This was a couple days before reading week, or before exams, and we had these Senior Dinners. My grandma had made beaded graduation stoles for the seven Native grads—she made eight stoles, just in case one broke. I took them to the Native American Senior Dinner, and I was giving them out to people. My professor said, "Ashley, are you ready for law school?" I told him, "I'm not going. My time in Connecticut's over." He asked, "What do you mean?" I told him, "My mom's sick. My family has made a lot of sacrifices for me to come here, and it's time for me to go home."

My graduation in 2007 was really awesome for me and my family. I was the first one to graduate from college and my grandma got to see me walk. She's always wanted to see an orchestra, and Yale has a beautiful symphony. I took her to brunch, and then we went to watch the Yale Symphony. I remember being really happy and feeling like I did something good, even though it was a bittersweet ending. I didn't have any big goals. We were happy, and we were away from all the bad stuff in my community, in my family, all the stuff that we had gone through. It kind of felt like my degree wasn't just mine, like it was all of ours.

WORKING FOR THE TRIBE

I moved back home, and I didn't know what I was going to do. All I had was a Yale history degree with a focus in tribal government. I'd come home right after tribal election. We had a new chairman. About a week later, I got an invitation from the new tribal chairman to come to his office. So I went. We started talking, and he asks, "Have you thought about working for the tribe? I need help with funding. I need a grant writer." I thought, *Well, I've had a couple research grants and I'm pretty good at writing, so I'll apply for that.* The application was accepted. I was twenty-two and in the executive administration of the tribal government.

My first year home, my mom was still sick. The specialist said that she needed an operation, and we had to try to get her operation-ready. In the spring of that year, she was okayed for surgery. I took her to the hospital. She had an emergency situation on the operating table. The nurse said that there were complications. They had warned me that surgery might not go okay, and I remember thinking, *This one time, give my mom a break, you know? She doesn't even have to be completely healed. Just let it go right, and we will do the radiation, we will do the chemo, we will do whatever.* I remember feeling so angry. Because when you try to do everything right and things still go wrong, it makes you feel like those good things weren't meant for you. I remember walking outside the hospital and screaming, "Come on! Just come on! Give me a break!" I finally just broke down and started crying. I got a phone call saying that the doctors needed to speak with me. They said, "We thought we had lost her for a little bit, but she seems to be okay." I was able to take her home a couple days later.

That fall, my mom got her radiation treatment. We had a final doctor's visit with the specialist and we got the results back. She was cancer-free. In February, for my mom's birthday, we did a birthday month. We did everything—we went to concerts, gambling, shopping, traveling, powwows. Whatever she wanted to do, we did.

Once my mom got cleared from treatment, I wondered, *Do I go back to law school, or do I stay here?* I felt good in my job; it felt good to be home. I decided to apply to graduate school part time at University of Nevada, Las Vegas, and commuted to get my graduate certificate in nonprofit management and my master's degree in public administration.

At school, I was a government specialist in a field that scholars and academics don't take seriously. Then I'd go home and have people question my credentials and my ability—people who have a high school diploma or a GED.[19] At that point, people who worked for the tribal government were tribal members who didn't really live in the community. I'd ask them to meet a deadline and they wouldn't meet it because, according to them, I didn't know what I was talking about. I was like, "No! I'm on your team. I think your program is good. I think it's needed." That's what I struggled with the most: I was here and people were fighting with me because I'm different. I was younger, I was female, and I was from a family that lived in the community.

AN ASSIMILATION PROCESS THAT
HAS FRACTURED MY COMMUNITY

My role was to maintain increased external funding so that our government expenditure didn't eat away at existing financial resources. The idea was that there'd be a larger amount of resources for the council so that we could offer programs such as education scholarships. The education department, teen council, tribal government, different policy actors, boards, everyone agreed as a nation that each tribal member, no matter what age, could go to school and could get a four-year degree free of charge.

In our first five years, only one person went to a four-year college. One person out of fifty kids. The others have all graduated high school, so that's promising. Some have gone to vocational schools, tech schools, but many drop out. But we've also seen a lot of young people just not want to go to school, and it occurred to me that even though we have resources now, it would be like giving a lot of money to a war-engulfed country and then expecting people to go and become doctors and lawyers and nurses and pediatricians and what

---

19. General Educational Development certificate.

have you. Even though we're not at war, we have gone through an assimilation process that has fractured my community, and it hinders the younger generations from breaking out.

"Assimilation" refers to a set of policies developed by both the United States and Canada during the period 1870 through 1920. The goal of these policies was to incorporate Indians into the settler economy, to eliminate Indigenous lifeways that obstructed settler expansion.[20] Toward this aim, Indians would be relocated to reservations, converted to Christianity, and pressured to adopt farmwork as their livelihood. In the United States, these mandates were implemented through treaties in which tribal leaders were coerced into ceding all but small tracts of their land, called "reservations," which their people would then be confined to. Treaties also required that Indians send their children to government schools, designed to blot out Native language and culture in favor of Anglo and Christian traditions.

Assimilationist values of individualism and private property ownership were further promoted through the General Allotment Act of 1887, which made it possible to privately own once communally held reservation land. The act promised each tribal member 160 acres for farming, with all remaining land sold off as "surplus." Unsurprisingly, the lands that remained in Indian hands were not often quality farmlands, and Indian families struggled to survive. By the 1920s, the failure of assimilation policies was clear. The US had fragmented tribal lifeways without supporting the conditions for Native survival by alternate means.

My grandmother lived through a number of the assimilationist policies the US used against Native American tribes. In her lifetime, you can see the fragmentation that happened to people who went through these programs and the effect on their families. For example, my mom and her siblings knew a very different version of my

---

20. For more on the history of assimilationist policies in North America, see appendix essay 1.

grandma than my brother and I know. When she was raising my mom and her siblings, she was resolving all the stuff she had been through and not doing a very good job of that.

Of course, she always had a house, stuff to eat. But alcohol was a factor for her. So my mom had a very different upbringing with her than I did. My brother and I were really my grandmother's second-chance kids. She was able to share how to pray for someone in our language, how to care for someone in our language, what it means to feel as a Mojave. She wasn't able to share with her children then what she can now—now that she's more comfortable expressing who she is. When I talk about assimilation and fragmentation in my family, you can see it within just three generations.

At work, we push resources to counter assimilation's effects, but it's like putting a Band-Aid on a gunshot wound. You don't have the right tools to take the bullet out, and so that bullet keeps hurting you no matter how hard you're working.

The benefits of working for your tribe far outweigh any other job that you can imagine. You're a part of something that helps another little girl or boy keep building. By being there, being different, it's letting people know that it's okay to be Indian. It's okay to be educated. It's okay to know how nontribal people live and to help use those best practices to help us live better. And that doesn't mean that you've assimilated. It just means that you can speak someone else's language, and you can translate it to a world that doesn't have quite as many interpreters, a world that doesn't have quite as many people listening from the outside.

For the last five years, I've been Mojave's tribal administrator. I've noticed that a lot of adults a little older than me are embarrassed that they don't know as much about the culture, or don't speak the language. So my work has really been about opening up access points for people who are Mojave that want to learn, and who can walk in that identity. I come from a traditional family, and sharing those values throughout our tribal departments is the thing I'm most proud

of. We've come to understand that things here are not fucked up because *we* are fucked up; it's because we are dealing with a lot of heavy
history that we haven't untangled yet as a community.

*On our drive around the reservation, we stopped to see the new play-
ground at the Arizona Village, a housing development where a lot of the
tribe's young families live. The playground here was the first community
development project that Ashley worked to fund when she moved home
after finishing school. The park, just a few years old, looked good: bright
and inviting. It was a Saturday afternoon in the desert spring, and there
was not a single person there. However, a few minutes after we arrived,
a couple of girls who had been sitting in a yard across the street picked
up their basketball and made their way to the park's court. They started
to play. Later, when we returned to the car, we noticed the girls started
leaving too.*

We have people who you'd think would want the park to thrive, but
because there are so many issues on the reservation, people are just
trying to survive. They're having a hard time with basic needs, with
substance abuse, with domestic abuse. So you have this festering
of things that thrive in this habitat: people who sell drugs, people
who are violent; those things take up the space. And then you have
a playground that's in a community where no kids are playing in it.
There needs to be recognition that forced assimilation breaks down
a people. In my work, I'm trying to put together a common thread
to hold community together, to rebuild community. I meet a lot of
people who are looking for a past. I am looking for a future.

ERVIN CHARTRAND

MÉTIS/SAULTEAUX
INDEPENDENT FILMMAKER
BORN IN: 1973, Winnipeg, Manitoba
INTERVIEWED IN: Selkirk, Manitoba

Ervin Chartrand was born in a Métis community in Camperville, Manitoba.[1] He moved to Winnipeg with his mother when he was two years old. One of six children in his family, Ervin lived what he described as a transient lifestyle, moving every two to three years between his mother's reserve and the city. He said he grew up without a feeling of protection or mentorship and gravitated toward street kids because "those were the only kids that I could really hang out with and understand." Ervin

---

1. One of three recognized Aboriginal peoples of Canada, the Métis are the descendants of Cree, Ojibwe, Saulteaux, and Menominee peoples and French, Scottish, and British settlers.

joined his first gang at fourteen and was arrested at seventeen on a count of mischief he did not commit.

I met Ervin at his home in Selkirk, Manitoba. The sunlit and airy space where we sat contrasted starkly with the darker days he remembered. Ervin spoke about how he was thrown into the justice system with a lack of proper representation and offered a choice—one he says is common—to plea out in order "to get it over with, start the sentence, and get out of prison." While Canada's crime rate has been dropping for years, the numbers of Indigenous people in its prisons are way up. To draw a comparison, in the United States, Black men are six times as likely to be in prison than white men, while in Canada, Indigenous men are ten times as likely, and in the province of Saskatchewan thirty-three times more likely to be imprisoned.[2] Ervin's own incarceration also prompted thoughts about how his mother's experience at an Indian residential school is linked to the Canadian justice system's treatment of Indigenous people today.

CEREMONIES WERE BANNED

I was raised in Camperville, which is about 450 kilometers north of Winnipeg. It's probably about one and a half hour's drive from Dauphin, Manitoba. It's a Métis community, near a First Nations community, Pine Creek Reserve. It's also near another Métis community, Duck Bay. My mom is Ojibwe from Pine Creek. I consider my dad's family more Métis, and he was from Camperville. I grew up more on the Métis side and understood the Métis culture. Being Métis also meant going to Catholic Church. My mom made us pray almost every night. I considered my mom's side of the family more spiritual/cultural, involved in ceremonies, powwows, and stuff like that. Back then, with the residential schools, traditional ceremonies were banned

---

2. For more on high rates of Indigenous incarceration, see appendix essay 2.

on reserves.[3] I remember my mom telling me how her family had to hide their cultural practices. So they'd practice their ceremonies deep in the woods. I was told when I was a kid that if I didn't pray, if I did bad things, I'd go straight to hell. I was really scared of burning in hell then, but for some reason I continued to do bad things. I guess burning in hell was tame compared to my living conditions.

My father died of stomach cancer when I was six months old. My mom had to raise the six kids: Paul, Sidney, Loretta, Ernest, Patrick, and me. We moved to Winnipeg when I was two years old. We moved in with my aunt Leona, who liked to drink a lot. When my mom was around my aunties, her sisters, they all drank together and partied.

Every time we moved to the city my mom started drinking a lot after the move. She drank and drank. There were parties all the time. We lived a very transient lifestyle, went hungry a lot. We barely ever stayed in one place longer than one or two years. We'd move back up north, to Camperville, where we wouldn't go hungry. My mom would straighten herself out because we had the support to get us by. Then she would get bored again, and we'd move back to the city. The parties would start up and we'd go hungry again. We'd always live fine for the first month or two, but all my mom's alcoholic friends would eventually find us and the cycle would start again. As my mom got older she started to slow down, but my older brothers picked up the pace, keeping the parties alive.

As far back as I can remember, I had no one there to protect or mentor me. The only person who was there most of the time was my brother Ernest, who was four years older than me. He showed mentorship, but he also showed me violence right through my childhood. He'd be happy with me one minute, playing street hockey

---

3. The Indian Act of Canada forbade First Nations people from practicing their traditional religions and declared cultural ceremonies illegal. In the 1951 amendments to the act, the banning of dancing and ceremonies was removed. For more on the Indian Act, see the timeline.

or just hanging out, loving me, and the next minute, when he was drunk or high, he'd kick the shit out of me. I didn't care because he was probably the only person who really paid any attention to me, though it was the wrong kind of attention. My mother, maybe she tried, but she was never there for me. She was never home. I'd sit at the door or the window crying for her, but she'd go out and party anyway.

A LOT OF DISAPPOINTMENT

Winnipeg is home to Canada's largest urban Indigenous population (and the second largest in North America after Anchorage by proportion). Its Indigenous population is three times as likely to be living in poverty than the rest of the city's residents.[4] The city is also home to two of Canada's three poorest postal codes, both predominantly Indigenous neighborhoods in the city's North End. The area is infamous for its substandard housing, poor financial and retail services, and high levels of violent crime, which are associated with poverty and the presence of Indigenous gangs.

We moved into a new neighborhood on Young Street when I was around ten years old. One day, I was sitting on my front stoop, and this other Native kid walked by. I vividly remember what he was wearing—jeans ripped at the knees and torn at the bottom. He had no T-shirt on, no shoes, nothing. His hair was messy and dirty, even his skin was dirty. He walked by once and he walked by again, then he said, "Hi." I said, "Hi" back, and he came over and started talking to me. Chris was his name.

Another day when I met up with Chris, I was shocked at how clean he was. He had on new clothes. We talked, and he took me to his place. It was beautiful—fridge full of food, everything a kid

---

4. This is based on percentage of the population living below the poverty line.

could want, lots of toys. We played with his toys all day and night, so I decided to sleep over. My mom was probably out drinking so she wouldn't miss me. In the morning, Chris's mom woke us up, and she took us out shopping. She goes, "Let's go get some breakfast." So she took us to a corner store, and she went down one aisle, shoving stuff into her pants. She winked at me. I went down another aisle, and I see my friend's brother, Burton, also shoving stuff down his pants.

Chris was telling me to "keep six"—to watch out for the store clerk. Chris's mom paid for a can of soup or something, then we all left. She pulled out all this stuff, bacon, eggs, everything, and she cooked up this great big breakfast. And I stayed there for the day. Then she left and when she came back at night, I heard screaming. She was drunk, and she was angry. She was grabbing Chris, and Chris was screaming at me, "We've got to get the fuck out of here!" He broke free, we ran out of the house, and she came running after us with a frying pan or something in her hand. We took off down the alley into the darkness.

Chris and I became really good friends. Sometimes we'd steal bikes and wander the streets together, biking around the city, breaking into garages, going into freezers, taking food. I got arrested for the first time around then. The cops were going around with a paddy wagon picking up kids on stolen bicycles. There was a convoy of cop cars and kids sitting in the back and they would point out, "Oh, there's another kid that steals bikes." I guess one of the kids pointed us out and they came to our home. We had so many bikes in our garage, and they charged my brother Pat and me with theft. I don't remember what happened with those charges—I guess they were stayed or dropped because we were so young.

When I was around twelve, we'd play street hockey, which I always looked forward to. I'd always gravitated toward street kids, because those were the only kids that I could really hang out with and understand. Good kids come from good homes and most of the time their parents wouldn't want me to hang out with them. Growing up in poverty, I didn't invite any of my friends over to my house because I was embarrassed about the way we lived. We barely had any furniture, no pictures hanging on the walls, a broken TV, a couch that was ripped, chairs that were mismatched, holes in the walls, and no food in the fridge. So inviting friends over wasn't really an option—unless they grew up in poverty like myself, then they wouldn't discriminate because of their similar situation.

So there was a lot of disappointment, from not having a mother there for me and not having a father, to having to look to the people of the streets or my older brother as a mentor while he's in a gang. Ernest always brought his gang friends over. They'd party hard. After the party calmed down and everyone left, he'd be physically abusive to me, my brother Pat, and on occasion my mom. He'd always want to fight. As he got older, bigger, and tougher, he'd pick fights with my older brothers Sid and Paul. My brother Pat was never home for this reason. So it was just me, my mom, and Ernest at nights. I was getting tired of being a punching bag so when Ernest came home drunk, I'd take off and go find my friends on the streets or at their houses. If that didn't work out, I'd keep wandering until I found an open apartment building. I'd pull on the door handle and if it was open, I'd walk down the hallway, find the stairs to a lower level, and tuck myself in. I'd sleep under the stairs for the night, just to get away from all the yelling and violence.

I JOINED MY FIRST GANG WHEN I WAS FOURTEEN

Aboriginal street gangs in Winnipeg exploded in the late 1980s, as local organizations were fortified through partnerships with motorcycle gangs, like the Hells Angels, that were making their way across Canada. Limited economic opportunities on the province's reserves were compounded by hydroelectric projects built from the 1960s to the 1980s, which flooded and devastated traditional hunting and fishing grounds throughout the province, driving increasing numbers of Indigenous people to the city in search of better economic opportunities.[5] However, with a lack of appropriate training and education to transition to urban jobs, or services and resources to support them through the transition, some new residents and their children were particularly vulnerable to the promise of money and employment that the gangs presented.

Ernest had started this gang with Chris's other older brother, BJ. This was probably in the early eighties. It was my first introduction to gangs. They used to roller-skate around the city. They'd tie their shoes to the side of their belt loop while they roller-skated through the streets. They called themselves "the Night Walkers." My brother Pat eventually joined a gang called the Main Street Rattlers. It was a really big Aboriginal street gang back in the eighties.[6] I joined my first gang when I was fourteen years old, mimicking my brothers. Over twenty street kids formed the Junior Rattlers; we were mostly the younger brothers of the Main Street Rattlers. Back then, it was just about territory, and we'd get into fights with other gangs. We'd meet in parks and back alleys with bats, chains, fists, or whatever. Nobody ever got killed. It was just fighting, a bunch of kids fighting each other over territory or girls.

When I was about sixteen, I became a drug dealer, selling drugs in downtown Winnipeg arcades. In the beginning, I was working for someone, just a runner making five dollars a bag. I realized how easy it was to make money, so through one of my best friends—his dad was a biker who sold large quantities of marijuana—I bought an ounce for myself. With my brother's street cred, I got a spot on the street selling my own drugs and had my own runners making five a bag. I was in and out of school at the time, selling on the streets and sometimes in school.

---

5. For more on Manitoba's hydroelectric projects, see James B. Waldram, "Native People and Hydroelectric Development in Northern Manitoba, 1957–1987: The Promise and the Reality," *Manitoba History* 15 (Spring 1988).

6. *Aboriginal* is another term used to refer to Indigenous or First Nations people in Canada. For more on the term, see the glossary.

THEY ARRESTED ME FOR MISCHIEF

In Canada, Indigenous people are drastically overrepresented in the criminal justice system. While there are no studies that quantify the exact numbers of wrongfully convicted, Indigenous people are also thought to be wrongfully convicted at higher rates and less likely to get help following a conviction. Reasons for this disparate experience include institutional racism, language barriers, and mistrust of the legal system, which prevent Indigenous people from seeking help.

When I turned seventeen, I got arrested again. I had some friends who weren't in gangs. I used to hang out with them from time to time. I was at this house party, and one of my friends from school was so wasted. He went across the street to take a piss by this run-down garage. We heard something smash, and he walked by us, trailing drops of blood, and back into the house. Then, a few minutes later, cops pull up, lights come on, everybody scatters. I stayed. I remember thinking to myself, *Why run? I didn't do anything.* So I didn't run. The cops grabbed me and tossed me hard on the hood of their car. They said I fit the description of a kid with a leather vest and long hair who looked Indian. There were six other kids who looked like that. They roughed me up and arrested me for mischief—for breaking a garage window.

I got thrown into the justice system. I didn't have a lawyer. I didn't have anybody telling me, "Oh, you've got to show up to court next time or this is going to happen to you." No one ever gave me this kind of information. I just assumed it would go away. I was young. I got five breaches for missing court on five different occasions.[7] Those five breaches turned into a fine, which I got community service for. I went twice, never went back. It was like $300 for the garage window and $200 for the breaches, which totaled $500,

---

7. Not making a court date is considered a breach of contract, or the conditions the court places on an individual facing charges.

I think. Then I got picked up again for breaching my fine option. Back then, you could work off your fine in prison. The courts would take your fine in consideration for the time spent in remand, or they would add it into your sentence. I got sentenced to sixty days. This was my first time in prison. I was eighteen.

I went to the Annex B. That annex is minimum security in Headingley Prison.[8] There were a lot of people I recognized from the streets. I thought this was very odd. I became part of the Dutch Elm Bush Crew. My brother Ernest had a lot of cred on the street, and these guys respected him. A couple of guys asked if he was my brother, I said yes, and they gave me some cigarettes and canteen junk food. So from that point on, I started making connections in prison. I got out in twenty days for good behavior and started selling larger quantities of drugs with known gang members. Once you do time, that gives you more cred on the streets, and it makes you look more solid. I started selling cocaine in the bars. I was making a lot of money.

My reserve, Pine Creek First Nations, opened a bar that used to be called the Pink Flamingo on McPhillips and Notre Dame in 1990. They bought it and turned it into the Pine Creek Inn. They needed bouncers, so they called my brothers Paul and Sid to be head bouncers and to hire security. They immediately hired my brother Ernest, my brother Pat, myself, and some of our cousins. So there were like thirteen of us doing security. We had these black, silky jackets. They had the words "Warrior Security" on the back with a big emblem, like a starred Indian head, in the Four Directions colors.[9]

---

8. Headingley Correctional Centre is a minimum-, medium-, and maximum-security facility in Manitoba. Located just west of the town of Headingley, it occupies twenty acres of land beside the Assiniboine River.

9. The Four Directions are represented by the colors yellow, red, black, and white on some images of the Medicine Wheel. Also known as the Sacred Hoop, the Medicine Wheel image has been used by generations of Native Americans of many tribes. The wheel is meant to signify the four directions, which among other things, can also represent the stages of life, seasons of the year, and elements of nature.

Paul and Sid eventually quit because they couldn't handle the drugs and violence. This guy named Joe came in with my cousin Brian, and Joe became the head bouncer. The place was hopping with a lot of money to be made so we started attracting all types of people who wanted a cut of the action. Indigenous and non-Indigenous from different gangs trying to sell drugs started to come into the bar. Everyone was getting their toes stepped on, and we didn't know how to handle the situation. One evening, in 1996, Joe called a meeting. With the amount we were all selling, he told us, he could get drugs cheaper, but we needed to do something about the gangs cutting into our business. We had to create some kind of alliance. We agreed to create a gang.

We all sat at this meeting wearing our "Warrior Security" jackets. Everyone said, "We need a name." "Warriors," someone said, "Why don't we call ourselves the Manitoba Warriors?" After this was finalized, my brother Pat got my mom to sew the Indian head symbol and the lettering on the back of a leather vest. Everyone followed, asking my mom to do the same to their jackets. We started making actual patches that read "Manitoba" on the top, the symbol in the middle, and "Warriors" on the bottom. We voted in a president, vice president, sergeant at arms, treasurer. We became the thirteen OG members.

As soon as we set up, we started making ourselves known. We hit almost every drug operation there was in Winnipeg. If there was a gang selling drugs out of a location we wanted, we'd go in and take it over, with a lot of beatings and drive-by shootings to show that we weren't to be messed with. Once we took over locations, we'd put in our own lower-level guys who wanted to make a name and earn their full patch.[10] So people knew we were serious at the street level. We had the strength and the juice to carry it forward.

In 1997, I went to jail for pointing a firearm at a police officer as well as for drug convictions. I got an eight-month sentence. While I was in prison my daughter was born, Alexis Love Marsden.

---

10. To earn a full patch means to become a full member of the gang.

I got out not too long after, she was maybe a month old. And it was a strange feeling to hold her. I felt like I didn't know how to be a father. I stayed with her for about a week when I got out, but I just couldn't accept the responsibility. So I was barely around when she was first born.

My ex-girlfriend, Alexis's mom, was an alcoholic and drug user like myself. We were always partying, drinking, and using drugs. It wasn't good to be around each other. She was violent. I was in a gang and selling drugs and living this lifestyle. We would be on and off, but when I got picked up for Operation Northern Snow, the relationship was pretty much over.

FIFTY-TWO PEOPLE GOT ARRESTED

Operation Northern Snow was an investigation by the Winnipeg Police and the gang unit in 1998.[11] I was twenty-seven. Larger motorcycle clubs were moving in to patch over clubs in Winnipeg. Those larger clubs were "interviewing," you could say, other clubs like the Manitoba Warriors. At that time, a lot of violence was happening throughout Canada and in Montreal with the two rival motorcycle clubs.

We were very organized and had a lot of solid members at the time. We were slowly gaining control of the drug trade on Winnipeg streets and in the prisons. I think that's the reason we were arrested in Operation Northern Snow: we were drawing too much heat, getting greedy. It was a perfect time to infiltrate us.

We had this president who came in shortly after Joe retired. He had inside intel. He said there were two undercover cops within our organization, that everybody should lay low and not do any kind of business. But we thought he was crazy. So he eventually dropped out,

---

11. Operation Northern Snow was a police investigation initiated by the Winnipeg Police Service's Street Gangs Unit in 1998 to confront the Manitoba Warriors' increasing involvement in drug trafficking and prostitution.

and we voted in a new president. We just went on with our business, and meanwhile, the cops are collecting all this intel on us. When we got arrested, I found out through court documents that the two undercover police officers were female, and that there were over a hundred informants. Fifty-two people got arrested on November 4, 1998, with two full-patch club members rolling over.[12]

I was looking at two and a half years in the beginning. I really wanted to take this deal because the police didn't know I was the vice president at the time of my arrest; they just had me as a regular patch member.[13] When full-patch member Chummy rolled over, he gave a one-hundred-and-fifty-page statement. After his statement, the Crown came back to my lawyer stating they now had me as the vice president of the gang.[14] I was then looking at fourteen years. I started thinking, *I'm now looking at a lot of time in prison because of this fucking rat. They didn't want me taking a deal. Well, fuck this. I'm going to drop out, I quit.*

I dropped my colors in prison—and there was no turning back.[15] When I was finally sentenced to Stony, I got jumped in my cell, death threats every day.[16] After all this, I could've checked myself into protective custody.[17] But I decided to stay in general population, because it really didn't matter where I went. You can find protection in PC, but eventually you're going to be on the streets, and you're still going to be running, could be for the rest of your life. I was going

12. "Rolling over" means to cooperate with the police.

13. Ervin had become vice president of the gang in 1996.

14. Crown attorneys are the prosecutors in Canada's legal system.

15. "I dropped my colors" is another way of saying he left the gang.

16. Stony Mountain Institution is a minimum-, medium-, and maximum-security facility approximately twenty-four kilometers north of Winnipeg.

17. A form of separation carried out by prison officials to protect a person from threats that other prisoners in the general population pose for that person. In many jails and prisons, prisoners held in "PC" status are kept in the same cells and units as those in administrative or disciplinary segregation.

to bump into these guys sooner or later. I wanted to face it and deal with it in that moment.

I started doing ceremony in prison; I was twenty-eight. I'd never been to a sweat.[18] I didn't really know anything about Aboriginal spirituality or culture; I was just curious. *Why were people going to the lodge?* There were four sweat lodges on the spiritual grounds. Back then, you were free to roam through breezeways as long as you had a pass. I had access to go to the sweats and speak with the elders. My two uncles, my mom's brothers, were elders in Stony Mountain. My first sweat I just cried my eyes out. I bawled like a little baby. They say it's like being in your mother's womb. It felt like someone poured a bucket of water over me and the water was taking all this pain away. I felt this flood of emotion being lifted from my body. All this stuff just coming up to the surface. That was the beginning of something. From that point on, I continued going to sweats and tried to get that same feeling back. The next sweat was just as rewarding, and it taught me a lot. I think that's what kept me sane in prison, the ceremonies, being connected to the elders and the lodge.

HOW ANIMALS FEEL WHEN THEY'RE CAGED UP

Hobbema, Alberta—that's where I started my journey after leaving Stony Mountain.[19] That was 2001, and I was thirty-one. The first day I got to Hobbema healing lodge, before getting off that Greyhound bus, I felt like I was in a movie, you know that one with Nicholas Cage, *Con Air*, where the plane gets hijacked by prisoners and all the other prisoners are shackled in separate little cubicles.[20] They have you seated two prisoners to each caged cubicle on the right side

---

18. A "sweat" is a ceremony used as a ritual means of purification.

19. Hobbema was renamed Maskwacis in 2014.

20. The healing lodge in Hobbema is called the Pê Sâkâstêw Centre. Aboriginal healing lodges, run by Correctional Service Canada, are institutions that use Aboriginal values, beliefs, and traditions to design programs for incarcerated

of the bus, and on the opposite side, there's one small cubicle with room for one prisoner. I was shackled on the right side, along with this other guy. We're both shackled at our waists and our ankles are shackled to the floor. It was so tight. We were going from Stony Mountain Institution all the way to Hobbema, which is like eighteen hours if you were driving by car, but we were on the con bus, so it took even longer. We had to make all these stops to drop off other prisoners. It was so fucking hot and cramped. When we had to use the washroom, they wouldn't take the shackles off. Think about trying to get your zipper undone while your hands are shackled to the side of your waist, the bus swinging back and forth and all the while, you trying to relieve yourself, trying to get your balance, piss flying all over the place, and while all this is happening, there's a guard watching you through a small window at waist height. I actually thought the driver was intentionally swerving the bus.

Midway through, I thought the single cubicles looked more comfortable. I think we were in Saskatchewan. We'd dropped off a lot of guys, so the bus had started to empty out, and I'd had it with this other guy next to me. So I asked one of the sheriffs, "Can you put me in one of those smaller cubicles?" He said, "Yeah, sure." He threw me in a single cubicle, and it was so fucking small, so tight. I wouldn't recommend it if you're claustrophobic, it's not a good place to be. It was so uncomfortable, oh my God. When I got out, I could imagine how animals feel when they're caged up. I just wanted to run around and shake off all that stink and sweat.

I arrived at the healing lodge at around three in the morning. I went to bed immediately. I woke up and I felt like I could breathe again. I wasn't exactly free, I was still in prison, but that's what it felt like for me. I did a lot of ceremonies, but I had a lot of time to myself because the elders were all Cree and they always spoke Cree, which I didn't understand. I sometimes sat in the elders' office with a

---

individuals. For women, healing lodges may be minimum or medium security, and for men they are minimum-security facilities.

bunch of other prisoners just to listen to them. I never really understood what they were talking about, but it was a happy environment.
They were telling jokes. Sometimes one of the prisoners would sort
of translate what the elder was saying, but most of the time, I just
liked to be around the laughter.

I remember going to a four-day fast, sort of a transition for
prisoners, up by Rocky Mountain House, Alberta. Fasting in the
mountains was amazing, even though there was the threat of wild
animals—cougars, bears. The morning we were leaving, as I was
walking out on my way to the van, I glanced at the television. That's
when the planes were hitting the Twin Towers in New York on 9/11.
I stopped and then saw the second plane hit, and I swear I thought
it was a movie. When I got to the van, everybody was silent. I think
someone said, "You think it's going to be the end of the world when
we come out of the fast?" I was like, "End of the world? What's going
on?" And then there was just quietness after that.

I SURE DIDN'T WANT TO WIND UP BACK IN PRISON

I was there for seven months. I didn't think going back to Winnipeg
was a good idea for me. But Alexis, my daughter, was there, and I
started to miss her and my family, so I decided to go back. I wanted
Alexis to be in my life. I had everything set up. My auntie had giv-
en me a pamphlet about the Aboriginal Broadcast Training Initiative in Winnipeg, and I thought that would be an interesting job. I
started that program in January 2003. But I think once a prisoner is
released, it doesn't matter how solid his supports are, you're going to
fall through the cracks eventually. It's easy to slip up and go back to
drinking and maybe go back to hanging out with your gang friends.
I wound up going back and hanging around with the wrong guys.
When I came out of prison, I felt having a kid was a burden on me,
interrupting my business. I wanted to go out and be with the boys
and sell drugs and party. Meanwhile, I had a kid who needed me to

care for her, but for some reason, I just didn't care. My mother was never there for me, and maybe I looked at parenting the same way. I felt drugs, alcohol, the gang, and everything else was more important.

And then something happened to me. I got jumped at this house party that year. I thought, *What am I doing?* That was it. I sure didn't want to wind up back in prison. I had all these other guys, some from the Manitoba Warriors and some solid guys I knew from the streets, wanting to go retaliate. I still had a lot of respect on the streets. I decided to send everyone home. I said, "No, it's not worth it anymore." It's just a vicious cycle. You go retaliate, then you're stuck in the same kind of situation you were in before, and you have no choice but to go back to the gang because you need the backup. You need that protection. After everything calmed down and I got my bearings, I went to the hospital, got sewn up, and that was it. I never went back. And I finished school that December. After graduating, I went to work for Lisa Meeches at *The Sharing Circle* for a couple of seasons.[21] I ended my parole while working there. It was the support I needed.

I did my first two films while I worked there. This was in 2005, and I won a new talent award at the Aboriginal Film Festival for a five-minute film about this guy coming to grips with his past as he's about to leave prison. It was titled *504930C*, which was my prison FPS number.[22]

I've always been told to write what you know, because it's hard to tell someone else's story. I usually do crime drama. My films tend to be on the darker side of reality and revolve around crime, the justice system, and prison. They convey the struggle of being raised through poverty, alcohol, drugs, gangs, and violence. In *504930C*, the character has his gang family on one side and his real family on the other,

---

21. *The Sharing Circle* (1991–2008) was a Canadian documentary series and the country's longest-running Aboriginal television series.

22. An "FPS number" is a Finger Print Serial number. Individuals convicted in court for an offense under Canada's criminal code are assigned a number, which is attached to their criminal record and backed up by their fingerprints.

and it just kind of ends like that. That's pretty much the reality of it. We all have choices and we all struggle from time to time.

YOU CAN'T LEAVE THE TRAUMA BEHIND

Canada's Indian residential school system was a government-sponsored network of boarding schools established to assimilate Indigenous children by attempting to remove their language, culture, and connection to family. The intergenerational impact of this mandate has cast a long shadow over the lives of Indigenous Canadians, who are more likely to live in poverty, more likely to live with chronic illness, more likely to have their children apprehended from them, and more likely to be incarcerated than other Canadians.

In 2007, the implementation of the Indian Residential Schools Settlement Agreement began. The largest class-action settlement in Canadian history, the agreement was reached by the legal counsel for former students, legal counsel for the churches that ran some of the schools, the Assembly of First Nations, other Indigenous organizations, and the government of Canada. The Truth and Reconciliation Commission of Canada (TRC) was one of the agreement's five components. Its mandate was to inform all Canadians about what happened in the country's Indian residential schools. Between 2007 and 2015, the TRC heard from more than 6,500 witnesses throughout Canada.

I just learned about my mom's abuse, physical abuse, in the residential schools not too long ago.[23] I didn't know people suffered abuse in residential schools. When the Truth and Reconciliation Commission came out and did this whole investigation, they began to get statements from abused people, and my mom was one of them. My

---

23. Between 1874 and 1996, approximately 154,000 Indigenous children were separated from family and culture to attend Indian residential schools and often suffered physical and sexual abuse while there. For more on the legacy of the Indian residential schools, see appendix essay 2.

brother Paul took my mom down to see a lawyer to give her state-ment in 2010. She didn't want to go. When they came home, she ran into her bedroom and locked the door and stayed in there all night. She was really traumatized. The next morning, she said she didn't want to do that again. I was a little upset that they pressured her to go. But I think it's important too. So that people might understand the trauma that those kids went through.

She'd never, ever spoken of it to me or my family. I didn't know that she was abused; that she'd been slapped, punched, and had her hair pulled. Her sisters experienced the same thing. I just thought she had an alcohol problem. I started realizing where this alcoholism came from, the life we'd lived, and why she abused herself and us through her drinking. Now, I understand where all the hurt came from; it was all the trauma that she experienced from the schools, which led to the alcohol abuse and that kind of trickled down to us. We were abused by a person who'd been abused.[24] I want to know more; I just don't know how to talk to her about it. But I understand now why we moved around so much. My mom was searching and wanting to start over—make a fresh start. In my mind, that's what she was doing. But you can't leave the trauma behind, it's always going to follow you.

My daughter knows that my mom went to residential school. But we haven't had a conversation about it yet. I'm sure it'll come up eventually. I want her to understand where the violence came from—the alcohol abuse, the drug abuse, the neglect, her feeling abandoned. I guess you experience it, you pass it on.

These institutions are all the same, right? Like for instance, the residential school: kids are apprehended and thrown into a religious school system. They're forced to learn a different language and a dif-ferent way of life, a European culture. The child and welfare system: they have kids thrown into group homes, youth centers, whatever. Same principle of apprehension. And the prison system, sort of the

---

24. For more on intergenerational trauma in Native communities, see appendix essay 2.

same thing: they apprehend adults, throw them into the justice system and then into the institutions.

I'm actually in the investigative stages with the National Film Board on a documentary on the overrepresentation of Aboriginal people within the prison system. We're trying to understand why there are so many Aboriginal people incarcerated in Canada. More than half the prison population throughout the prairie provinces. Across the nation, I think it's over 26 percent.[25] That's crazy. So many people being incarcerated are Aboriginal.

I look back at my personal journey, like when I got picked up, when I got apprehended off the street. If people took the time to investigate the situation, they would've known that I wasn't the kid who put his fist through a broken-down garage window. I was taken someplace against my will. No matter what I said, it didn't matter, they were going to arrest me. The prison systems are filled with people who are just in for the first time and in on misdemeanors—vandalism or getting intoxicated in public, or mischief—just petty, petty crimes. They're flooding the courts and the prisons with Aboriginal people. People like me, who didn't understand the justice system, people coming from northern communities who get thrown into the system—they don't even know why they're there. They're not getting answers that they need. They don't have proper representation. They end up pleading out. Everybody pleads out just to get it over with, to start the sentence, to get out of prison. But then, you're in the justice system from that point on. It's like a revolving door that you can never get out of.

---

25. For more on Indigenous incarceration rates in Canada, see appendix essay 2.

JAMES FAVEL

PEGUIS FIRST NATION
EXECUTIVE DIRECTOR, BEAR CLAN PATROL
BORN IN: 1968, Scarborough, Ontario
INTERVIEWED IN: Winnipeg, Manitoba

James Favel grew up in Winnipeg, one of a handful of Indigenous kids in his community. He was bullied from the age of five. At fifteen, James pursued a relationship with his father, who lived on Peguis First Nation, about 190 kilometers north of the city.[1] He was embraced by his father's extended family but fell into what he called "a series of self-destructive behaviors" after his father passed away just two years after they met.

I met James in downtown Winnipeg. His tattooed arms burst out of

---

1. Peguis First Nation is the largest First Nation community in Manitoba. Members of its population of ten thousand are of Ojibwe and Cree descent.

his black Bear Clan Patrol T-shirt.[2] He seemed to survey the room as he entered it, and he projected enormous energy and a sense of efficiency—the stories and information he shared would have taken most people twice as long to convey. James spoke about his young adult life working as a drug dealer in the city's Native bars, leaving that world to pursue his trucker's license, and how his life shifted toward activism after he bought a house in the city's North End. James recalled his family's first years in this new home where his wife, Shannon, could not tend the garden in the front yard without being solicited by men for sex, and his daughter, Mandy, did not feel safe coming home alone from school.

In 2014, the body of fifteen-year-old Tina Fontaine (Sagkeeng First Nation) was found at the bottom of the city's Red River, wrapped in plastic and a duvet cover and weighted down with rocks. James's urgent need to do something for the security of his community led him to bring back Winnipeg's Bear Clan Patrol, which served the neighborhood for several years after being formed in 1992. The group's work began with efforts to drive men in search of prostitutes out of the neighborhood but quickly expanded as its members came to see how much broader the needs of the community really were. Today the organization trains volunteers to patrol the neighborhood at night, to protect its women, children, elderly, and other vulnerable members.

I'M BROWN AND SHE WAS WHITE

I grew up one of five Indigenous kids in my community, in my school, in my grade. It wasn't easy. There was a lot of bullying. It was confusing to me, because I didn't understand why people were mad at me. Kids kept telling me things like my mom wasn't my mom, because I'm brown and she was white. My mom's English, my father's Indigenous from Peguis First Nation. I would walk to school with

---

2. The Bear Clan is a community-based solution to crime prevention, providing a sense of safety, solidarity, and belonging to both its members and the communities they serve.

the same group of boys who, on the way home, once they got with the others, would chase me and try to kick my ass.

My experience with bullying was atypical, because I was bigger and stronger than most of the bullies. Normally the bullied boy goes home with a bloody nose. For me, it was the other way around—I'd send *them* home with bloody noses. Afterward they'd tell me their parents gave them a hard time and said, "Why can't you beat him? Go back, you're better . . . fight him again." So, from the time I was five years old, more or less, I was fighting on a regular basis, and it turned me into a kind of anti-bully.

Otherwise, my childhood was kind of normal. I was a free-range kid doing everything, going everywhere, seeing all kinds of stuff. My mom's second husband worked for the Fisheries and Oceans Department at the University of Manitoba; my mother worked there as well. So we did some traveling when I was young, to Mexico, places like that.

What was weird was my family, my mother's extended family, wanted nothing to do with me at all. My cousin, he was white, so he was invited to all the family gatherings, but I wasn't. My mother said that she was protecting me from them because they were all of that mindset and there was no point in me associating with them. But she was part of that family, so when those functions happened, she'd go.

But my mother loved and cared for me. There was a stable home for me. There was always food in the fridge, clothes on my back. I didn't have to worry about those things. Many of my friends were in Child and Family Services care and foster homes, and I'd always bring them home with me. If they were in need, I'd bring them to my mom, because she'd make everything right.

I FIRST MET MY FATHER WHEN I WAS FIFTEEN

I was raised in the white world, away from my family on the reserve, until I was about fourteen, and started asking questions like, "Who's my dad?" I first met my father when I was fifteen, at Peguis. The two years I had with him was mainly him drinking and me tagging along as much as I could because I just wanted to be near him. It wasn't good. I remember waking up at parties on the reserve and him asking me to give him his insulin injection. But I didn't spend a great deal of time out there. I think the longest stretch was about three weeks. I would know where my dad was, but he wouldn't know where I was for the most part. Mom kept me away.

The extended family on my dad's side just swallowed me up. They wanted me to be there. It was a wonderful thing. My aunts and uncles, they all really took to me right away. My uncle "Boogie" Gerald Favel, for example, acted like I was just another kid in the house. The door was open, I'd come in. It was really refreshing to have family in that way, considering what I'd known in the past.

My dad died when I was seventeen, from complications of diabetes brought on by alcoholism. And I went into self-destruct mode at that point, acting like, "I'll be dead by the time I'm twenty-five. I'll live hard, party hard, and die fast." That's how I conducted myself for a long time.

Peguis was a growing community when I was there in the late eighties, early nineties. But there wasn't any kind of job I could get out there; there wasn't a lot of productive activity. It was a lot of dull times. I didn't have my driver's license. I didn't have a car. If you don't have those things on the rez, you're just stuck. I was about just having fun, partying a little bit when my father was alive, but then after he died, I disconnected again and came back to the city, and I dove into some really self-destructive behaviors. I was just angry at the world.

I PICKED UP THE PISTOL

I started selling drugs. School wasn't a priority, because why would I sit in class when I could go down on the corner and make $200 a day selling hash? We were young and naïve children playing these adult games, doing some really stupid stuff. People got hurt.

There were three of us in the main group—me, Greg, and Dale—and I was kind of the leader. They always asked me what to do. One of my friends went out and stole some weapons. He came back with these three guns and gave one to each of us. We had the guns, but we only had six bullets for two revolvers, and he didn't have any bullets for his nine-millimeter automatic. So we put three bullets in each of the revolvers; the cylinder had every other one empty, and we'd have them set so if we shot them, they would've gone *click, bang, click, bang, click, bang.*

I was going to school, at Technical Vocational High School, but we'd party all the time. I didn't work at that point because I was the head drug dealer and I had all the money. We'd party all night, then Greg would go out to work in the morning, and he'd come back. He was laying on the floor one afternoon, and I'd just gotten out of the shower. I came downstairs, and he said, "I'm fucking tired after working all day." I picked up the pistol and pointed it at him and said, "I should shoot you and put you out of your misery." And he grabbed the pistol and put it on his chest, and said, "Go ahead." Just a kid playing with a loaded weapon; I pulled the trigger. When he had grabbed it, he must have knocked it so that the cylinder rotated and the bullet lined up with the barrel. I shot him in the chest at point-blank range, but because he moved the barrel over just that little bit, I think that saved his life.

I got arrested. He got arrested. In the end, all I did was two months' open custody at the youth center. "Open custody" meant you could get a pass, called a "temporary absence," to go out if you went looking for work. I thought, *Okay, I'll do that.* I took my yellow sheet—the temporary absence—and I went running out there looking for jobs.

I got hired by Pic a Pop and I was working there for a couple of months while my grandfather and mother were both helping to support me.[3] I got my driver's license. My grandfather helped me get my first loan, and I bought my first car for $900. I was driving, and it was pretty good. I left the job at Pic a Pop for a job with Lucas Fluid Power. It was more money and more responsibility. I was really starting to feel I was doing good.

By that point I'd been out on bail for about eighteen months. I think it was close to my nineteenth birthday by the time they incarcerated me. I met this woman, and I was weak. And stupid things happened. She wanted to stay out all night, and I went because I wanted to be with her so much. That was a mistake. I couldn't be at her place at three in the morning and at work at seven in the morning consistently. I got charged with impaired driving. And then I got a charge for trafficking. I got charged with possessing a restricted firearm and drug possession. I ended up losing my job.

Every time I got in trouble with the law, I reevaluated my circumstances. In preparation for my court date, I tried to change so I wouldn't present poorly. I started changing my pattern again, looking for work, applying to university, and my life started changing. My band, Peguis, was paying for me to go. I had a generous allowance of $375 every two weeks from the band, plus, after my first year, there was an Aboriginal internship program with the federal government. It was at the Canada Employment Center, and I was a file clerk. I was there three summers in a row. I was doing well in university, getting closer to my bachelor's, and had my job with the federal government. In the last year, after the end of the season they kept me on part time.

Back in the Filmon era, the government was trying to save money.[4] When Filmon axed sixteen thousand federal positions for low-

---

3. Pic a Pop was a popular drink company in Manitoba for several decades.

4. Gary Filmon was the premier of Manitoba from 1988 to 1999. In 1990, he embarked upon an austerity program, increasing taxes and cutting government jobs and services.

end guys like myself, my job disappeared. I got a job with ADM Flour Mill when I was twenty-seven, and it was decent money, but they'd only give me shifts once in a while. It wasn't enough, and I ended up losing my apartment.

SELLING DRUGS IN THE BARS

I started doing security in bars as a bouncer. I was at the Stock Exchange Hotel, the Westbrook Inn, C-Weed's Cabaret before that—only the Native clubs in the city. I started going to those bars and drinking there. I met Shannon when I was at the Stock Exchange. She was a customer, and she had a daughter, Mandy, who was four. When we first started dating, I think what really struck me was we laughed so much. It was refreshing. We were a good fit together.

But from the time I was about twenty-seven till about thirty-four, I was working as a bouncer and selling drugs in the bars and drinking all the time. And because all the people in those bars were Indigenous, I started learning about my culture, kind of back-asswards, through alcohol. It seemed like they were more caring and forgiving and giving, whereas the family on the other side, my maternal grandparents' world, was all about pretenses, always worried about what the neighbors think, keeping the grass just right, those things.

After several years of crazy behaviors, I got arrested again. The officer who arrested me, Brian Chrupalo, was part of the gang unit. We had a lot of gang activity in the bar, so he'd come in on a weekly basis to see how things were. I was not a typical drug-dealing douchebag. I was open to speaking with the cops about things that were going on. I let them know when this guy tried to rob that guy, this guy slapped this one. I was not afraid of reprisals because I wasn't a gang member. That was my responsibility, so I did that willingly.

In the summer of 2002, Brian pulled me over. I was traveling to work in a cab, and I think I got ratted out as being a dealer by somebody who knew me. I see the brown car behind, and I see the lights go on, and I'm like, *Fuck. I've got a big bunch of dope in my pocket.* Brian was like, "Sorry, James, this sucks, but I have to do what I have to do." I said, "I get it." He cuffed me and took me downtown.

I got that charge and I was out on bail for three years awaiting trial. And during that time—I guess it was in the winter of 2004— one of my friends who worked for a trucking company said, "Get your Class One, I'll show you how to drive." So I started doing that.[5]

By November 2005, I had my full Class One driver's license. I quit selling drugs and being a bouncer, and had been working as a truck driver for about eight months by the time I went to sentencing. I was looking at three years in a federal penitentiary, but because of my job and because Officer Chrupalo came and spoke on my behalf, I was given two years less a day serving the community.[6] They essentially put me on house arrest. I had a temporary absence that said I could be out every day as long as I was working.

I think that was where the real shift happened in my life and my own being. I thought, *Now I'm going to make a go of it. There are no other chances for me. If I get caught again for doing something stupid, I'm done. I'll be in prison. I don't want to live that way. I don't want my family to have to go through that.*

NOW I WAS A STAKEHOLDER

I started looking for property in 2005. But every time I got close to finding something, I'd find out somebody lied about something, misrepresented something, and it was frustrating. So I took a real estate licensing course. Around 2008, my great-aunt passed away,

---

5. A Class One is a professional truck driver's license.

6. "Two years less a day" is a special legal expression. This kind of sentence (of two years or less) means a less drastic sentence of serving the time in a provincial jail rather than a federal prison.

and she left a bunch of money for my mom. My mom wanted to help me to buy a house.

When I was looking for property in 2009, I was in my second phase of the real estate course. There was a house for sale on Stella Avenue and a vacant piece of city property next door. I bought both on April 1, 2009. That was the start of my shift toward activism because now I was a stakeholder.

There was a private Catholic school behind my house, and parents would park on both sides of the back lane and block me in. One day, I go to my mailbox, and there's a paper from the Dufferin Residents Association. I thought, *Maybe the association will be able to help.* I went to the meeting and the woman was like, "I don't think there's anything I can do to help you, but you might be able to help us." She said, "Why don't you come and be on our board?"

So, I went. I'm proactive; I like to get things going. Right away we started building a community housing plan. We also started doing bylaw sweeps through the community.[7] Bulky waste was a real problem in our community. So I started using my computer and camera, taking pictures, documenting, and making reports and sending them to the city so they would come take away the garbage. I thought, *Wow, this is great.* After the first year, they elected me to be chairman of the board.

When I first went to work with the Dufferin Residents Association, we had probably two dozen boarded-up, vacant buildings in our community. Landlords weren't taking care of properties, leaving them abandoned. They became flophouses, used for drug activity; people were having sex in them, drinking. You had people in there starting fires to keep warm or for fun; some floors didn't have the structural integrity to support a person.

The predation on our women was just rampant. And because the exploitation was going on unchecked, we'd have to meet Mandy

---

7. Bylaws are rules and guidelines that a local authority or community sometimes creates to regulate itself. The "bylaw sweep" James describes was an effort to address the discarding of waste that contravened his community's bylaws.

at the bus stop every day when she was coming home from school. Some guy was trying to solicit her. Shannon would pick weeds out of the lawn around the fence on our property, and some guy would drive by and offer her twenty bucks. I don't think there's a woman in our community that doesn't have a story like that, and that's one of the things that drove me wild.

With the Dufferin Residents Association, I was all about john traffic bylaws, trying to get people to do the right thing.[8] Trying also to get the police to do the right thing—address our needs and give us the respect that we deserve as community members. Because I lived right there, I'd see a car drive by and pick up the prostitute on the corner, and I'd take the license plate number down. I'd call 911 and say, "Look, I just caught this guy picking up a woman," and they were like, "So?" I'd call the non-emergency number, 986-4222, and they'd say, "Well, without a complainant, you don't have a crime."[9] Since I'm just a private citizen, they didn't take me seriously. That was one of the things that I wanted to see addressed.

That was the crux of why I got involved in the first place. I lived in a household with two women. And they were both badgered by unwanted sexual advances, by predators. And in my daughter's case, after a couple of years, in 2012, she had enough, and she left. My daughter, my baby, my child moved away. She took off. I wanted her to stay at home as long as she was comfortable, and she became uncomfortable because of these turds outside the house.

Mandy moved in with a friend of hers for a while, out of the neighborhood, in Tyndall Park, and she ended up falling in with a young man who wasn't good for her. He was a drug addict and eleven years her senior. They ended up having a baby. He's gone now thankfully, but she went through a lot of trouble with that relationship.

---

8. "John" is an informal noun used to describe a prostitute's client. James worked to promote knowledge and understanding of the neighborhood's john traffic bylaws to encourage people to report incidents as they occurred.

9. 986-4222 is the city information phone number for Winnipeg.

In August 2014, the body of fifteen-year-old Tina Fontaine was found in the Red River. She had been in the care of Manitoba Child and Family Services when she was reported missing, and reports written in the aftermath of her death show that the supports and interventions that she desperately needed went unfulfilled.

When Tina Fontaine was found, we'd already been talking about a community patrol model.[10] We were looking at COPP—the Community on Patrol Program—and Neighborhood Watch. Those are both administered through the state. They have a lot to offer—bells and whistles, jackets, flashlights, backpacks, first aid, and training. But the state does the vetting of the personnel. I wouldn't be qualified to be part of a watch because of my criminal history.

And so we were looking for another option, and when Tina's body was found in the river, it started a conversation with my wife in bed while we were watching *The Daily Show* one night. It was part of our daily routine. We'd discuss the issues of the day. And as chairman of the Dufferin Residents Association, I was preoccupied with crime in the community. Mandy was away at that point, and Shannon and I were always strategizing a better way forward. Not only for ourselves and our family but for the people around us. We had a moment of inspiration. We said, "We should get the Bear Clan Patrol back."[11]

IT WENT OUT AT SIX ON THE NEWS

My truck was in for service one morning just after Tina's body was found. We went down to the Alexander Docks to show our support.

---

10. Tina Fontaine's death is seen as a key moment in the call for a National Inquiry into Missing and Murdered Indigenous Women and Girls (MMIWG). For more on MMIWG, see the historical timeline and appendix essay 2.

11. The Bear Clan was first formed in Winnipeg's North End in 1992. After several years of community service the patrol went on hiatus, but was revived in 2015.

When we got there—I think it was August 18—there was just a news camera and a sacred fire.[12] The reporter came over right away and asked me some questions. That was the first time I said anything about the Bear Clan out loud, outside of the house, and it went out at six on the news.

One of my colleagues in the Dufferin Residents Association managed to arrange a meeting the following day with two of the original members of the Bear Clan. I met up with them that afternoon and I asked them for permission to carry on the program. They said, "Go for it." I wanted to see the Bear Clan Patrol restart. But I had no intention of running it. I had a career. I was a professional truck driver. I didn't have time. Because I was on the news, the original clan members said, "It's your baby. You take it and you do it." It took nine months from the time of that first meeting. We met every Tuesday for two hours until May. And in May 2015, we had our kickoff event.

That spring, I was in the car with Shannon driving toward our house. It's 5:45—the sun is going down, it's cool already, and it had been raining. And there's this girl lying in a fetal position on the concrete stoop of a dentist's office. She's kind of half in a puddle, with a backless shirt, no shoes, no jacket, with her back to the road. I'm like, "Fuck, fuck, turn the car around," to my wife. We get out of the car and ask the girl, "Are you okay?" She goes, "No, I've been robbed. I got beat up. They took my stuff. They left me here." I said, "How long have you been here?" She goes, "I've been here for an hour." Rush-hour traffic, cars and buses going all over the place, but nobody stopped to check on this girl for an hour. That's that disconnect. People see somebody injured and say, "Not my problem." People are too scared to step up and say and do the right thing. So I'm trying to set an example and fucking do it. It is your responsibility. These are your community members. That should be worth something to you.

---

12. A sacred fire is believed to open a doorway that allows communication with the spirit world. It is often lit to start a ceremony or sacred event.

One of the things that I've experienced myself is that as a stakeholder, certain things are more important. So I've been trying to convey that to the larger community—that you may not own anything, but you're a stakeholder because you've got to walk these streets every day. So that's what I'm focused on when I'm on patrol. We're trying to rebuild that feeling of the village. We're trying to reconnect our community members.

MORE WOMEN WENT MISSING

We started patrolling in June. We realized we were making some mistakes. Our first patrol, we had children out with us. Grandmothers came with their five-year-old grandchildren. We're out on the street. There are intoxicated persons, exploited persons. There's drug use going on. It's not something that five-year-olds need to see. Plus, too many flip-flops were coming across needles and broken crack pipes. So we said, "This isn't right. We've got to slow down." We stepped back and made a policy that there should be no one under the age of eighteen and that you need proper attire when you're out. And then we got a little more focused on nonviolent crisis and prevention training because we wanted to make sure that we weren't going to have cowboys out there trying to bust heads. In July 2015, we committed to patrolling four days a week, Thursday through Sunday. Sometimes it was small, four or five people, but we just kept going. It took us about a year before people really started taking us seriously. But after that, our work spoke for itself.

In November 2015, there was a fire at the social housing project right across from my house.[13] It went up in flames, and there were twenty-nine people—seventeen children, twelve adults, seven residences—that lost everything in that afternoon. I put out a call for donations on our Facebook page. We got enough donations to meet

---

13. The Social Housing Rental Program is subsidized housing provided for low-income Manitobans.

the needs of the families that were affected. They all got into new accommodations and with our assistance, they were able to get all of the housewares that they needed.

By January first, all the families were resituated, and we still had a 52-foot semi-trailer full of housewares that we had collected over that period. On the twenty-fifth of January, we got access to the Indian and Métis Friendship Centre, a great big bingo hall. I just backed that 52-foot trailer up to the door and we put everything out on the tables. And then at ten in the morning we opened the doors and let the community come in. Some of the first people were Syrian refugees who had just arrived. They had a place down the street. I let them pick whatever they wanted, loaded it in the back of my truck, and drove to their house to unload it. We did a lot of good that day; 450 people, not counting children, got all kinds of free stuff.

The first year the Bear Clan was operational, I was trying to do four nights a week on patrol, possibly in bed by like nine, and getting up at 4:30 in the morning to get out and haul gravel. I wasn't going to be able to do both for very much longer. And that year I finished hauling gravel in October. It was early, we usually don't finish until about mid-November, so there was going to be a shortfall in my income. I needed more. The Bear Clan board and one of our advisers kept on telling me salary dollars were going to come. At the beginning of January, they said, "Don't worry about it, James," and so I didn't truck that winter. I stayed in town and worked as a staff member for Native Clan Organization and did what I could with the Bear Clan on the side.[14]

In February 2016, Cooper Nemeth went missing. He was a non-Indigenous boy. There was a rumor that Cooper was last seen at Siloam Mission, which is right across the tracks from our community. So I said to the patrollers, "Tomorrow when we start looking,

---

14. Established in 1972, Native Clan Organization is a nonprofit whose mission is to provide services to Indigenous offenders and ex-offenders to support their reintegration into the community.

we're going to be focusing on the area around the tracks, underneath the bridges." Sadly, our efforts were largely symbolic because he was never in our community. He was dead the night that he went missing. But we gave the family comfort in knowing that we were out there looking for him. It wasn't just us; it was people all over the place, but somehow the focus was on us. I think that was the year that we were labeled the most racist city in Canada.[15] So the news really liked that, the Indigenous organization in the North End helping out the non-Indigenous community. Our Facebook page went from 20,000 people to over 210,000 overnight.

That spring, things started getting crazy. Azraya Kokopenace, then Catherine Curtis—more women went missing.[16] We were looking for all of them. I was basically working a hundred hours a week just on Bear Clan stuff, making the patrols. A little bit of money started coming in. I started taking a salary from Bear Clan, and then we were incorporated that summer. I'm now the executive director of a nonprofit. It was like, *Holy fuck, what happened?*

In June 2016, I had a meeting with Devon Clunis, chief of police here in Winnipeg. He was asking about my salary and said, "What would it take to keep you here?" I said, "Well, I'm used to pulling down $5,000 every week in my truck. But I can survive on about a grand a week." He said, "We'll get you that." He said that he would have it by September. It didn't happen. I got a $10,000 grant from University of Winnipeg Community Renewal Corporation to pay my salary for that period. I was only getting $1,500 biweekly at first. I almost lost my house in the fall of last year; I had to pay my house taxes off. But I managed to pull it out.

When we first started on the patrol, it was in response to violence against women. It was a response to what happened with Tina

15. See Nancy Macdonald, "Welcome to Winnipeg: Where Canada's Racism Problem Is at Its Worst," *Maclean's*, January 22, 2015.

16. These Indigenous women and girls are among Canada's missing and murdered. For more on this, see appendix essay 2.

Fontaine, so I was focused primarily on john traffic. We would go out at night with a pen and paper and take down license plates of johns and file them off to the detective. But once we got out there, people came up to us and asked us for food. We had people asking us for first aid. We had people asking us for condoms. We had people asking us for sanitary napkins, for toilet paper.

So we started thinking about that. Now we go out with backpacks full of care kits, first aid kits for people on the street. Seventy of our members are trained to use Naloxone.[17] We have an opioid overdosing kit. We've got an AED.[18] About 120 of our members are trained in first aid. We're building up their résumés.

Now Bear Clan Patrol is well beyond anything I'd ever imagined. There's so much good coming out of it. In this world, we've been trained to think that there are this many jobs and that's all there is, and if you don't fit into that paradigm, then you're out. But there's more than that. People have gifts. The people in our community aren't recognized the way other people are, but they have their own skills and abilities. We're trying to help them find their way. That's what we're offering.

GENERATIONS OF ADULTS WHO NEED TO RELEARN HOW TO LOVE

My community is 75 percent Indigenous. Now we have a large newcomer presence as well. A guy from Eritrea was giving a speech at the Bell Tower last year.[19] He said that the handlers that come over from Canada to their countries to get them to emigrate tell them stories about Indigenous people. And he says they were told that the

---

17. Naloxone is an opioid overdose reversal medication.

18. An automated external defibrillator is a portable device that can be used to treat sudden cardiac arrest.

19. "Meet Me at the Bell Tower" is a Friday evening community gathering in Winnipeg's North End.

Indigenous people are lazy. They're drunks. They're drug addicts. They don't work. Stay away from them. Well, you hear it from one guy, whatever, you move on. But I've been working with a lot of people now. I've been working with them to build community patrols for their people in our communities. I ask them, "So is that true? Are people saying that to you?" They all say yes. But it's Indigenous people they're working alongside in the community and they're seeing a different side. They're seeing a new reality, and I'm working hard to see that grow.

I've come to some realizations: The intergenerational trauma inflicted by the residential school system has produced generations of people who grew up taken from their families, so they were raised by strangers, by people who didn't love and care for them. They were treated as a commodity, abused, neglected. And so now we have generations of adults here who need to relearn how to love.[20]

Working with the refugee communities—a lot of Somalis, Syrians—one thing I noticed is that they're very demonstrative. They're family. They love. They're always together. And I noticed that that's what's lacking in our communities, that connection. But also, what I'm seeing is that they all have their culture. They all have their own language and they're unified. In the Indigenous communities, we've lost our languages. We've lost our cultures. All levels of government need to really step up; eradicate poverty for us so we can get our heads up out of the sand for more than five seconds.

I was at Stony Mountain in May for a resource fair.[21] They brought in all the social services that prisoners can expect to see when they come out. And you know, you hear the provincial numbers: 70 percent incarcerated are Indigenous. But it's one thing to hear it, it's

---

20. For more on the legacy of intergenerational trauma in Native communities, see appendix essay 2.

21. Stony Mountain Institution is a minimum-, medium-, and maximum-security facility approximately twenty-four kilometers north of Winnipeg.

another thing to witness it. Guys come walking in there, and they're all my guys that I know from the street. It really hit home then. *Yeah, I fucking feel that.*

Today we have eleven thousand kids in Manitoba in Child and Family Services care. Of the apprehensions, only 13 percent of them are for abuse; most of the apprehensions are poverty related.[22] There was a story last summer about a young woman and her baby, members of Ebb and Flow First Nation.[23] It was a very hot summer day when the social worker came to visit her. The mother had gone through the CFS system herself, so it was expected they would check on her. She had gone through parenting classes, taken all the right steps. But when the social worker stopped there that day, they wanted to take custody of the child because it was *hot*. She's going to take this woman's child away, at great cost, for something that could've been remedied by spending ninety dollars on an air conditioner? Thankfully, the chief and the council got involved and they put the kibosh on that. But again, they were just looking for some reason, some cause to take that child. It has become part of their budget. CFS is given something like $4,500 every time they apprehend a child. If you're incentivizing the destruction of our families, in 2019, that's a problem.

A child in care, as a commodity, has a daily value that the government will pay to outside organizations or foster homes to look after. But they'd never pay that same kind of money to keep the family together, to give that support to the family. And that's one of the functions of the Bear Clan out there. We deescalate situations so that CFS doesn't have to come in, so police don't have to come in, so the fire department and the ambulance don't have to come. When we come across a domestic disturbance and there are children involved,

---

22. *Apprehension* is the official term used in Canada for the removal of children from their homes by child protection agencies.

23. Ebb and Flow First Nation is a community about 240 kilometers northwest of Winnipeg.

we will on occasion take children from the home, to a family member. Many times these community members aren't strangers to us, but even if they are, we'll take their children to a safe space so they don't get apprehended. That's what we're doing. We're getting in the way of these fucking system trends. There's so much going on. I feel responsible for all of it, and I can only do so much.

MARIAN NARANJO

SANTA CLARA PUEBLO
FOUNDER, HONOR OUR PUEBLO EXISTENCE
BORN IN: 1950, Tooele Ordnance Depot, Utah
INTERVIEWED IN: Santa Clara Pueblo, New Mexico

Santa Clara is a Tewa-speaking pueblo located along the west bank of the Rio Grande, about twenty-five miles north of Santa Fe. The area has been inhabited by the Pueblo people since the late fourteenth or early fifteenth centuries. In 1598, Spanish conquistador Juan de Oñate founded the colony of New Mexico for Spain and continued the process, already begun in nearby regions, of subjugating the locals; imposing taxes paid in crops, cotton, and work; and attempting to dismantle the Pueblo peoples' religion. The Pueblo people were forced to labor for the colonizers and sometimes sold into slavery as the conquistadors let their cattle overgraze Pueblo land, which eventually led to drought, erosion, and famine. In 1680, the Pueblo peoples conducted a successful revolt against the Spanish and drove them from the region. Santa Fe was re-conquered in 1692 by Spanish forces.

I met Marian in her home at Santa Clara, and she spoke about the challenges her people have faced in their stewardship of the land. In 1941 and '42, the US government used the First and Second War Powers Acts to grant itself permission to build the Los Alamos National Laboratory on Pueblo land that contains or lies near more than twenty-four Native reservations and sacred places especially important to the Santa Clara, San Ildefonso, Cochiti, Pojoaque, and Jemez Pueblos peoples. Acting without permission from the Indigenous peoples whose ancestral lands they occupied, Marian says, "they planted themselves within the west wall of our church." The lab, which produces weapons of destruction, has polluted the land and water, preventing Pueblo people from accessing the places that are integral to their cultural practices.[1]

A mother of four and grandmother of eight, Marian has spent the last twenty years focusing on the resulting environmental and health is-sues in the region, including high rates of radionuclides found in tradi-tional food staples grown nearby and high rates of cancers in neighboring communities. As she describes it, her people believe that "the Creator placed the first people on this earth with a plan and a way of being in a particular place that form lifeways of sustainability, through giving thanks for the Creator's gifts of land, air, and water."

THE LIFEWAYS OF OTHER PEOPLE

My two younger brothers and I grew up on an army base in Utah—Tooele Ordnance Depot, where my dad worked. When I was little, we'd go back and forth from the army base to Santa Clara, where my father is from. Here at Santa Clara, there were no-plumbing adobe

---

1. For more on this injustice, see "Environmental Injustices for Pueblo Communi-ties Near Los Alamos National Laboratory," *Environmental Justice in the Southwest*, November 17, 2016, https://sites.coloradocollege.edu/ejsw/2016/11/17/environmental -injustices-for-pueblo-communities-near-los-alamos-national-laboratory/.

homes.[2] But the cultural aspects of the village were just so beautiful, and it was a whole different world compared to where I was born. We'd come for special events, and my relatives at that time here spoke Tewa.[3]

One of the first lessons I learned in elementary school on the base, which stayed with me my whole life, was in fourth grade in 1960. We were supposed to write about what we did for our summer vacation, and we had to present it in front of a classroom. I wrote about the preparations here at Santa Clara for our feast day, August 12, which is also my birthday.[4] I'd watched the women make fifty pounds of flour into dough and bake them in the outside ovens. I remember all the cooking, and the beautiful corn that our Winter People would bring out for that day.[5] I started talking in front of the class about my summer vacation. And my teacher stopped me, and she says, "Marian, you have to talk about something that really happened, that you really did." I was a little embarrassed because I'd gotten interrupted, the only one in the whole class who got interrupted, couldn't finish, and thought, *She's supposed to be my teacher and she doesn't know that this is real.* So, a day or two later, I redid the assignment, wrote about a fake summer vacation, and got an A on it. That was my first lesson about the educational system and how you weave your way through it. I did very well in school with that.

2. Adobe is one of humanity's oldest building materials. Traditionally a mix of earth, clay, water, sand, and an organic material like straw, it can be poured into molds and shaped like bricks. Pueblo people stacked adobe blocks into walls to form their homes.

3. Tewa, also known as Tano, is one of three Kiowa-Tanoan languages spoken by Pueblo people of New Mexico.

4. Part religious and part secular, feast day celebrations combine elements of Catholicism with Pueblo culture. Feast days include traditional dances, cultural activities, food, and arts and crafts. Unlike strictly religious activities, they are open to the public.

5. Santa Clara Pueblo clans are organized into two complementary units, known as the Summer People and the Winter People.

I am the eldest and there were nine of us, so a lot of my childhood was spent helping at home. You know, feeding and rocking babies to sleep, helping to clean, those kinds of things, and the whole school part was almost like entertainment to me—my chance to get away from the family responsibilities. And I was really interested in people. When I was in the sixth grade, there was this one gal in particular, Deborah, and we connected so well at school. She was of German descent, her father was a high-ranking officer, so their living quarters were across the tracks, and she was an only child. We would play jacks together, or double-dutch, and we became friends. One time, the bus was late, and we had a little bit of time to spare. I knew she didn't want to just wait at school, and I lived maybe four blocks away, so I invited her over to my house. And of course, you know, my house was all kids playing and my mom cooking and conversation, all different levels going on, and Deborah had never experienced that. Another day, I snuck down with her to her house. They had this nice, clean, shiny floor, with everything in proper order—we had to take our shoes off at the door—and it was just uncomfortable to even *be* in this perfect scenario. We talked about those differences as little girls. It always stuck with me that the lifeways of other people were sometimes more enticing than my own, but at the same time, I was in a place where I accepted my lifeway and was open to sharing it.

When I was in junior high school, the civilian base closed down and all the civilian workers—including my dad—had to move. So we came here to Santa Clara and stayed with two different households of relatives.

I lived with an aunt, Escapula, who was a traditional potter. I got to go with her to Santa Fe, to the Palace of the Governors, where the Santa Clara potters would sell their wares.[6] Because I could speak English, I would do a lot of the selling. People would come,

---

6. The Native American Vendors Program at Santa Fe's Palace of the Governors occupies the north side of the historic plaza. Vendors travel there from forty-seven communities throughout New Mexico to sell their arts and crafts.

they'd look at the prices marked, and they'd try to lower those prices, to get it for almost nothing. And by the end of the afternoon, you need to buy gas, food; that's your purpose, that's your livelihood. And it didn't feel right. I knew all the work that went into making these pots. It's long and tedious—the skill, the spirituality, that one has being a potter—and it was like, *No, you're not gonna do this to my aunt.* And I figured out a good way to talk to these tourists. I'd tell them about all the work that went into making the pots and explain, "That's why they're priced like this."

I'D RELATE DNA MOLECULES TO OUR CORN DANCE

The schools that I went to, Española Junior High and Española High School, were in the township of Española, a Hispanic community.[7] I did very well in school because of what I'd learned earlier and because I was interested in learning. I also learned about the internal political system here at Santa Clara, who our leaders were—governor, lieutenant governor, and all of the elected officials. We also had our traditional leaders in our kivas.[8]

I'd always do these mental exercises to connect our traditional practices with Western knowledge. I'll give an example: We go into the kiva four days before our Corn Dance.[9] When the Corn Dancers come out of the kiva, there are two lines, two lines of men and women. The beautiful dance would come out and it just had such a strong connection to the land, to each other. One heart, one body, one mind. In the classroom, in science class, I'd relate DNA molecules to our Corn Dance. The double helix and the acids that make up this DNA and the beautiful dance—it was the same thing. So I realized

---

7. Española is a city of around ten thousand people in Rio Arriba County, New Mexico. It is located 1.5 miles north of Santa Clara Pueblo.

8. A kiva is a sacred building, usually built underground, used for spiritual and religious ceremonies.

9. The Corn Dance is one of Santa Clara Pueblo's traditional dances.

in junior high school that our Native religion and science were both based on natural law; it was just expressed very differently. Relating to our own ways of knowing was just so right on, and it helped me through a lot of science and math.

By the time I got to eleventh grade, I was very well recognized by teachers for my math and science skills. There was this program at the time where the National Science Foundation, along with the Atomic Energy Commission, gathered high school juniors to go to different universities throughout the United States to do science projects for three months. And it was competitive. Well, I got chosen from Española, and I went to Bowling Green, to Western Kentucky University.

All the students were divided up into biology, chemistry, and physics groups to conduct experiments. So as part of a biology group, we seined a pond. We used a net to take the fish out, a number of catfish, and then we built these two cement walls and an outdoor swimming pool, filled them with water and fish. The physics people made concoctions of radiated fish food for the biology people. Our job was to feed the different doses of whatever concoction they'd made to these fish. The end result was the fish were highly radiated, revealing different amounts because of what they ate, and yet their fecal matter contained zero radiation. So high school kids proved that when fish eat radiated matter, it stays in them. That was our project.

When I graduated from high school, I got offered a permanent position to work at Los Alamos National Laboratory. I worked at the Dosimetry.[10] People at the lab had to wear film badges to indicate their exposures to radiation, and in the Dosimetry we'd read the badges and document their exposure rates in the database. There was a man whose job it was to stand behind a window and watch five women work, to make sure we weren't talking. That didn't feel good. We kept logs of how much exposure the workers were getting from the different sites and logging that, and we had to tell certain workers

10. Radiation dosimetry is the calculation of the dose of radiation absorbed in tissue resulting from exposure to ionizing radiation.

or scientists when they had too much exposure. I had a decision to make: Keep this job long term, which I was being encouraged by my father and my mother to do, or go to college. My choice was college, the University of New Mexico in Albuquerque.

It was the sixties. I was running with a group of Native people in Albuquerque, and I met a man from Michigan. Ernest was a beautiful man—a guitar player, fantastic artist, who was not enrolled at our school but was there hanging out with the same little crew for a few years. I was swept off my feet and took off with him. We left town and headed to Michigan.

That was a time when there was a lot of drugs and alcohol in all of our lives. I kind of lost who I was for about five years. We had no money, and I remember friends going into stores, going in with no money but coming out with food—potato chips and baloney and bread—and I couldn't eat it because it was stolen. And Ernest would get mad at me because I wouldn't eat it. I lost a whole lot of weight. We went to sell our blood a lot. I have B positive blood, so my blood was worth more. That was a big thing. So sometimes they'd take me to go sell my blood so that people in our group could eat.

I wanted to come home to Santa Clara. And Ernest came with me. We hitchhiked back, and my dad and mom, everybody, cried because I wasn't the same girl as when I'd left. I was twenty-two and we got married by the justice of the peace two weeks later and had a little gathering with close family. We had four beautiful children, my daughters Emily and Cecilia, and my sons Raymond and Ernie.

I didn't know until after we were married that Ernest worked undercover with drug dealers in Albuquerque. We traveled around quite a bit and one of the reasons was because he'd gotten several people busted and so was always hiding from people who'd look for him when they got out of jail. He eventually revealed the whole thing and took me on a drug bust. It was in Arizona. After the bust, we were told to meet the undercover cops in this alley, and they paid him half in marijuana and half in cash. I had to seriously look at that, and I gave him an ultimatum. I couldn't raise my kids around that, and I'd decided that Santa Clara was my home no matter what.

KEEP YOUR EYES, YOUR EARS, AND YOUR HEART OPEN

Today tribal enrollment criteria are determined by tribes, and are articulated in the tribal constitutions, articles of incorporation, and ordinances of individual tribes. However, the tribal enrollment process originated as part of a strategy toward solving the "American Indian problem." Indians interfered with Western expansion, and settlers saw their assimilation into Euro-American society as the solution to this problem. For the federal and state governments that introduced it, the agenda behind tribal enrollment was to manipulate enrollment so that Indians might eventually be defined out of existence. When that happened, the federal government would be freed of its "Indian problem."

Another reason Ernest and I argued was the rules and regulations of tribal enrollment. Back in 1932, our village adopted a constitution and the law had changed here to say, "If you are male and one-half Santa Clara, your children are members of the tribe. If you are female and one-half Santa Clara, and marry outside the tribe, your children are not members." So that was my situation. We were married and had children, yet my children could not be members here. My husband could not be head of the household.

Ernest stayed for thirteen years. But then it ended really ugly, very badly. I got beaten up and went to the hospital. And he did that in front of the kids when they were little—two, four, six, and eight. I had to say, "It's done."

When the children started school, I began connecting with the potters of Santa Clara, using my traditional knowledge to become a potter.

When you're learning, your first pots are these ugly, little lopsided things. And when you have four babies, you need milk and diapers yesterday and the money is in Santa Fe and you have no vehicle and you're already humiliated with what has transpired. So you hitchhike with your ugly little pots and find someone to watch the kids, beg people to buy these pots, go through the whole humiliating circuit and take whatever you get, and come home and cry and do it again. Well, my mentor, Christina Naranjo, bless her heart, lived right across the road and she became very, very close to me, and I would cry to her. And she'd say things, like, "Marian, I see you out there! Every morning throwing your cornmeal and I'm hearing and watching your problems, your story, and I see what's missing.[11] Tomorrow, when you go outside and you do your prayer, you ask them—they already know what your problems are—but you ask them to help you keep your eyes, your ears, and your heart open and pay attention to what they send you daily. Just start doing that." I had no clue, really, what she was talking about, but the next day, I did that.

I went outside—our house was at the end of our road—and I threw my cornmeal. I looked up as I'd just finished, "Help me to keep open to what you send me," and I'll be darned, people in a car saw me out there and stopped, and they said, "Oh, we're from back east, and we came here to Santa Clara and the pots are so expensive. We're looking for very inexpensive pieces that we can take home to remind us of our trip." And it was like, *Oh!* So I got it, you know. From that day, I started living like that. Every day. And things would happen like magic all the time.

OPENING THE MOUTH OF THE FIRING DRAGON

I listened to Christina's stories about when she was a little girl and her great-grandpa was a *kasiki*, one of the spiritual leaders. There was no governor, and she overheard stories of the US government coming here, and how our people couldn't revolt, retaliate, as we

---

11. Marian is referring to offering cornmeal to the spirits as part of her prayer.

had when the Spanish came.[12] She said when the US government came here, it was via anthropologists, Edgar L. Hewett and Adolph Bandelier, who wanted to do digs in our ancestral sacred sites. We were warned not to uncover any of our sacred sites from Mesa Verde on down to Chaco Canyon, or the Puye Cliffs.[13] If we uncovered them, we'd be opening up the mouth of the Firing Dragon. Nobody knew exactly what it meant, but at that time, you always listened to what the elders told you because there was no such thing as lies. The anthropologists did the digs here, and after they did, Los Alamos National Laboratory opened, in 1943. And if that's not opening the mouth of the Firing Dragon, I don't know what is.

The US government, with the War Powers Act, gave itself permission to come and plant itself in our sacred place. And it conducted the Trinity Test, the first atomic blast that went around the world.[14] Who was here? Native people, Hispanic farmers, and Anglo ranchers, all the land-based people.

In the 1940s, the US government requested that the San Ildefonso Pueblo give up part of their land for military purposes. The San Ildefonso Pueblo conveyed the land with the understanding that it would be returned after World War II. However, in 1943, the area became the

---

12. In 1680, nearly a century and a half after Spanish explorers and missionaries had settled in New Mexico, the Pueblo people rebelled, driving the Spanish out of New Mexico. This rebellion is called the Pueblo Revolt and lasted for twelve years.

13. The Mesa Verde region is located in the Four Corners area of the Southwest. The Pueblo people migrated from this region to Arizona and New Mexico in the late 1200s. The Puye Cliffs are the ancestral home of the Santa Clara people. Chaco Canyon was a major cultural center for the Pueblo people. The first evidence of human settlement there dates to the third century CE.

14. The War Powers Acts of 1941 was an emergency law that expanded the powers of the American president during World War II. (It was followed by the passing of a Second War Powers Act, in 1942.) The Trinity Test was the outcome of a top-secret program of nuclear testing and development at Los Alamos. In July 1945, its scientists exploded the world's first atomic bomb.

site of Los Alamos National Laboratory (LANL), where most of the research and development for the Manhattan Project, which produced the world's first nuclear weapons, took place.[15]

The land taken for the project is at the base of the Jemez Mountain range and the top of the Pajarito Plateau in northern New Mexico. This area is culturally and spiritually important for Pueblo peoples; many sacred sites are rooted within the landscape and the land is scattered with crucial ceremonial materials like spring water, medicines, minerals, and clay.

For fifty years after the development of LANL, the Pueblo peoples living near the lab and downriver from it had no knowledge or input about the dangerous pollutants being leaked and dumped into the air, water, and land. As a result of the bomb tests and nuclear waste disposal, which consistently showed a lack of environmental ethics and respect for Pueblo land, sacred sites have been destroyed. The environmental injustices perpetrated by Los Alamos have been an affront to the Pueblo communities that can no longer visit or practice their traditional lifeways or ceremonies on these sites.

For Indigenous people, not just here, but everywhere on the earth, there's an order to the universe that's instilled in us by the Creator, and it's the plan for how our lifeways are to be lived. Our whole reason for being is to be the caretakers of the air, the water, the land, and each other. That's been the constant. We had these places, and those who wish to live here should learn what it takes to live in these places: the woodlands, the rivers, the deserts, all of our nations, all of our sacred sites. How do we redo our education, our way of being, to pass that down? If we don't, we're going to be the dinosaurs. That's all there is to it. We're destroying ourselves. We're the delicate ones. Mother Earth is so powerful. She knows how to clean herself.

---

15. "Environmental Injustices for Pueblo Communities Near Los Alamos National Laboratory."

WE WERE THE SUBJECTS OF THE EXPERIMENT

My highest honor in pottery was to hear from the potters who have passed, who taught me so much say, and to be told, "Marian, you're a good potter." But all potters reach this time in their lives when their backs get bent and their fingers curl. They'd say to me, "When you start feeling the aches in your neck and your back and your fingers, remember that you are an educated woman. Use that."

My kids grew up, they all left to live their lives, and then I was here by myself. In 1998, I was feeling the aches in my neck so I did a spiritual walk up on Tsicomo Peak, and it was like my whole life passed through my mind, and I thought, *Here I am. What do you want me to do?* The following day, an old friend of mine from Tesuque came over, and he said, "Hey, let me take you to lunch tomorrow. I really want to introduce you to some people." So he picked me up, we went to Santa Fe, and we walked into this meeting with an environmental group, Concerned Citizens for Nuclear Safety (CCNS), which had just won a settlement agreement from Los Alamos National Laboratory, for it not being in compliance with the Clean Air Act.[16] We were the only Native people there. And they were having their negotiations. Part of the settlement was that CCNS had to hire a Native outreach director. And they had to form a relationship with the University of New Mexico. I applied for that position.

But first I had to get the blessings from the elders, to say this is the work that I'd do now. I'd never even opened up a computer; I'd been doing pots. Everyone I would work with there at CCNS were Anglo people and a whole new world to me. But the environmen-

---

16. The Clean Air Act of 1970 is a federal law that regulates air emissions. One of its goals was to set National Ambient Air Quality Standards to protect public health in every state. In 1994, CCNS sued LANL to force it to comply with the act. The lawsuit cited the lab's failure to disclose all its sources of radionuclide released emissions and to install appropriate monitoring equipment on its vapor-release stacks. For more information about this settlement, see CCNS's website: https://nuclearactive .org/news/041300.html.

tal issues around Los Alamos were so clear, given my background in science. And it was coming full circle somehow. When I went to get blessings from the elders for the outreach position, I asked them, "How do you feel about Los Alamos National Laboratory being in our sacred place?" And it just opened up these voices that had seemed bottled for their whole lives. There were stories after stories about people's experiences when the lab opened here. It was so secretive. It was also a chance to make money. Many of the stories from the women were about when they became maids for the scientists. But they didn't know what was going on at the lab, only that they had an opportunity to make money. And then later on, when they were elderly, they realized the truth of what was happening when they were young people—that our air, our water, and our land were contaminated by the existence of the lab in our sacred place.

I got the blessing from the elders at Santa Clara to take the job later that year. My work was to find the information from the lab's own environmental impact statements and to educate people here about the contamination. Part of the work was reading documents. I found this book that was written on past radiation experiments, and lo and behold, I learned that in 1967, the National Science Foundation and the Atomic Energy Commission gathered high school kids to do low-dose radiation experiments.[17] At the time, I'd felt very honored that my school had selected me to do this venture. I was young. I was naïve about a lot of things. But I learned from that book that *we* were the subjects of the experiment.[18] All these years later to find out! It made me reevaluate the experience. My part had

---

17. Experiments performed on human beings without their knowledge or consent have occurred throughout US history. Unethical and often secretive human radiation experiments, which occurred throughout the twentieth century, were performed to understand the effects of radioactive contamination on the human body. In many instances, information was not released about them until many years following completion of the studies.

18. Advisory Committee on Human Radiation Experiments, *Final Report* (Washington, DC: Advisory Committee on Human Radiation Experiments, 1995).

been to seine the pond and to feed the fish, and different amounts of radiation were put in that fish food. My roommate and I would walk in that water to feed the fish! We didn't have protective gloves or anything!

I tried desperately to call Rodes-Harlin Hall, the dormitory where I had lived then. I tried to get information. But there were no records, nothing. Like it never happened. Discovering this after years had passed and after starting my environmental work for a paycheck? It was like a shock and awe moment, like, *Wow. This was me. I did this. Is this real?* It was just too creepy, and it matched with how the atomic age started, how it was so secretive.

I've thought about the secrecy because we as Native people were forced to go underground with a lot of our spiritual ceremonies a long time ago. Fairly recently, I realized that by maintaining secrecy we're losing out on passing knowledge that is so vital for our younger people.

And this leads me to think about the nuclear stuff. This knowledge is not really secret anymore; it's known around the world. So why are people not being forthright with the information? We have a right to know what has transpired in our sacred places, what has been released and how much and where. And to hold the government accountable for the damages that have transpired. Our people have a right to know; that's how I feel about it. That secrecy is no longer viable. People need to be accountable for the atrocities that happened.

HONOR OUR PUEBLO EXISTENCE

There were issues at the CCNS workplace. It was like watching a ping-pong match of these white activists and the laboratory going back and forth, over my sacred land. It was like, *Wow, how ugly is this?*

My prayer from the beginning of my work with CCNS was that at least one pueblo village would make substantial comments on Los Alamos' environmental impact statement. It took twelve years, but

Santa Clara finally did it. Twenty-two pages. The main comment was that the site needed to be recognized as our Mecca, our sacred place. And that we don't have access to that area anymore, which was a very important part of our lives growing up. In 2011, Los Alamos forced the Los Conchas Fire to go north, to our watershed, to save the lab. So we don't have access to that area anymore—the sacred sites were washed out.[19] People would go to the canyon area in summertime, or if you felt bad, you'd go and visit the many sacred places up there, marked places that are now gone. That brings tears to many elders now. We can't share how we grew up with our grandchildren because it's gone. A lifeway was lost.

I started having conversations with my oldest son, Raymond, about what I'd do next. And we thought, *Well, be director of your own organization!* Since he was twelve years old, Raymond wanted to become a chef, and the whole reason was that he remembers when he was little how some days, we didn't have any food. And sometimes he'd walk around the whole village and eat well because of what the trees were growing. When my youngest son, Ernie, was a little boy, he'd say, "Mom, how come you have to go to school and graduate and get a job to make money to buy a car, to go to the store, to eat? Why can't we just eat?" That stuck with me. It was just so simple, *there it is.* This little innocent person, who knew what it was to not have food some days, was so clear.

Honor Our Pueblo Existence came together in 2004, and it was based on trying to go back to our traditional knowledge and our culture and re-implementing our order to the universe, to address the environmental and health issues we face.[20] Since 1998, all the nuclear sites in the nation have done dose reconstruction, except for where it was born, right here in Los Alamos.[21] So we did a congressional

---

19. The Los Conchas Fire, the largest wildfire in New Mexico's history, burned more than 156,000 acres. Several watersheds in the area were heavily impacted.

20. To learn more about Indigenous resurgence movements, see appendix essay 3.

21. Dose reconstruction is a process used to estimate the level of radiation that individuals or populations have been exposed to.

delegation, the whole shebang, to demand the Centers for Disease Control and Prevention do a dose reconstruction. It was supposed to take five years. Well, it took thirteen because of a lack of records, permission, and the lab's secrecy.

In the meantime, I helped cofound other organizations so that we can work on all these issues going forward. One, Las Mujeres Hablan, The Women Speak, is the organization that used the dose reconstruction from the Trinity Test to bridge the environmental work and the health of the people. Finally, there will be documentation from the US government that says, *This is what that test did to the health of the people.*

Data show that nuclear fallout and leaked radioactive waste have polluted the land around, downwind, and downriver from Los Alamos with radionuclides, findings that likely explain the high incidences of thyroid and other cancers in these areas. In 1998, LANL completed a comparison study measuring the extent of exposure to radioactive chemicals in the canyons and downriver communities, reporting that the concentrations of six radionuclides in three staple foods (pinto beans, squash, and corn) grown within neighboring communities were considerably higher than those grown outside the area.[22]

WE NEEDED A SACRED SPACE

One of the other things I work toward is balancing the village, putting stuff back. So we built the Buwah Tewa house here in 2005. Buwah is our first ancestral bread used for ceremony and sustenance, and the whole process of growing, harvesting, shucking, and grinding before actually getting to the point of making bread is vital.

---

22. For more on this, see P. R. Fresquez et al., "The Uptake of Radionuclides by Beans, Squash, and Corn Growing in Contaminated Alluvial Soils at Los Alamos National Laboratory," *Journal of Environmental Science and Health, Part B* 33, no. 1 (1998): 99–121.

My daughter, myself, another gal from here, and women from San Ildefonso and Tesuque got together, and we started learning how to make the bread. We knew that we needed a sacred space for women to ground ourselves. Building the houses was part of a dream I had when I was talking to the elders about the loss of access to our canyon area, our sacred places around Los Alamos. The dream was to create sacred places that we have access to.

We had a traditional art class, which was run out of the Institute of American Indian Arts, come every Friday through the whole month of April to help us build the houses. Every Friday the institute students used forms to make seventy adobe blocks. We also had a Native men's rehabilitation center come here every Tuesday to do the same because it healed them so much. We talked to them about how to handle wet adobes: you treat them like babies, and you hug them, and you're gentle with them. They connected to this tenderness, to how they were not treated right. And then every weekend we'd have the young girls and boys from the Pueblo come. And spiritual leaders would talk to them about relationships with one another, their relationship with the outside world, and being connected with who we are. That's how that house got built.

BLAINE WILSON

TSARTLIP FIRST NATION
FISHER/HUNTER
BORN IN: 1969, Nanaimo, British Columbia
INTERVIEWED IN: Tsartlip First Nation, British Columbia

I met Blaine through his sister, Tracy, an academic coordinator at the University of Victoria's Indigenous Student Support Centre. Her face lit up as she described her brother as "a bear" who lived off the land and said he was the only person of her generation she knows who truly does. When I arrived at his home on Tsartlip First Nation, Blaine was washing his white pickup truck in front of his one-story home. Tsartlip is located on the Saanich Peninsula, in Saanich, or W̱SÁNEĆ, territory. Its 824.8 acres of reserve land lie about twenty-three kilometers north of Victoria on Vancouver Island. And its one thousand members make up one of fifty First Nations on the island.

Blaine offered me a seat in a camping chair under a small overhang in front of his house. A few toy cars and an old car seat were evidence of Blaine's fatherhood; a pair of antlers nailed to the house's outside wall, along with fishing gaffs leaned against it, were evidence of his livelihoods. A sign reading "Douglas Treaty Supersedes Modern Treaties" was nailed to the side of an old fish smokehouse that sat across the driveway, and beside the house there was also a new, larger smokehouse. Another sign, which read "Our Time Is Now," hung from a fence.

Saanich has been home to its Indigenous residents for thousands of years; its colonial history began in the 1840s with the arrival of the Hudson's Bay Company (HBC). The British had granted the company a ten-year lease to govern the island. In 1849, when the British government granted Vancouver Island status as an official colony, Sir James Douglas, the HBC's chief factor, needed to find a way to secure land for the immigration and European settlement that this status would encourage. With an exchange of cash, blankets, and clothing, Douglas negotiated fourteen treaties over the next four years. No band received more than about $9,000 in today's money. There is much evidence to support the Saanich people's claim that their ancestors understood this as a peace treaty, an agreement to co-exist with the British, not a purchase agreement. As viewed by the British, however, the treaties essentially removed Aboriginal title from the nations that signed them but promised continued and perpetual rights to fish.

While we sat under the big, gray West Coast sky, Blaine explained that his passion for hockey had given him his smile—a big gap in the place of his two front teeth. His face lit up as he described his love for hunting and fishing, his sons, and their traditional way of life. Blaine spoke about living by the seasons, how each one physically prepares him for the next. Blaine lives the same way his father and grandfather did, and he is teaching his sons to support themselves and contribute to the community the same way. He also described how the distraction of digital technology is threatening the intergenerational transfer of knowledge and how environmental changes are endangering his family's livelihood.

WE PRETTY WELL KNOW
THE WHOLE AREA FROM FAMILY

I've been here at Tsartlip since 1977, when I was eight years old. I got two sisters, a brother, and a lot of cousins who are just like brothers and sisters. Big, big family, lot of aunties, lot of uncles living in Kamloops and Musqueam.[1] We pretty well know the whole area from family, from going there to visit them. We traveled a lot, our whole family in a van, a 1966 Chevy. Oh yeah, it was nice. If it broke down, we fixed it. Once we'd get some place, we'd wake up, and we'd know where we were because we've been there. We've been going there all our life. We'd be all over to see our aunties and our cousins.

My Indian name is Sluxsthet. It was my great-grandfather's name. It was my father's Indian name, and is my first son's Indian name. Each family in the area has an ancestral name. It helps us. We see each other, we call each other by that name. It's like our ancestors are with us. It's how we represent our ancestors—to be a family person, to be caring for your community, to be here for the people. A lot of people recognize our ancestral name and when people call our name, we answer. Our name is what brings us alive, what ties us to our land because it ties us to our history here. And that's still the same today. Our friends, when they want some help, we can help them. I feel fortunate to be able to do things with my hands, with skill. Neighbors say, "We need help." I say, "My son's coming!" I go out there up the road and my neighbors say, "Thank you for chopping my wood." That's a good thing about being with family. We don't have to worry, we got help on the way.

Mom knits. She could knit anything you wanted. She knits toques and mitts and sweaters. Sweaters sell for big money, like hun-

---

1. Kamloops is a city in south-central British Columbia with a population of close to 104,000 people. It sits at the confluence of the two branches of the Thompson River. The journey from Tsartlip takes about six hours by car and ferry. Musqueam is a First Nations band in British Columbia whose reserve lies within Vancouver's city boundaries.

dreds. When we get wool, we sell knitting. That's part of being from around here. All of our people from here can do it like that. When we were kids, she'd have so much knitting. There was a clothing store, the Golden Rule, in Bellingham, Washington, that wanted her knitwear, so they'd close the store and let us shop. She'd put a shopping spree on for us. We'd all get new clothes from her knitting. She made a sweater with a buffalo design that brought us good money. Around here, they like whales. Other places we traveled, they like buffalos. But we know what comes from knitting. If you have a hard time, the knitting will put you ahead. You'll stay warm, and people will give you money for it.

My dad taught me about the chainsaw, driving, hockey. He had a vision for me to be a hockey player and saw an ad in the newspaper for an arena at Okanagan.[2] We traveled over there and for fifteen years, I played ice hockey. Still live the dream. I was really lucky to have a hockey career here. Our community helped us. I'd go door to door, tell neighbors I'm doing a skate-a-thon, and they'd give me free skates. I won free registration for ice hockey. I skated with the best people. Through hockey, my friends are many.

My dad passed away around 1984, when he was forty-two. He was a residential-school survivor and he took in a lot of alcohol, so probably alcohol took his life.[3] And he was just far too amazing to have a short, short life. He taught me the roads, going to communities to help people having hard times, traveling to see family, to gatherings. My dad's friends and relatives, elder guys also teach me different things. Working together, we form a crew to go get wood. A lot of people have these tools, like the chainsaw, ax, and wedge, but the way we use them, nobody knows besides us. We use the young maples and the cedar. We burn the maple and alder for smoking fish,

---

2. Okanagan is four hundred kilometers northeast of Tsartlip, on mainland British Columbia.

3. For more on the residential schools, see the glossary, and for more on the intergenerational effects of the schools, see appendix essay 2.

and we use the cedars for hanging bears and use the fir for the big fires. We make trails when we go into the forests, and it looks like a sidewalk, we've made such a good trail. Sometimes the younger people come along, so we slow down and show them, or we let them pack wood, and let them feel what it's like to get that heavy wood up on their shoulders. They thrive.

In Canada, Aboriginal rights are protected under the Constitution Act, which guarantees status and non-status Indians, First Nations, Inuit, and Métis the right to participate in their traditional activities on their ancestral lands. In the words of the Union of British Columbia Indian Chiefs: "Salmon are a resource treasured and shared by all Indigenous Peoples within British Columbia. They are born in one area, grow to maturity in another, and live their adult lives in marine waters, to return to the place of their birth for their life cycle to continue. All Indigenous Nations [in the province] have territories which include either oceans, rivers, streams or lakes so salmon are seen as binding all Indigenous peoples in British Columbia together. When salmon are threatened, the livelihood and way of life of all Indigenous Peoples are threatened."[4]

In addition to the Douglas Treaties, which confirm the right to "carry on fisheries as formerly" for Blaine's band, the right to fish was reaffirmed by the Supreme Court of Canada's decision in R. v. Sparrow *(1990), a defining moment for the country's Aboriginal fishing rights. In that case, the Musqueam Nation asserted its right to fish; the government of Canada claimed that First Nations' only rights were those granted by the Fisheries Act. The court ruled that Aboriginal rights could be taken away only through clear and explicit legislation, and that the Fisheries Act had never extinguished them. Sparrow defined Aboriginal peoples' right to fish for food, social, and ceremonial purposes as a right to be given priority over all of the fisheries uses, aside from conservation.*

---

4. See Union of BC Indian Chiefs, "Fish Farms, Zero Tolerance: Indian Fish Don't Do Drugs," www.ubcic.bc.ca/fish_farms_zero_tolerance.

WHEN I TAKE MY SONS FISHING, THEY LISTEN

My son Michael is twenty-eight, Austin turned nineteen, and Bobby, he'll be eighteen this year. We live seasonally, hunting and fishing; everything comes seasonally to our lives here. Like now, in January, we're going to clear the way for the new year; we're going to physically get ready, strengthen up to go fishing in the springtime. It's a really good time of year. We got about three boats that we like to go fishing on and once we start, we go for months, we're never home. We just head out here and do some cod fishing. We head to the mainland and do some crabbing with our cousins, and then we do the Fraser River and we fish eulachon. And we fish spring salmon. And the sockeye's really good when it happens. Then we fish the Goldstream River for chum salmon. We get fish from Port Alberni to Nanaimo to Duncan, Merritt, or Kamloops, and anywhere in between. We go to the mainland, and because we have prawns and clams, people we trade or sell to there ask, "Where've you guys been?" They want all of our fish because they don't have the salty fish. That's just a part of being from here. We prepare ourselves to get out there, to stay away from home, to be ready if it rains, for the winds. We have to be alert, to be ready to get out of the way of Mother Nature. We have to pay attention.

When I take my sons fishing, they listen. It really makes them happy to learn the way we do it, so they can teach their friends all the things that we do—crabbing and fishing and hunting. Once we've done the work of one task, we can go to the next. I've trained my son on the fishing rod. He's younger than everybody else and he'll out-fish them. When we're catching fish, it gives us strength to go get a deer. We're not tired and weak, we've already been busy, that's what gives us the strength. We use the same strength that we've been building to go to the next part of the calendar year. That's what we carry around.

Once we get the fish, we have to start getting wood, collect good smoking wood. We get maple or alder—I favor those, it's how I was trained. And once we get that fish home, we start getting the sticks to hang the fish. You get all the tools and you form a team to help cut the fish. And then you get to smoking the fish, and it's like the fish are still alive. They all move when the fire starts.

It's ten months fishing and in September, we get some time off. It slows down. In September and October, we can get some hunting in, and that's a whole other way of living. We get deer and ducks. We only get to use our guns for a little while, and then we've got to put them away because we hunted already and we got no more places to put our meat. We're not overloaded, but we got some of each.

I do this for my food, for my living. Our friends are always saying, "You guys got the fish?" And that is part of living the treaty, because that's our connection. We can get the fish and it helps us in our daily living. When we have the fish, we're going to do good. We make fish and chips. Oh, you're going to spend fifty bucks? No, we got it right here. We bring our own fish and chips. It's good for all of us that I swap fish. That's our medicine. Last time I didn't even take one home, I gave it all out. All my fish went out, so it all had to be good.

IT'S NOW CONTAMINATED

Industrial resource extraction and sources of pollution severely impact Aboriginal title lands and waters, degrading coastal areas. Today water in the area is contaminated, poisoning salmon, shellfish, and other marine life. Traditional harvesting grounds, like the clam beds around Brentwood Bay where Blaine's family gathered clams, are also poisoned and destroyed.

We had the best places in town to sell our clams, but we won't do it anymore because of the contamination. We don't want to hurt the tourists. Private land owners lease the land to businesses and the run-off of everyday life—the stuff that comes from the junk yard, the scrap yard, the lumber mill—has done a lot of damage over the years. All the contaminants going into the ditches, and the ditches run down to the water, and down to the clam beds at the beach. It's bad for the whole area. It kills the ground and where the fresh water used to run, it's now contaminated. Because it's private land we can't regulate it or tell people what to do.

I would say the problem started twenty-five years ago. We used to be able to pack three-hundred-pound bags of clams. And now we don't do that at all. When we do the clam digging now, there's almost nothing there. A lot of people don't have a car or a boat to go to the other places where it might be better, so we need our local beaches.

There's lots of change. There's no more canoe races. The canoe paddling, it should start now, because it's a change of season and the days are longer, and it's time to start running and training to get your wind and get your strength to paddle.[5] You have to be in shape, and the diet's really strict. You can't have the drive-through diet, and you have to have water and less sugar intake.[6] Training has to be done daily. You have to be in shape to be on the canoe. You have to be pure to get in the canoe. And it's a good life because you end up going to all the different areas, to the different reserves that host the races. But people don't do it as much today. It has to be picked up. It's time to do it now, start running, and form the team, the committee, team dinners, fundraisers, so they can travel the canoe. It takes the full effort for everybody to do it. You need a whole community. Today there are less canoes because there's more to do. Cell phones and computers, it's tough to beat them.

A lot of people have technology with them now. If they get in

---

5. Blaine is referring to the tribal canoe journey, an annual celebration for Indigenous people of the Pacific Northwest. Dozens of communities participate, with representative groups traveling in oceangoing canoes and visiting other Native nations on their way to each year's final host destination.

6. He is referring to a fast-food diet.

trouble, they ain't gonna go ask Grandpa, they're gonna ask their iPhone. The only thing they want Grandpa for is a ride, or money. They're going to say, "How do you fix the car?" and their phone will tell them. And that's how people work now. If they didn't have any of this phone stuff, they would say, "Okay, work tomorrow?" And more things would get done like that, together. Back in the day, there'd be houses full of ten kids each. Today, people quit at two and three kids. And how do you get two or three to match up to ten kids? Lots of areas around here, work is affected. Nobody hand digs the garden in the spring. And you don't see anybody cut wood, you don't see anybody make a canoe. They say, "Okay, well, I'm going to phone somebody and get somebody else to do it," never mind doing it themselves. I wouldn't want to just *have* all that.

EVERYBODY WANTED TO FISH FOR A MILLION

The decline in the province's wild salmon population is attributed to a number of factors, including overfishing, pollution, and rising water temperature due to climate change. The federal Department of Fisheries and Oceans has been criticized by some researchers for consistently allowing too many fish to be killed in its commercial and recreational fisheries. Other research suggests that fish farming along the sockeye's maritime migration routes is transmitting pollution and diseases to wild salmon. Fish farms pollute and damage the marine environment surrounding the net pens, and lights submerged in the waters can attract wild salmon, increasing their risk of being harmed. One concern is a parasite called sea lice, which attach themselves to the fish, weakening or killing them. Opponents of fish farming are convinced it increases the number of lice in the open ocean. For the province, the farms are a big business, with around $1.5 billion in revenue and 6,600 jobs tied to the industry.[7]

---

7. See Greg Rasmussen, "It's Wild Salmon Health vs. Money and Jobs as B.C.'s Fish Farm Fight Comes to a Head," *CBC News*, June 18, 2018, www.cbc.ca/news /canada/british-columbia/fish-farming-bc-leases-1.4704626.

In January 2019, the Dzawada'enuxw Nation filed a claim as-serting that the farming of Atlantic salmon in their traditional waters constitutes a violation of Aboriginal rights. If they succeed, the lawsuit would force closure of the fish farms that affect the Dzawada'enuxw Na-tion, and it could serve as legal precedent for other First Nations looking to shut down farms across the British Columbia coast.

When I was twenty-five, thirty, there was more salmon, and I was fishing every other day. Now I'd be lucky to go once a week. Why would there be less salmon? Because everybody wanted to fish for a million. Everybody wanted to make a million bucks, so they got out there, fished like hell, and now there's no more fish. The fish are not laying enough eggs because everybody caught the fish. They got big-ger bins, bigger nets, more nets, bigger boats. It's bad for the whole cycle, and it's never gonna get better. In our own lives, it's what we've seen. You can't bring it back.

The fish farms lead to contamination and pollution. Our water goes straight to the farms. One of their nets broke last year, in the States, in the San Juan Islands, an hour away on our boat.[8] Every-thing that those farms leave in the water gets on our fish. Also, the water is warmer—the fish will mob around, and if the river is too warm, they won't come up. Not only the river but the land changed, too. The new growth was cut. And what they planted is now big and they can cut again. So the trees went just like that—right in front of us. They grew up and they're cut down and they grew up again and they're cut down again. That's how much they log here.

We just have to be after it all the time, taking care of ourselves. If you get a taste of our fish, you wouldn't want to go buy it from the store. You'd want to get it yourself. And it's pretty hard to be generous when you can't even get it for yourself. We have our own kids sit right there and say, "Want to have some fish and chips, then?" If we don't

---

8. The San Juan Islands are in northwest Washington state.

have it, that's another shock to the whole family, when we ain't got no fish!

WE HAVE TO SPREAD THE TREATY

They want to put us in boundaries. But we're treaty Indians here. The Douglas Treaty protects us in more ways than just hunting and fishing. The outside world is encroaching on us. You don't have to go far—you've got businesses over there, you've got businesses coming here, and the treaty has held a lot of it off. Businesses could easily look at our land and want to take it; they want to do stuff here.

We have the oldest existing treaty in British Columbia, the Douglas Treaty of 1863.[9] All of my life, every day—that treaty is alive in me and that's what I live by. It's always, "Oh, thank heaven I'm a Douglas Treaty Indian." Now we have to go bigger. We have to spread the treaty more. We were given that a long time ago so we have to save it for more than just our own kids. I was born into the treaty. I actually live it, and it leads back to my sons. I've put a lot of the teachings in them. I really hope they'll continue to make a living this way because it's been a really, really good life. I don't see this way of living going away. Hunting and fishing—I believe in it. I can use my fish, my deer, my elk, and my moose, and have a feast with people. I have too much, I can't eat it all myself. The kids—they want to learn that and we want to teach. I hope my kids are re-

---

9. The British government declared that only the Crown could acquire land from Indigenous people, which was to be enacted through the negotiation of treaties. However, unlike in the rest of Canada, much of British Columbia's land was never ceded or signed away through treaties made with the Crown. Ninety-five percent of British Columbia remains unceded. The Douglas Treaties covered parts of Vancouver Island, and Treaty 8 (1899), made between First Nations and the federal government, included part of the province's northeastern corner. Together these areas make up the 5 percent of ceded land in the province. For more on the Douglas Treaties and modern treaties in Canada, see appendix essay 1.

sourceful so they can teach whoever they come across. It's quite the challenge if you aren't resourceful or you don't live by the treaty or you don't have ways of catching stuff. We don't just think, *Oh, we're going to wish for this.* We make a lot of effort to get what we're after. You know the song "Huntin', Fishin' and Lovin' Every Day"?[10] He's singing about me! Everything that I do every day is in that song. My sons and I love it.

---

10. The song is a 2015 recording by country music artist Luke Bryan.

ALTHEA GUIBOCHE

MÉTIS/OJIBWE/SAULTEAUX
COMMUNITY ADVOCATE
BORN IN: 1974, Swan River, Manitoba
INTERVIEWED IN: Winnipeg, Manitoba

Originally from Duck Bay, Manitoba, Althea is a celebrated citizen of Winnipeg's North End. Known as "the Bannock Lady," Althea advocates for the city's homeless population.[1] She started the organization Got Bannock?, which serves meals to about three hundred people twice a month, in response to the constant need she saw around her. This is a need that she understood firsthand, having lived through a period of homelessness with five of her children in 2011, when her three youngest were three, nineteen months, and four months old.

---

1. A staple food of many First Nations, bannock is a large, round bread prepared from flour, baking powder, sugar, lard, and water or milk.

We began our conversation in the lobby of Winnipeg's Humphry Inn and continued it the following evening over dinner. As we said our good-byes, Althea told me not to take a taxi back to my hotel. Instead, she tried to find me a lift with an Indigenous safe-ride service, which was founded in response to threats to Indigenous women's security in local cabs, some of whom report they have been propositioned for sex while using the city's taxis.[2] Even more report that drivers direct sexual comments at them and others. These services and the work of other organizations, like the Bear Clan Patrol, align with Althea's vision to work "in honor of the village we once had."

During our meetings, Althea spoke about her traditional Métis up-bringing, how that way of life was fractured after a move to the city, and the poverty and eventual homelessness that followed.[3] In her work with scholar Jesse Thistle, Althea has helped to develop a definition of Indigenous homelessness in Canada that considers the structural issues contributing to the disproportionate number of Indigenous people among Canada's homeless.[4] As the definition states: "It is clear that being with-out a home via an Indigenous worldview is not simply a lack of accom-modation, but rather is a web of relationships that involves connections to human kinship networks; relations to animals, plants, spirits, and elements; relationship to the Earth, lands, waters, and territories; and connection to traditional stories, songs, teachings, names, and ancestors. All these aspects of the circle of interconnectedness are known as "home"

---

2. Kelly Geraldine Malone, "'I Felt Unsafe: Indigenous Safe-Ride Service for Women Can't Keep Up with Need," Canadian Press, www.cbc.ca/news/canada /manitoba/winnipeg-safe-ride-service-ikwe-1.4621212.

3. The Métis are of mixed European and Indigenous lineage and trace their descent to Cree, Ojibwe, Saulteaux, and Menominee Indigenous peoples and to French, Scottish, and British settlers. They became one of three recognized Aboriginal peo-ples of Canada via the Constitution Act of 1982.

4. To learn more about how Althea contributed to this definition of Indigenous home-lessness, see Jesse Thistle, "Reframing the Discussion: An Indigenous Definition of Homelessness," Homeless Hub, www.homelesshub.ca/blog/reframing-discussion -indigenous-definition-homelessness.

in Indigenous societies and worldviews."[5]

Althea spoke passionately about rebuilding the traditional village, based upon respect, honor, and love, in which each member of the tribe contributes toward its survival, and wealth is measured less by what one has than by what one shares.

WE LIVED THE TRADITIONAL LIFESTYLE

My traditional name is Whistling North Wind Woman, and I come from the Ojibwe/Saulteaux tribe, the Mahkwa Clan.[6] I was born in Swan River, the third born of four.[7] Our extended family was about thirty members strong, and all of us basically lived at home. My mom's family, her brother Arnold, their aunties and uncles, and the whole extended family were together. We lived in Duck Bay.[8] We lived the traditional lifestyle, and we migrated with the season's changes. As kids, we were taught how to forage. We could live in the bush all day and not have food to eat except the berries and nuts that we found. We would go hunting. Those camps in the bush, at Kettle Stones Provincial Park, were always active.[9] There was always something going on. That's how we made our living, in the traditional Métis way, harvesting from the land.

My grandpa, Henry D. Chartrand, had two farmsteads: one was

---

5. Thistle, "Definition of Indigenous Homelessness."

6. "Mahkwa" is Anishinaabe-mowin for "bear."

7. Swan River is a city with a population of around one thousand and is 525 kilometers northwest of Winnipeg. For more information on the terms *tribe* and *clan*, see the glossary.

8. The community of Duck Bay, which has a population of around 350, rests on the western shore of Lake Winnipegosis. Its inhabitants are mostly Métis of Ojibwe and French ancestry.

9. Kettle Stones Provincial Park is located on the north side of the Kettle Hills, in the Swan-Pelican Provincial Forest, seventy kilometers northeast of the town of Swan River.

right in Duck Bay and the other one we got to by boat. It seemed like we were a well-off family back then, like we were entrepreneurs. We lived off our land. We had all kinds of farm implements. We had six working horses, ten ponies, a hundred cows, a hundred chickens. My grandpa used to sell cream made from our cows, so that was another source of income. We had a taxicab company for a while. We sold gas and had a little store. We were doing very well. We always helped all the neighbors.

Some families didn't have as much as we did, and they had lots of kids, so whenever my family would hunt, they'd get like ten moose and butcher them up and take parcels of meat to other families, or we'd invite the ones who didn't have the means we did to go out hunting. It was really instilled in me from a young age to share and care about your neighbors. We also were taught to respect the land, respect the water, to leave the land the way you found it. That was part of growing up.

In the bush, everybody had their own roles and responsibilities. Even the dogs had roles. There were some that stayed in the kitchen, usually older dogs that didn't really have much pep. Then there were some sent with me and the smaller kids. I was old enough to pick berries, but they needed someone to watch the younger ones, so that was my role, and a dog was sent with us. The berry pickers took dogs, the hunters took dogs, and so on. We had about eight dogs. They all had different roles in the camp. That was just amazing to me.

My grandpa was in the army; he was a sapper, a part of the logistics team in the army. After I learned all the things that a sapper did, the way he did things meticulously began to make so much sense. He would lay out all his blades, he'd lay out all his different files according to shape, he'd put his gloves on, put his handkerchief around his neck, and all day I would watch him, filing his tools. They'd begin preparing for the camps in the summer. They'd start in the spring, pull out all the tents, make sure everything was repaired. They'd stock up on grub, make tons of lists of what was needed, and make sure that it was all good to go. They'd go through their guns, start stocking ammunition. It was so organized. I can only imagine how much stuff was needed for thirty people in the bush.

The family blazed a trail one time from Duck Bay to Kettle Stones Provincial Park, where our traditional picking and hunting grounds were. We could have gone by the highway, but we took the horse and wagon. My grandpa probably felt they needed the horses in the bush, so we transferred the whole family through the bush as well. My grandpa knew how to make bridges—that's where that sapper experience came in—so we were never stuck. He'd just say, "We'll make a bridge."

In the winter, we lived in town. I remember staying briefly in the house across the lake on the weekends to hunt. But we also had to go to school, so we'd have to stay in town for that. The family was always busy. My parents, my aunties and uncles, everybody was into something. We had this really long table, and I remember sitting there in the morning and everybody's eating porridge, asking each other, "What are you doing today?" And they'd lay out their day's plans.

CULTURE SHOCK

We lived, I think, not on the reserve, but on the Métis side, and we grew up in the cities, in Winnipeg, Brandon, Thompson, so I experienced schools both on and off the reserve.[10] We had to fight our way, no matter where it was, to be accepted, to be involved. At the white schools, the other students were always really surprised about me and my brother, like, "Oh! You guys are smart." *Yes, we are. Really, we're probably smarter than you.* My mom, Audrey, was very educated, very serious, she lived sober, and school was just everything to her. She used to make us read; it didn't matter if we had kids over. Kids would be at my house, and they'd say, "You mean I have to

---

10. A First Nations reserve is a piece of land "reserved" for the exclusive use of an Indian band under the Indian Act and treaty agreements. For more on reserves, see the glossary.

read?" and I'd be like, "Yes, here—quick, pick a book and be quiet. She's going to test you later." They were all like, "Oh no, I didn't sign up for this." And I'd say, "Shut up and read." We'd all line up, and my mom would say, "Okay, what is the book about? What is the plot? What is the setting?" So she really instilled that in us, reading and learning and always trying to get educated. And then she'd let us go off and play.

During our time in Duck Bay, my uncle Arnold went missing, during the winter of 1984–85. I was ten. Everybody was searching for him the whole winter. They found him in the spring thaw. He drowned in the lake. It completely devastated the family. Arnold was like the glue that held the family together, and then when he was gone, *poof*, everybody just kind of parted ways and continued to survive and cope the best they could. I've asked myself many times what it was about him. He just brought so much life to everything. He was a jokester, always in the thick of everything, the plans, the work. He was everybody's favorite person.

It felt like us kids were on our own that winter because our parents and grandparents were so involved with trying to find Arnold. If some of us had been just a little bit older, we probably could've kept the family farm going, but we were just too young. And then when they did find him, they basically sold everything we owned for whatever they could get, and everybody moved to Calgary. There were some relatives already out there. Some of the parents and grandparents became bedridden and sickly. We were on welfare all of a sudden and that was a new thing for us. We were living off the food banks. It was a real culture shock to go from being a thriving entrepreneurial family to one that's completely poverty-stricken.

According to the definition of Indigenous homelessness in Canada provided by the Canadian Observatory on Homelessness, the relocation of Althea's family to Calgary can be seen through a lens of "cultural disintegration and loss homelessness," a homelessness that "dislocates or alienates Indigenous individuals and communities from their culture and from the relationship web of Indigenous society."[11]

My mom developed shingles that year. She was selling makeup for Avon, and I remember asking her about it one day. I remember her saying, "Oh, if only I could deliver brochures, I could be getting orders," and I was like, "Well, what do you need to do?" She goes, "I just need to take these books and some samples and go hand them out." I said, "Get them ready. I'll do it." I took my little red wagon full of Avon stuff, and I started canvassing the neighborhood. I can only imagine the sales pitches I gave: "My mom's sick and she's bedridden." People were like, "Oh, my God, yes. I'll order!" There was lots of interest and questions. I don't know how much money I made, but I think I was bringing in a good income. We actually mapped out my route, and it was huge. My mom was given an award for highest Avon sales in the whole western district of Canada.

We came back to Manitoba, to Camperville, for my high school years, and my mom got past her shingles, but her health was never the same.[12] She was very depressed, always sleeping. My dad, Edward, got his journeyman papers for carpentry, and he was gone for work a lot of the time.[13] So instead of being that big, close family we once were, it seemed like we all went our own ways.

I was rebellious in high school, but my mom always stuck up for me no matter what trouble I got into. It wasn't like really terrible trouble. I was just known to have a big mouth and a sassy attitude. The teachers would pick on me and blame me for stuff, and I'd be like, "No, no, I didn't do that. You're not blaming me. I'm going to

---

11. Jesse Thistle, "Definition of Indigenous Homelessness in Canada," Canadian Observatory on Homelessness, 2017.

12. Camperville is a northern community with a population of around eight hundred. Primarily a Métis community, it sits on the western shore of Lake Winnipegosis.

13. Journeyman papers, or a journeyman's license, is a tradesman or craftsman's certification of graduation from an apprenticeship training.

call my mom," and so she'd come in. She'd be like, "Stop trying to blame Althea for everything. I know my daughter. If she said she didn't do it, she didn't do it." Then she goes to me, "You didn't do it, right? If I'm going to stick up for you, then you better make damn sure you're innocent." She gave me the power to be myself.

I WAS VERY DISCONNECTED

I had Jordan, my first child, just after I turned seventeen. He was a gift for me. But I was in an abusive relationship, so life was basically about trying to survive and trying to go to high school. My boyfriend at the time didn't want me to leave the house, so it was a constant daily battle.[14] I was living on welfare, arguing with the welfare people, constantly having to go see them. I did a lot of walking with my baby. That's basically the life of a poor person: walking, walking, walking. You can't afford bus fare so you have to walk everywhere. I was living here, in Winnipeg. My dad would often babysit. I would leave at 8 a.m. and walk five kilometers to school, then go to work and come back to take care of my baby and to the abuse that I had to endure. My boyfriend was a really horrible person. He was just wrong in the head—mean, petty. He'd slap me and spit on me, pull my hair out. It was terrible. But it took me a long time to leave and we eventually had two sons together, Christopher and Alexander.

School brought out a part of me that I thought I'd lost. I went to Children of the Earth High School, which is a traditional school.[15] They teach you the culture and the language and that solidified a lot in my mind about who we are as Indigenous people. It helped carry me through a lot of hard times.

I worked hard at that time, too, but of course the only jobs

14. Jordan was not this boyfriend's child.

15. Children of the Earth High School offers Aboriginal Languages programs in Cree and Ojibwe.

available were like internships, so basically I made no money. I graduated high school at twenty-three years old and got the Governor General's Academic Medal.[16] Jordan was six, Christopher was three, and Alexander, one. I'd won five scholarships. But I was very disconnected, very isolated, very alone.

When I was twenty-five, and Jordan was about eight, I realized I had to get him out of my house due to the abuse that both he and I were taking, because unlike the younger two, he wasn't my then boyfriend's child. I asked Jordan one day, "Do you want to go live with Koko and Papa?"[17] He said, "Okay." I walked him downtown to my parents' house, about twenty minutes away, dropped him off, then went back home.

My boyfriend was always telling me to throw myself away, throw the kids away. On and on. So I kind of became suicidal. I took off one day, and I went to Waterfront.[18] I'd heard it's dangerous there. You could get hurt there. So I went hoping someone would hurt me.

I was walking along, crying, and I fell down because it was all flooded. While I was laying in the mud, I saw the light glinting off the water, and I thought, *I'm going to throw myself in.* I got up to do that, and when I stood up, all of a sudden, a bee went by my ear. Then it went into the tree. Then the tree went *swoosh*, with all the leaves. And then this butterfly came out, and it flew by me and went into the grass. The grass went *swish*, and then this dragonfly came out, and it went around me and into the water. The water again was glinting, and I was just like, *Ohhh.* I got the shivers. I didn't go in, I just stood there and looked at it. All those little things—the bee, the butterfly, and the dragonfly—they basically saved me. The wind, the

---

16. The Governor General's Academic Medal is awarded to a Canadian high school, college, or university program's graduating student with the highest grade-point average.

17. Koko is short for "kokum," which means grandmother in Cree.

18. Waterfront Drive is a road in Winnipeg. Partly bordered by green space, it runs adjacent to the Red River.

trees, the water, and the grass—all of a sudden, something just connected. That was a transformational moment, and then I went home.
I just felt like it was okay, and there was nothing my boyfriend could
do to me. I was just like, *No. You're not hurting me anymore.*

I was thirty-three when I left. By then I had my daughter Victoria, too. After I left I decided to go to Thompson Crisis Centre, so
I was bused up there.[19] I was there on the emergency floor. It wasn't
long, maybe a week or so, but I felt, *Oh, look at how low I've come.
I'm in a women's shelter.* I felt so ashamed to be there. But it was a nice
facility, two levels. The top level was the transitional housing, and
Christopher, Alexander, Victoria, and I moved in and paid our own
rent there. The units were furnished, and we had to provide our own
food and whatnot. We were basically independent but in a secure
building. And I got to attend group counseling and individual counseling. We went on field trips. I got close to the other women there.
We really supported each other and became good friends.

While I was there, the center staff took us out to Paint Lake. I went
for a walk, and I just said out loud, "You know what? I need a clear sign
that I'm doing right with my life, that this is going to turn out good."
And then I looked up, and *wow.* I was on one of those beaches with
a rocky shore with grass and driftwood. There, in a pristine patch of
sand, was this little tiny pointy thing sticking up out of the middle. I
was like, "What's that?" I picked it up; it was an arrowhead. I was like,
"Oh my God!" I was just freaking out, running around the beach yelling and happy. "That's a sign!" I said. I ended up staying at the center
for seven months and, ultimately, it really changed my life.

The center gave me the tools I needed—for anger management,
stress management, counseling. I was able to come to terms with myself and learn how to spend time on my own. And I would remember
stuff, like, *Oh, I used to do that craft. Why did I stop? Oh yes, because*

---

19. With a population of almost thirteen thousand, Thompson is the largest city
in northern Manitoba. It is located on the Burntwood River, 739 kilometers north
of Winnipeg.

Asshole didn't like it. Well, I'm going to start again. I'd keep discovering pieces of myself.

I HAD THREE BABIES UNDER THREE YEARS OLD AND I WAS HOMELESS

From the crisis center, I came back to Winnipeg, and right away my ex figured out I was home and was after me again. So I ended up leaving once again, this time for Norway House.[20] Soon after, my dad was diagnosed with cancer, and I was able to spend the last six months of his life with him. He was an amazing person. He gave me a lot of the teachings, a lot of why I am the way I am, the way I treat people. Like, *I'll help you and I'll share with you, but just don't be an asshole or I'll have to kick your ass.*

I had my youngest three kids after I lost my dad.[21] I had those three little ones all in quick succession: Justin in 2008, Jaxtynne in 2009, and Aralyn in 2011. I was so depressed and sad. I felt suicidal, and I drank a lot. It was just a terrible state. I think if I didn't have my wee three, I would've given up. Finally, one day, I thought, *I can't live here anymore. I've got to get the hell out of here.* My sister and cousin lived in Ochre River, so I decided to go there. Ochre River was a little ten-lane town.[22] It had a half-Indigenous, half-white population. There was a bar, a school, a post office, fire hall, community hall. *The Manitoba provincial government, driven by its priority of protecting farm and pasture lands from flooding, decided on a course of action*

---

20. The northern community of Norway House is about three hundred kilometers south of Thompson, Manitoba.

21. Althea's abuser did not father these children.

22. Ochre River has a population of around nine hundred and is located twenty kilometers southeast of Dauphin, in northern Manitoba. While not exclusively Indigenous, the community of Ochre River has a large Native population, which is not uncommon in small northern towns where Indigenous people live in rural areas near their homelands.

that artificially raised the water levels of Dauphin Lake, thereby cre-
ating the conditions that allowed summer storms to flood surrounding
towns. In particular, the government had sought to minimize the flood-
ing of farm and pasture lands where the Assiniboine joins the Red River
downstream, near Winnipeg. It achieved this by raising lake waters by
way of the Portage Diversion, a 29-kilometer long channel, which di-
verted river water there and caused the floods.

In 2011, the floodwaters were hitting the Brandon area. In an effort to save farmland near Winnipeg pasture land, they diverted the
waters toward Lake Dauphin, where I lived. The house we lived in
wasn't directly on the shores of the water, but that diversion created a
lot of groundwater. My crawl space filled up with water, shorted out
my wiring, submerged my water pumps. The first day, there was only
water. Then about three days in, it started to smell. I looked down
into the crawlspace and you could see sewage floating; the sewage
line had broken. So at that point I had to get my kids out because I
could smell it everywhere.

　　The landlord didn't help because he had his own flooded house
to deal with. So I went to the rural municipality (RM) of Ochre
River, but they referred me back to the landlord. Then I went to the
city of Dauphin, and they referred me to the RM of Ochre River.
Manitoba Housing didn't provide emergency housing. I had three
babies under three years old and I was homeless. The welfare office
knew I was homeless, and the director of the department said, "Keep
me informed." At the Dauphin Friendship Centre, one of the ladies
laughed at me when I asked for help.[23]

Althea petitioned the provincial government and various emergency
service providers for housing, but these agencies did not have adequate

---

23. Friendship centres are community organizations that serve urban Inuit, Métis,
and First Nations people in Canada, providing various forms of assistance including
youth programs, health services, and housing, employment, and cultural programs.

emergency plans for effectively responding to the crisis. Furthermore, according to Althea, the service providers she reached out to were racist and placed her case at the bottom of a long list of priorities. The flooding was compounded by these bureaucratic obstacles, which together caused her homelessness. This "emergency crisis homelessness," in Jesse Thistle's words, "has affected vast swaths of Indigenous peoples across Canada. . . . The 'system,' it seems, is not built, or is unwilling, to house large populations of displaced Indigenous Peoples in crisis situations."[24]

Dauphin is a very racist town. It was hard to get past receptionists once they knew I was Indigenous. It was that attitude time and time again—that I was lesser, not important. I went to ten different social service agencies, all created to help people, and not one of them helped me. Time after time, I was turned away and rejected. The Red Cross didn't even call me back. When I said to Child and Family Services, "Take my kids. I'm homeless, take them," they replied, "We don't do that." Office after office had no clue how to help me. "That's not what we do" was their answer. The staff at the women's crisis shelter said because I wasn't facing domestic abuse, I didn't qualify, and I was like, "Well, let me go get a beating and I'll be right back." I told them they needed to change the name of their shelter to include "domestic abuse" and take that "crisis" word out of there.

The hardest part for me to get over was, How come nobody cared? How was I homeless with these babies? Like, what the hell? That was the most hurtful part for me, how society just allowed us to be homeless, and it took so long to find somebody to help, somebody to care, somebody to advocate for us. How in the heck can Canada have homeless babies? Justin wasn't even three yet. Jaxtynne was fifteen months. And Aralyn was a newborn. For a single mother with a tiny newborn baby just to be left like that, I was like, *Oh my God.* My mom basically drove eight hundred kilometers from Nor-

---

24. Thistle, "Reframing the Discussion: An Indigenous Definition of Homelessness."

way House to Dauphin, and picked me up off the floor and brought me and my kids to Winnipeg.

I stayed with my other sister for four weeks, and it was just hell. I had no rest; we were stuck in one bedroom. It was terrible. I went back to Dauphin, stayed there with a friend for three weeks. That was a terrible hellhole situation as well. Then finally I found a place to rent. I was really devastated, really sad. I stayed there about a year; I wasn't sure where to go. Winnipeg was the only other place where I knew people. I decided to give it another chance, going against my decision to never, ever come back because of my earlier life here with my ex. And right after I came back, I noticed all the people on the corners, and I was like, *Are these people all homeless?*

Instead of killing myself—what would that prove?—I became angry and I declared war on homelessness. I realized that homelessness was a bigger issue than just me and my kids. I decided that I was going to do everything in my power to let Canadians know that we're not this great nation, that we've got women with children going homeless. There's something really wrong happening here, and we need to fix it.

I was also trying to find my own healing solutions. I couldn't access any mental health care. My mom connected me with traditional healers who took us out to Bannock Point, so it was there that I was able to offer tobacco to the grandmothers and the grandfathers.[25] I asked for guidance and told them I needed to find my purpose.

A BATCH OF BANNOCK

I was eating eggs one day, in 2013, and I was like, *Oh, I wish I had bannock.* Then I thought, *What's wrong with me? I'm wishing*

---

25. Indigenous people have used tobacco for ceremonial and medicinal purposes for centuries. It is sometimes used as an offering to the Creator or to another person, place, or being when asking for guidance or protection.

for bannock! I'm a neechi; *there should be bannock everywhere here!*[26]
*That's it! I'm going to go out and buy the ingredients, and I'm going to
keep practicing until I become a master at baked bannock.* I kept trying
and trying. "This is an ugly bannock." I would throw it in the yard.
"Stupid bannock." I tried again, and I was just sitting there all frustrated after my fourth bannock that day. Then I heard squawking.
What the heck? I looked out my window and there were like fifty
birds. I thought, *What are they doing?* They were fighting over my
bannock. I thought, *Well, it can't be that bad.*

Then my friend came over. She was doing her laundry, and I was
giving her a bunch of groceries to help tide her over. I made her a
batch of bannock, and I was going to drive her home. It was minus
fifty degrees out. God, it was so cold. We stopped for gas, and while
I was gassing up, these two guys came over and asked, "Do you have
any change?" I was like, "No, sorry. Got fourteen dollars, and I need
gas." They asked, "Do you have any food?" I was like, "No. Oh, wait
a minute," I said, "I've got bannock." I gave them about three pieces
each, and a can of soup. I drove away and thought, *Wow. Bannock. I
gave them bannock that I made.*

Around this time, I started going to Idle No More rallies and felt
so inspired by the one that Buffy Sainte-Marie sang at.[27] I thought,
*Wow. This is how we've sounded for thousands of years. We're still here.
This is amazing.* I got a whiff of sage smoke, and it looked like hair
weaving through the people, like white hair. I was standing on the
stairs and all those big, round globe lights at the legislative building
were glowing orange. And when I yawned, my eyes watered, and

---

26. *Neechi* means "friend" in Ojibwe and other Algonquian languages. It is also
slang for a First Nations person.

27. Idle No More is an ongoing protest movement that "calls on all people to join in
a peaceful revolution, to honor Indigenous sovereignty and to protect the land and
water." Buffy Sainte-Marie, born in 1941 on the Piapot Plains Cree First Nation
Reserve, is a celebrated singer-songwriter and activist. For more on Idle No More
and Indigenous resurgence, see appendix 3.

from my watery, squinty eyes, it kind of looked like the lights were campfires. And then I heard the drum. People were dancing, they were doing their round dance, and this felt so good—very reaffirming that this was the way of our people.[28] The village is still here.

"IN HONOR OF THE VILLAGE WE ONCE HAD"

The day after the concert, I asked the ancestors for help. Right before I mixed together all the flour, the salt, and the baking powder, I said, "Ancestors, help me. All the best bannock makers, now in heaven—Mary, Dad, Granny, Grandpa, Rita—everybody! Get into my hands and help me."

Two days after I met those guys at the gas station, I went out with nineteen servings of bannock and chili, and I drove all over the city. I found one person here, another person there. I passed it to one person, they were sniffing and they kind of tried to hide their rag, and I was like, "Don't worry, I'm not here for that."[29] And then I pulled up to Dufferin and Main Street, which is between the Yale Hotel and the Northern Hotel, in a very derelict part of Main Street. I set up there and *boom*, all the food was just gone, and everyone was talking to me. And they were just making me laugh, and there was a lot of camaraderie. One woman—I handed the food to her outside of the Bell Hotel on Main Street—she asked me, "Who do you work for?" I said, "Nobody. I work for me, I work for you, for us." And then it just came to me. I said, "In honor of the village

---

28. Round dances, thought to have originated in the Plains, are now performed by Indigenous peoples throughout North America. The dance serves both social and ceremonial functions. Round dances are friendship dances. At social gatherings and powwows they are a way for many people to dance together, where positive energy is created and shared through hand-holding and shared movement around the circle.

29. People who sniff or huff gas sometimes place a gas-soaked rag over their mouth and nose, and this person may have thought Althea was with law enforcement.

we once had." She said, "Oh, from our people? *Meegwetch*, sister."[30]

That's become my motto, and I use the bannock as a reminder of the powerful village that we were before colonization, before this genocide, the stereotypes and stigmas, and these labels and names that have been placed upon us.[31] I try to remind people that we're more than all that. This is who we used to be, and it takes them back to the tables that they used to sit at with their own families, when they had a home, when they had loved ones. My friend Jesse Thistle says, "I'd say my own name to myself, just so I didn't forget who I was." That's why I try to remind everybody who we are.

We make warm lunch for probably a dollar a head, but we also provide water and baked goods and fruit—people donate all that. We're a registered charity. I have a treasurer, Dougald. I have a head chef, Sonya, who takes care of all our volunteers. She shows them how to prepare the meal. I do the bannock. There's another group that brings the fruit. The Treat Winnipeg group does the baking. They founded themselves just to support us!

We got a grant one winter and from that we fed about four thousand people and supported ten grassroots agencies with direct donations. But we're always struggling, like everybody else.

I used to drive around to find people to give food to, but that was getting costly, so I went back to Dufferin and Main. I set up there and people got to know me. They were the ones that named me "the Bannock Lady." Today they're waiting for me. Rain or shine, hot or cold, all winter we stand outside with them as equals.

The population varies according to which day of the month it is. Around the first, everybody's got their relief checks, so it's kind of sparse, and then around the fifteenth, there's like a hundred strong at least, lined up waiting for us. If it's around the day family allowance comes, it's mostly older people who don't get family allowance, who

---

30. *Meegwetch* means "thank you" in Anishinaabe.

31. Althea is not alone in her efforts to rebuild the village. For more on this movement toward Indigenous resurgence, see appendix essay 3.

are trying to make it to the end of the month.[32] When I was a kid, the outlook was, "When you retire, those are your golden years"—there's no such thing anymore! These people are literally starving. They have to choose between rent, medication, or food. Our elders are starving, and it makes me so angry.

On the street, I have to keep the peace. Sometimes we'll get a belligerent person. I don't care if they're drunk or intoxicated, whatever condition they're in, as long as they come and behave themselves. Sometimes we get somebody who doesn't, so then I have to go and talk to them and say, "Hey, straighten out. We don't accept this behavior here." We have the Mama Bear Clan members coming to help out.[33] I also have the beat officer coming by. He's become one of my friends. Various members from the community will step forward and say, "Hey, you leave the Bannock Lady alone." They straighten each other out. And the whole line, if someone's messing around too much, will tell them to smarten up. They say, "Sorry, Bannock Lady, sorry." I tell them, "It's okay. Just so you know next time, we're behaving ourselves here."

INTERGENERATIONAL TRAUMA THAT'S BEING CARRIED FORWARD

Winnipeg is home to Canada's largest Indigenous population, and one that is quickly growing. Migration from Manitoba's northern reserve communities contributes to this increase. Indigenous people, the fastest-growing demographic in Canada, are often driven from their reserves by poor housing conditions, long waiting lists for accommodation, overcrowding

---

32. Family allowance, or the Canada Child Benefit, is a tax-free monthly payment made to eligible families to assist them with the expenses involved in raising children under eighteen years old.

33. The Mama Bear Clan is a group of volunteer women who patrol the streets of North Point Douglas, Winnipeg, with food, medicine, and clothing for the city's homeless.

at six times the rate of off-reserve housing, and in some instances, a lack of running water. Other people have been compelled to leave their reserves after flooding or wildfires. These poor housing conditions force a choice between subpar housing on reserve and insecure and increasingly expensive housing in Winnipeg and other cities. And while many residents struggle to find appropriate accommodation in Winnipeg, Indigenous people make up more than 50 percent of the city's homeless population and are more likely to experience homelessness in the city or to live in accommodation that is overcrowded or in poor condition.[34]

Additional barriers to finding adequate housing include poverty rates that are double that of non-Indigenous peers and the reality that in transitioning to an urban center, as Althea's family did when she was a child, they have to adapt to a new culture and new way of life. Finally, as Althea experienced, Indigenous people are more likely to experience discrimination while attempting to navigate the complex bureaucratic systems of housing, health, and social services, sometimes without a rental history, bank account, or government identification.[35]

One of the biggest challenges I see is that people coming from the reserve into the city aren't aware of what resources are available. They come here because of the lack of opportunities on the reserve, the lack of housing. They come to try to go to school, find a job, get opportunities, and what they're finding is the rent is too high, the challenges are too much, and they get tired of struggling. And it's like, are we preparing our youth for this? They're just floating around from here to there instead of accessing resources.

---

34. A 2018 survey that included 406 homeless persons in Winnipeg found that 71.4 percent of that population was Indigenous. End Homelessness Winnipeg, *2018 Winnipeg Street Health Survey*, https://endhomelessnesswinnipeg.ca/wp-content /uploads/2019/02/2018-Winnipeg-Street-Health-Survey-Report.pdf.

35. To learn more about Indigenous migration to Winnipeg, see Josh Brandon and Evelyn Peters, "Moving to the City: Housing and Aboriginal Migration to Winnipeg," Canadian Center for Policy Alternatives, 2014.

If you're a single mother, the one income is not going to cut it, especially if you're not in low-income housing. And it takes at least a couple of years on the waitlist to get that housing; I was on the waitlist for two years myself when I was on assistance. I'd worked when I was younger as a receptionist and as a volunteer coordinator, when I had my first three sons, but when I had the three younger ones I just realized that I was never going to make enough money to fully support them. I'm only going to have the amount that welfare gives me. So I decided to stay home. My family allowance check became my everything, my survival, which is not what it was designed to do.[36]

I'd like to see us learning financial literacy, to advocate for ourselves—how to speak, how to present ourselves—because you get frustrated being homeless, and being passed off from agency to agency. How do we address that and prepare these youth to come to this city in a better way? You see these refugee centers for newcomers to Canada—well, Indigenous people need that, too. Not a refugee center, but a resettlement center of some kind for when people arrive in the cities.

The definition of Canadian Indigenous homelessness that I coauthored with Jesse Thistle really speaks to our intergenerational trauma.[37] It speaks to the historic displacement. It speaks to the loss of *all my relations*, the loss of our languages, the loss of our places, of our spirituality. That's what I work on now, trying to get that out, trying to get changes made to policy accordingly, and it's a huge task.

My sister-in-law, Bonnie, started Bannock in the Park, in Brandon, and I helped talk her through a lot of things.[38] She was getting

---

36. Family allowance is a monthly government payment to families with children to help cover costs of childcare. It was introduced in 1945 as Canada's first universal welfare program.

37. Intergenerational trauma refers to the transmission of trauma from survivors to succeeding generations. For more on intergenerational trauma, see appendix essay 2.

38. Brandon is located in the southwestern corner of Manitoba. It has a population of around forty-nine thousand and is the second largest city in the province. Bannock in the Park was inspired by Althea's free bannock lunches in Winnipeg.

harassed by the city officials. They were trying to make her install some kind of porta-potty. I'm like, "What are they doing?" I phoned a city official. I was like, "How dare you? You should be putting your arms around this woman." I just reamed them out. They later backed off. I told Bonnie, "You tell me if they do that again." I was so mad. A porta-potty—like where were these people going before Bonnie wanted to serve them soup? It was just so ridiculous.

My three little ones were right there with Got Bannock? from the beginning, so I call them my little CEOs. I hope that my children grow up to be caring, sharing people. They still help me. When I used to take them to hand out the bannock with me, it was hard not to lose track of them at times. I said, "Where are my kids?" So I had people show up to watch them. It definitely takes a village to do all of this.

HOMELESS AGAIN

I spoke with Althea in October 2019 for an update. She had been honored with both the Senate of Canada Medal and the Meritorious Service Medal shortly after we met in 2017. After a series of health issues and incidents of domestic violence, she became homeless again the following year. These personal stresses and a lack of structural support led her to end Got Bannock?'s activities in March 2019. Althea is now living in Ochre River, the town in which she had become homeless eight years earlier.

In March 2019, I was abjectly homeless. I slept in my car a few times, stayed with friends. I had to leave my kids behind, with my mom.

I stopped the Got Bannock? lunches that month. It was really a lot of extra responsibility. I just didn't have it some days. Donations had slowed down. And come December, if I don't do anything, there goes the registered charity status. I'm trying to figure out what's next. There are people calling me to start a bannock business, maybe cater.

The Bannock Army was a large entity and I thank anybody that ever stepped up to help us in any way, shape, or form. People are asking me to come back. But I don't know. I did have a dedicated crew that would step in—Mitch Bourbonniere and Ogijiita Pimatiswin Kinamatwin.[39] Mitch would bring foster children as helpers. I didn't realize the relationship at first. He pointed it out and said, "The reason I bring these guys here is because they can see their families come through the food line and see there's nothing between them. There's no walls. There's no interventions. No agencies. It's just them." And I'd see it happen. "Look, there's my boy!" their parents said. "He's helping the Bannock Lady!" They were just crying and hugging. Oh my God, that was beautiful. That's exactly what I'd wanted Got Bannock? to be.

---

39. Ogijiita Pimatiswin Kinamatwin (OPK) is an organization that aims to nurture and support marginalized, at-risk, Indigenous young adults and their families.

VERA STYRES

MOHAWK/TUSCARORA
RETIRED SOCIAL WORKER
BORN IN: 1935, Six Nations of the
Grand River First Nation, Ontario
INTERVIEWED IN: Six Nations

Six Nations is the most populous First Nations reserve in Canada, with a total of 27,276 members, 12,848 of whom live on the reserve as of 2017.[1] The only reserve in North America that has representatives of all six Iroquois nations living together, Six Nations' 46,000 acres near the city of Brantford, Ontario, includes only about 5 percent of the original 950,000 acres the band was granted by the 1784 Haldimand Treaty.[2]

---

1. To learn more about the band, visit www.sixnations.ca.

2. A First Nations band is the basic unit of government for people subject to Canada's Indian Act. For more, see the glossary.

The Iroquois nations had long histories of trade with the British, with whom they allied to stop colonial American advances on their territories. Many Iroquois warriors fought alongside the British during the American Revolutionary War. However, after the colonists' victory, the British government relinquished all of its land in the colonies, including that belonging to Six Nations, without consulting them.

Vera's one-story home sits on a major road intersecting the reserve's vastly shrunken remaining land, at the far end of a wide lot shared with a gas station owned by her youngest son.[3] At both of our meetings, in December 2017 and May the following year, we drank tea at her kitchen table while the setting sun warmed our faces through a window above her sink. She spoke about her time at a residential school as a young child and how resuming her education through night school as a widowed mother of five set her on the path to becoming Six Nations' first social worker.

Vera recalled the racism she encountered in Ontario's Child and Family Services system, in which she said it was common for agencies to apprehend Native children because there were financial incentives to do so.[4] By 1977, approximately 15,500 Indigenous children were living in foster care. While Indigenous children made up less than 5 percent of the total child population in Canada, they were 20 percent of all the children in foster care.[5]

---

3. In both the US and Canada, Indigenous peoples have been forcibly moved to and confined within specific areas of land. Called a "reserve" in Canada and a "reservation" in the US, these are lands set apart by the respective federal governments for the use and occupation of an Indian band, First Nation, or Native American tribe. For more on reserves, see the glossary.

4. *Apprehension* is the official term used in Canada for the removal of children from their homes by child protection agencies.

5. Statistics based on a study by H. Philip Hepworth, "Foster Care and Adoption in Canada," Canadian Council on Social Development, 1980. Cited in Patrick Johnson, "The Ontario Superior Court Is Hearing a Lawsuit on a Dark Part of Our History—the Mass Removal of Indigenous Children by Child Welfare Authorities," *Policy Options Politiques*, July 26, 2016, https://policyoptions.irpp .org/magazines/july-2016/revisiting-the-sixties-scoop-of-indigenous-children/.

These numbers led Vera to participate in the development of Part X of the Child and Family Services Act.[6] The goal, she explains, was "to convince the powers that be that we can grow up just fine in our own community with our own people."

NOWHERE FOR US TO GO

I was born in January, 1935, at the Lady Willingdon Hospital right here on the reserve. My mother's name was Frieda Henhawk and my father's was Walter Mount Pleasant. My mother attended longhouse and my father was Baptist.[7] It was easier to accept the beliefs of the longhouse than what we heard in church because Christianity was all hellfire and brimstone. God was not a very loving God. He was a punitive God. You'll go to hell if you do this, you'll go to hell if you do that. At the longhouse, regardless of what you did, you were going to the happy hunting grounds.[8] We lived on a farm up until I was five years old, and then I'm not sure what happened, but my father was no longer there, and my mother couldn't manage the farm, and everybody just moved on.

We ended up at a canning factory in Winona, the E. D. Smith

6. In 1984, the Child and Family Services Act (CFSA) mandated Part X – Native and Indian Rights, or "customary care," a model of Aboriginal child welfare service. Customary care is defined under CFSA as "the care and supervision of an Indian or Native child by a person who is not the child's parent, according to the custom of the child's Band or native community." The last version of the Child and Family Services Act (of 1990) was repealed on April 30, 2018, and replaced by the Child, Youth and Family Services Act. Part IV of the new law addresses First Nations, Inuit, and Métis Child and Family Services.

7. The longhouse is a long and relatively narrow dwelling; various types were built by different peoples throughout Indigenous North America. There is also a religious tradition in which the longhouse plays a central role. Founded in 1799 by the Seneca prophet Sganyodaiyo, or Handsome Lake, the longhouse movement combined Iroquois belief with some elements of Christianity.

8. The "happy hunting ground" is the name given to the afterlife paradise of some Indian tribes in which hunting and feasting are plentiful.

canning factory.[9] My mother was a boarding house manager there. We had our own beds, in the bunkhouse for the workers. And she met up with a fella who I guess promised to take care of her and her four girls. So they got together and we moved back here, but there was no room for all of us to live in one place. My mother took us to work on a tobacco farm, and the accommodation for the help was the haymow in the barn above the horse stable. There was nowhere for us to go so she ended up sending my sister Iowne, who was born in 1932, and me—the school-age girls—to the Mohawk Institute.[10] With only two kids—my sisters Wilma, born 1938, and Romaine, born 1940—she was able to find accommodation for herself and them.

Throughout the history of the Indian residential school system in Canada, many children's attendance was mandatory and enforced by law. But for other families, the coercion to attend was less explicit. The same assimilationist policies and practices that dismantled economies that had served Native populations for generations were causing greater numbers of Indians to send their children to boarding schools. While earlier generations had effectively educated their children in their own cultural and economic practices, some parents, compelled to leave reservations in search of work in cities, or faced with a period of intense economic pressure, enrolled their children in boarding school. In both the United States and Canada, the policies that determined Indian education in its very earliest incarnation were an expression of two parallel views: the belief in white superiority and the Christian need to "raise Indians up to the level of the whites" and the political need to extinguish all Indian title to land.[11]

---

9. Winona is a small community that is officially a part of the city of Hamilton, thirty kilometers northeast of Six Nations.

10. The Mohawk Institute Residential School, in Brantford, Ontario, operated from 1885 to 1970.

11. Dian Million, "Telling Secrets: Sex, Power and Narratives in Indian Residential Schools," *Canadian Woman Studies* 20, no. 2 (2000): 95.

So that was a unique experience, going to the residential school.[12] In one way, it was good because we had nowhere to live and it was warm there. We didn't have to go out and cut wood and draw water because there was running water and central heating. There were about eighty-five girls and over a hundred boys at the Mush Hole.[13] That was in 1942, '43. I was seven and eight.

I learned how to roller-skate, how to ice-skate, a lot about what other people ate. Like I didn't know we ate sheep. I thought sheep were just for wool. And I didn't know that people ate all parts of a pig because my only experience eating pork before that was bacon. Even the different vegetables we ate there—I had seen them before but not eaten them. And going to church every Sunday and going to chapel, prayers every night—that was something different too. I learned a lot about the Bible and all the rules and regulations about how to get along with each other. But the people who were teaching the rules didn't follow them. And I wondered why. Like, "Honor thy father and thy mother," but they kept telling us what terrible people our parents were. Or "Treat everybody like your brothers and sisters," yet they told us how nasty and good for nothing Indians were. They contradicted everything they were teaching. It was confusing, really.

When we were admitted to the school in August, we had to get our hair cut and scrubbed down and doused with kerosene to kill the lice—even if we didn't have any.[14] I had this darker tan from being out in the tobacco fields and helping there before we went to school.

---

12. Residential schools were a network of boarding schools designed to remove Indian children from their families and culture to assimilate them into Canadian culture. For more on residential schools, see the glossary.

13. "Mush Hole" was a nickname given to the Mohawk Institute by students who attended it because they were forced to eat mushy oatmeal there.

14. For many Native tribes an individual's hair, including the practice of wearing it long, has specific cultural significance and meaning. Forced haircuts at Indian residential and boarding schools were part of an intentional effort to dismantle culture.

And the lady who admitted us tried to scrub the color off me and left a scar on my neck. It scabbed over, and then she scrubbed the scab off. So I wasn't just a dirty little Indian, I was a "scabby, dirty little Indian," and she said that as she was scrubbing!

My schooling was the same as any school—reading, writing, and all that. It was easy to me, but then school was always easy for me anyway, no matter how dumb they said I was. I couldn't eat a lot of the stuff they were feeding us, and I got real skinny. You know how you get those mealy worms in grain? We still had to eat the oatmeal even though there were mealy worms in there. They didn't really cook the oatmeal. It was put in these great big vats, enough to feed a couple hundred kids. They'd put the oatmeal and the water in and heat it up, but sometimes it wouldn't even be totally heated through, it would just kind of get mushy and slimy. The mealy worms could still move because they didn't get cooked. You'd have your plate and you'd see these little things moving. But most of the kids ate it because there was nothing else to eat.

My mom came to visit after the tobacco harvest, which was around the end of September, and she started to cry when she saw me. She said to the principal, "You promised me you were going to take care of my kids. Look at her—look at how skinny she is." And she punched the principal right in the face. So after that, they tried to look after us more. The principal came and force-fed me at breakfast every day, but I couldn't swallow the stuff, and if I did, it ended up a projectile sent right back on him. So he wore my breakfast every time he tried to feed me.

There were two floors of dormitories for the eighty-five girls. The younger ones were on one floor and the older ones were on the upper floor. And there were sections—six beds on that side, six beds on this side—as many as could fit. And they were all single beds. At home, we were accustomed to at least two in a bed. There, we got to have our own bed, which was not always as cozy as we would've been at home, but it was okay. Then sometimes there were bed-wetters who, needing to switch beds, would take yours. Kids were mean to each other. And if the bed-wetter had an older sister, then you couldn't do anything about it because she'd beat you up if you tried to force the little sister to take back her wet bed. It was kind of a survival of the fittest.

GOT YOUR OWN HOUSE? YOU CAN SURVIVE

We left the school when my mother got a place for us to live, with her new partner. That was down at Saint John's Corner.[15] And by then we had a brother. I got along with my stepfather. Coming home, I was expected to do chores. I got the outside chores and my older sister got the inside chores. So she got to cook and clean, and I was my stepfather's helper—cutting wood and carrying water and learning how to make a fire and all the things that the oldest boy would usually do. That was my job.

My stepfather was a hunter, a trapper, so he believed in the responsibilities of providing for a family; he did what he could. He worked in Hamilton, at the Hamilton Foundry.[16] But then, after the war, he didn't have a job there anymore so he worked on farms, picking strawberries, raspberries, cherries, pears, tomatoes, apples, tobacco—whatever harvesting had to be done.

The school for us was just down the road on the corner—Number Ten school. I guess it was the tenth school to be built on the reserve. We didn't have far to go. And then the church was on the other side of the corner. It was an English Anglican church. If you went to Sunday school, you got a gift at Christmastime, candy and an orange, so we went.

My sisters and I had to entertain ourselves because there were no toys. So we went exploring, climbing trees and digging up roots,

---

15. Saint John's is one of several named communities within Six Nations.

16. Hamilton is a city about thirty kilometers northeast of Six Nations.

finding things in the crick.[17] We'd have to go and get water anyway, so everybody would go.

We grew gardens too. We had to. Potatoes and carrots and onions. And there was a big patch of horseradish. And people who wanted horseradish would come and trade other edibles for it. Everybody traded whatever they were growing. And the farmers we worked for, if they had extra stuff in their fields, we could go and get whatever was left. They had machines that dug up and picked up the potatoes, and whatever the machines left in the field, we could go and get. There were times when we'd have to hire somebody with a pickup truck to go and get the bags of potatoes that we picked up. And we'd pay them in potatoes.

My mother had pretty strict ideas about what a man's responsibilities were and what a woman's responsibilities were. Like, it wasn't a woman's responsibility to put food on the table and feed her man— and if that's what you thought, then it was time for you to leave, or for her to leave. And this is what became of her relationship. My stepdad wasn't able to provide for the family anymore. He died from cancer when my second brother was four or five, so he must've been getting sick before then. He couldn't do the physical labor that was required to provide for six kids, so when they split up, three of us went back to the Mush Hole in 1946. Me and two younger ones. I was eleven years old.

My older sister stayed home to help take care of the two youngest, two boys. And my mother worked. During that time, my mom was able to get a couple of structures from what used to be army barracks in Brantford. She took them apart and put them back together as a house for us. So by the time that year was up at the Mush Hole, we had our own house. Now we didn't have to move. We had our own place to live and could survive without depending on a man. Got your own house? You can survive. And, of course, we had our garden.

---

17. Crick, or creek.

My mother discovered something else: she became a bootlegger. Native people generally weren't allowed to buy booze, but she knew that the army fellas—the veterans coming back from the war—*were* allowed to buy it.[18] So veterans bought the booze for her and she sold it to whoever happened to want it. She made a living that way, to provide for us kids so that we didn't have to go to the Mush Hole anymore. My mom taught me: you do for yourself. If you know what is wrong, then you do something about it. You fix it.

My mother was the "banker"; she took all the money from our strawberry picking, cherry picking, and any berry picking we did. There were no laws against child labor back then, so if you knew the difference between a ripe strawberry and a green one, then you got to pick strawberries. Any kind of work that had to be done, if you were able to learn how to do it, you did it. Strawberry money was used for buying summer clothes and new summer shoes, running shoes for everybody. Then money from picking cherries would be for school clothes for the fall. And then tobacco-picking money was for stocking up the pantry for the winter. We'd have sugar by the hundred-pound bags, flour by the hundred-pound bags. This was the time we had money, so we had to buy stuff—we had to provide for the winter when there would be nothing coming in. And all summer, we would can berries and make chili sauce and jams. We had cases and cases of canned goods tucked under our beds. When the Royal Canadian Mounted Police came and raided us, looking for booze, all they'd find was cans of Carnation milk and other canned goods. When powdered milk and margarine became available, we bought cases of that as well.

To get through the winter, we'd have the milk, the potatoes, all the canned stuff like pickles, chili sauce, and canned strawberries and tomatoes. We'd have tomato sauce on all kinds of things. We ate pretty good. And we'd make hot biscuits with the flour. My mother

---

18. The Indian Act prohibited the sale of alcohol to First Nations people.

figured out how much we needed to get us from December to April, so we had quite a stash.

My mother used to take me with her to different ceremonies where they needed someone to make a fire and keep the fire going and draw the water. I had to do all that while she was meeting with people. I got to meet all these medicine people too. My mother was also a medicine woman. She knew natural herbal medicines, and she would help lots of people. She would find out what was bothering them and fix up some kind of concoction and they'd get better. She was demonized by the men who didn't know how to make these potions—they called her a witch. It was these witches who had the formulas, and in order for the men to capitalize on what the women knew, they had to condemn the women and get the recipes out of them. Some people were afraid that my mom could use her knowledge for hurting them. There were people who were genuinely afraid of her, and I couldn't understand that because she made these things to help people, not to hurt them. She knew how to do abortions, but it was only people who wanted them who came to her. She wouldn't take your baby just because she was a witch.

SMART ENOUGH TO BE WHITE

When I was fifteen, in 1950, and then all through high school—besides working all summer—I worked nights at the canning factory. The bus would come around and pick us up to go to Brantwood Farms.[19] We'd work during the corn harvest. We'd go to school during the days and work nights. We'd get home about two o'clock in the morning or something like that—never had time for homework except if we did it on the bus. So we had to develop a pretty good memory to get through school. Every once in a while, I'd have to take a day off because I couldn't stay awake in school. It was hard

---

19. Brantwood Farms is located in Brantford, Ontario, about twenty-one kilometers northwest of Six Nations.

work. But that only lasted about three weeks. So it wasn't bad. It gave me spending money for the winter so I could go to the restaurant and get French fries with the other kids or buy an ice cream cone or something like that. And I could buy my loose-leaf paper, pencils, and erasers for school.

Enfranchisement, made compulsory by the 1876 Indian Act, was the most common legal process by which Indigenous people lost their Indian status. To reduce the size of First Nations tribes, enfranchisement was required of any male Indian over twenty-one "able to speak, read and write either the English or the French language readily and well, and [who] is sufficiently advanced in the elementary branches of education and is of good moral character and free from debt." An "enfranchised" Indian would not retain the "legal rights and liabilities of Indians" and would "no longer be deemed an Indian" but rather a regular British subject.[20] Through education and enfranchisement, Indians lost the right to their land. Throughout the colony First Nations governments immediately saw the implications for tribal survival. One leader remarked, it was an attempt "to break them to pieces" and some bands removed their children from the schools.[21]

The Indian Act changed in 1961.[22] Under Canadian law at that time, if a Native person graduated from university, you lost your Indian status because you were considered smart enough to be white.[23]

If you no longer had Native status, you couldn't live on a reserve,

---

20. "Act to Encourage the Gradual Civilization of the Indian Tribes in this Province, and to Amend the Laws Respecting Indians," 3rd Session, 5th Parliament, 1857.

21. John S. Milloy, *A National Crime: The Canadian Government and the Residential School System* (Winnipeg: University of Manitoba Press, 1999), 19.

22. In 1961, the government removed Section 112, known as the "compulsory enfranchisement" section, from the Indian Act.

23. The Indian Act forced enfranchisement, and loss of status rights, for any First Nations individuals admitted to university. Enfranchisement was the most

and you couldn't have any of the benefits of being on the reserve because you were overqualified to be Indian. A lot of the kids my age who went to longhouse didn't go to high school; the old folks said you would get off the band list if you went. All of these things were scary for us, like, *We won't be able to live on the reserve?* But we did know teachers and doctors and nurses who didn't lose their status, so I was wondering about that too—if it was really the law or just a myth the older folks were spreading to make the kids afraid to leave. I just wanted to go to school. I wanted to learn. Thankfully, in 1948, the buses started running to the off-reservation schools. It made it easier to get a high school education and showed me it was okay; I wasn't going to lose my status.

I always managed to be among the top five in each grade. But in grade twelve my mother got polio in November, so we were quarantined, and I had to miss school from November to the end of February. She was in the hospital, and us kids couldn't leave the house. People would bring food and leave it on the doorstep. I couldn't catch up in school after that, so I thought, *Well, I guess it's time to quit.* And I got a job at Westinghouse in Brantford. They were opening up the TV assembly plant, and I went and got tested to see if I could do any of the stuff that was required. They called me a "super operator." I could assemble anything. I got to be the inspector at the end of the assembly line, checking everybody else's work. That became my job.

Then I fell in love. Carl and I used to play together as kids. His family lived here on this property and my family lived down Fifth Line.[24] Our families used to visit back and forth. His parents broke up, my parents broke up, so they stopped visiting each other. But Carl and I went to high school at the same time. I used to walk from Saint John's to Sunday school at the Baptist church and he'd borrow

---

common legal process by which Indigenous people lost their Indian status under the Indian Act.

24. Fifth Line is a major road on Six Nations Reserve.

his brother's truck and pick me up. I'd be going the other way, and he'd take me home. If he couldn't borrow his brother's truck, he'd get his bicycle and ride along, keep me company going home.

We said, "We should run away together," get away from the reserve. His uncle Dan had a job picking cherries, in Williamson, New York. And Carl asked if we could go and work with him. So I quit my job at Westinghouse and went. That was in 1954, I was nineteen. After we finished picking cherries, we went to pick apples. From there we went to Rochester. Carl got a job in construction, and I got a job in a factory—a canning factory again. From there we moved to Buffalo.

My kids were born in 1956, '57, '59, '62. In 1959, we moved back to the reserve because my oldest needed to start going to school. We didn't want our kids going to school in the city. Our experience with kids from the city who came back to the reserve was that they were very aggressive; they thought they were better than everybody else. My husband called it Buffalo bullshit. We didn't want our kids to be like that.

My expectations were the same for my kids as my mom's were for me, in the sense that if they could learn on their own, with just a little bit of instruction, that's the way it would be. Because my mother made us do a lot for ourselves, we knew how to provide for ourselves and that prepared me for surviving the kind of life I would have later on.

I COULD PROVIDE FOR MY FAMILY

When my husband got killed in a car accident in 1963, I had four kids—and one on the way. The baby, Glenn, was born April 26, 1964, and I started tobacco planting in May that year. So at that point he would've been like three weeks, maybe a month old. I remember paying somebody twenty-five dollars a week to look after my kids while I went to work.

I can't remember a time when I didn't work. And when I was thirty-some years old, I thought, I better learn how to do something different. When I get older, I won't be able to work in the fields, so I'd better find another job to do. I started going to night school. By this time there was welfare and mother's allowance. In 1964, I think, they extended welfare onto the reserves.[25] But I already could provide for my family—I didn't need welfare. I could do it myself. Working in the fields, you could get unemployment insurance if you paid into it. As long as you had twenty-six weeks in, you could collect unemployment insurance for when you were laid off work. So that's what happened. I was able to stay home with my kids from January to May and collect unemployment insurance and provide that way, as long as I did what my mother did: buy all the stuff that I needed ahead of time. She taught me how to survive very well. That was the way I did it from the time I was twenty-nine, when Glenn was born, until I was around thirty-eight. Then I got my secretarial training and I got a job as a receptionist at a post-secondary school. But I took a drastic cut in pay. With the change from farmwork to secretarial work, my annual income dropped by almost ten thousand dollars. It was a shocker, like, *Hey, I'm supposed to have a real job now.*

My job was working with the education counselors. And the students would have to come to the office and talk with the counselors at different times, especially if they weren't doing well in school, or they were missing too many days. Sometimes they'd be crying when they came out of the office. They'd sit and talk to me, and then they'd go back to the classroom. The counselors told me that I was a natural counselor and that I should become a social worker. I decided to go back to school again. I went to Mohawk College and did a social service worker program. That's how I became Six Nations' first certified social worker.

---

25. The federal government approved the on-reserve income assistance program for First Nations in 1964.

Six Nations put me to work. I just had to jump in with both feet. There was no coddling or pampering or anything like that. And as the community got to know me and what I was doing, people were coming to me and saying, "This is what's happening. I need help." And I would identify the different services that were available for anyone who needed assistance.

WE CAN GROW UP JUST FINE
IN OUR OWN COMMUNITY

In 1982, we were in the process of developing Part X of the Child and Family Services Act. There were a lot of meetings happening in Toronto and Hamilton with the directors of social services. And I had a good strong voice—loud enough that I didn't need a microphone. I'd be asking questions, making suggestions, and after a while they just knew me by name. "Yes, Vera," or "Yes, Mrs. Styres, what do you have to say?"

And I'd say, "We need our own foster homes, we need our own people. We need our kids to stay with their own people. They need to stay in their own community." They argued that we didn't have suitable homes on the reserve to raise children. I replied, "Well, I grew up on the reserve. I did okay. My mother raised eleven kids. The majority of us are professionals. And we're raising our own families. I'm not sure what you consider a suitable foster home." They said each child needs their own room and their own bed. I said, "But they're not accustomed to that. Sisters sleep together in the same bed in the same room. Brothers sleep together in the same bed in the same room. Why would you put them in a place where it would be scary to sleep in their own bed all by themselves in a strange room in a strange house with strange people?"

So it took a lot of talking to convince the powers that be that we can grow up just fine in our own community with our own people. And it was difficult to convince non-Natives that we had suitable homes. I'd say, "Would you like to come to my house? Come on out—have supper with me. See what my house is like. I raised five kids. As a matter of fact, I still got one left at home. You can see how things are. You can talk to him, see how he feels about growing up." And they'd say, "Well, when is the reserve open? When do they open the gates so we can come and see?" Some lived in Brantford, some lived in Hamilton. But they had never been to the reserve because their idea was that it was surrounded by a palisade with big gates and a big lock on the gates. A lot of people seemed to have the idea that we were living on an animal reserve area, not a people reserve. People used to stop my kids when they were playing outside my house to ask them, "How far to the reserve?" I'm not sure what they were looking for. Tipis?

Another thing I learned when I started at Children's Aid was that agencies would take Native kids from their families to balance budgets. They would apprehend more Native kids because on top of their provincial grant per child provided by the feds, they got a 20 percent admin fee to provide for Native kids. Sometimes agencies would creatively describe the situation to justify what they did. And they'd laugh about it at these meetings: "Oh, we just got a family of five kids in Bruce or Simcoe County."

When I first started, there were seventy-five kids from Six Nations in care. I knew one family that didn't have a lot of money, and when we went to court to determine whether or not their two kids should be made wards of the Crown, I argued against it. And the judge leaned right over his desk and said, "Don't you want these children to grow up in a good home? Isn't it better for them if they grow up in a good home?" I said, "They need to grow up with their parents." I knew it wasn't good for kids to be separated from their parents.

Canadian child welfare agencies are accused of repeating the history of the Indian residential schools' removal of children from their families and communities, with disproportionately high rates of Aboriginal child apprehensions occurring across Canada. For decades, loving families that are judged "insufficient" in some way by non-Indigenous social workers have lost their children to the system instead of receiving support to care for them. The outcome of these policies closely resembles that of the schools: Indigenous communities are being drained of their youth and the opportunity to raise the next generation.[26]

It was all screwed up the way it went. We needed the service, we needed help. A lot of our families needed help to learn how to be parents because growing up in residential school, they didn't know how to be parents, because they had not been parented. And it was like, *Hey, this ain't fair.*

BACK TO SCHOOL AGAIN

I got tired of not having enough money to make ends meet. I could manage on very little money, but at Children's Aid I found out that I was doing the same work as my counterparts in the Brantford office, but they were getting fifteen thousand a year more than me because they had university degrees.[27] Well, what was I going to do? I wanted that pay. So I saved up enough money to go back to school again. I went and got my degree—two degrees, while I was at it.

I went to Saskatoon, to Saskatchewan Indian Federated College, in 1986. It took four years. My kids were grown, the youngest one was twenty-one. I then got recruited from university to work in child protection in British Columbia in 1990. We covered a hundred-kilometer radius from Chetwynd.[28]

I was learning more about how Indians were being treated all over

---

26. See appendix essay 2 for more on the legacy of Indian residential schools and high rates of Indigenous children in Canada's foster care system.

27. Ontario Children's Aid Societies are independent organizations approved by the province's Ministry of Children, Community and Social Services to provide child protection services.

28. Chetwynd is a municipality in northeastern BC.

the country. People were saying things to me that reminded me of what the workers at the Mush Hole said when I was a little kid: "Dumb, dirty Indian. Don't know how to do anything. Can't do anything."

The talk that would happen during coffee breaks and lunchtime at work—all the gossip would be about how bad Indian kids were, and how irresponsible and lazy Native people were. There were Native people who owned the beauty shop, who worked in the grocery stores, who worked in the bank. And yet, when they talked about Native people, it was the homeless or the ones out of work, or the ones who were seen in a bar. Those were the only *real Indians*. They even asked me if I was sure I was a real Indian, and if I was, how come I wasn't drunk?

I found that the further west I went, the more blatant the prejudice. My mother came to visit in Chetwynd, and we were in the village where I was working. I took her with me to the grocery store, and people would cross the street to avoid us on the sidewalk and that surprised me. At work, my supervisor told me that if she had a choice, she wouldn't have hired me. I said, "Why? Did I do something wrong?" She said, "No, but as far as I'm concerned there's not one Indian that's any good." It was just so frustrating, to think that no matter what I've done, what I've accomplished, what I've achieved, it doesn't make any difference because I'm not white. I can't change that.

But I also realized that Canadians didn't want us to have anything. It was institutionalized racism. It pleased them to see us in our place and keep us in our place. The thinking was, we should know better than to try and do anything different. And to me that wasn't right.

It seems to be just generally understood by anyone who's white that if you have any shade of color, you're not entitled to anything. You shouldn't have anything. Sometimes when I went to investigate as a social worker, the client wanted to know, "Since when did they let Indians be social workers?" And when Native people would come to our office and ask for me, my boss would say, "Why are they asking for you?" I said, "Because I treat them like human beings."

I'LL BE HOME

My mom got sick in 1981. I remember her telling us at different times, "I'm dying, you know?" And we'd say, "Can't you make medicine for yourself?" She'd tell us that the doctor gave her medicine for her cirrhosis, liver damage. But she also used her own medicine, and if she didn't take that along with what the doctor gave her, she probably wouldn't have lasted as long as she did. Because it seems to me, anyone with cirrhosis, not long after you hear about it they're gone.

In 1991, my sisters were calling me, saying, "It's your turn to look after Mother. You've been gone long enough; you've got to come home and look after her." I said, "Okay. I'll put my resignation in and I'll be home." I was home for a month before she died.

Everything that happened as I was growing up seemed like it happened to teach me what I needed to deal with. Like, I always had training in the sense that I knew how to deal with a situation when it hit me. Maybe it's because I was observant—I paid attention to other people, things happening around me, so I learned, *This too will pass*. My mother would say: "You can have anything you want in the world as long as you're willing to work for it and you don't step on anyone else to get it." She had all kinds of sayings about life. She was the one who taught me all that.

She used to make crepe paper flowers on a wire stem. She put leaves on there and dipped the flower in melted wax so that it would hold its shape. And if there was a death in the neighborhood, she would go out and pick pine boughs from the trees and form it into a wreath and make crepe paper flowers to put on there. And we always had to help because we had to finish it overnight. So that was a time to teach us how when you die, you go to heaven. She'd say, "This is what heaven is like. Always be good to people because if they die before you get a chance to say you're sorry for something you did, you're going to cry louder than anybody else. The people who have the most regrets scream the loudest, cry the loudest. If someone dies, and you got no regrets, you got no reason to cry." So many tidbits of wisdom that she would tell us, like, "The way you treat people, it comes back. Your kindness comes back tenfold. Your meanness comes back at you as well, so you've got to think about how you treat other people." Psychics talk about reincarnation and how you've got to treat that dog good because you don't know who that was before. And if a dog comes to your house and adopts you, don't send it away because—again—you don't know who that was. That might be your great-grandfather coming back to visit you or protect you or whatever. I often think about that. It sounds silly, like, *How can that be?* But then again, why take a chance?

GLOSSARY

Aboriginal: A term for people who are the first of their kind in a region. In Canada, *Aboriginal* is used to collectively describe First Nations, Inuit, and Métis peoples; it is rarely used in the United States. The term came into popular usage in Canadian contexts with the passing of the 1982 Constitution Act, whose Section 35 used *Aboriginal* to legally refer to the Indigenous peoples of Canada. *Aboriginal* is also a commonly used term in Australia.

adobe/adobes: One of humanity's oldest building materials. Traditionally a mix of earth, clay, water, sand, and an organic material like straw, it can be poured into molds and shaped like bricks. Pueblo people stacked adobes into walls to form their homes.

American Indian Movement (AIM): An American Indian civil rights organization, founded in Minneapolis, Minnesota, in 1968. Its original goal was to help urban Indians who had been displaced to cities after government programs drove them from reservations. AIM's goals later expanded to encompass a wider spectrum of demands, including cultural revitalization, the protection of legal rights, sovereignty over tribal areas, and the return of illegally seized lands.

band: Instituted in Canada by the Indian Act in 1876, a band is a governing unit of Indians. Defined in the act as a "body of Indians," 'each band has title to land, services, and money from the federal government. Today, many bands prefer to be called "First Nations."

band council: The governing body of a band. A band council usually consists of a chief and councilors elected by members of the community. It is responsible for governing band affairs, including education, housing, infrastructure, water management, and businesses.

boarding schools, residential schools: Commonly called "residential schools" in Canada and "boarding schools" in the US, these institutions were developed and run by the federal government and churches with the direct purpose of removing Indigenous children from their homes in order to eliminate cultural knowledge, languages, and kinship systems. In these institutions, children were forced to assimilate to settler culture and suffered intense physical, mental, and sexual abuse.

ceremony: An important aspect of many Indigenous cultures, a ceremony occurs for many diverse reasons, from healing to observing rites of passage, and can include prayer, singing, stories, and drumming.

clan: A group of people who have kinship responsibilities to one another and are usually determined by shared lineage. Often a clan is a smaller part of a larger Indigenous nation or group.

Declaration on the Rights of Indigenous Peoples: Since 2007, the UN Declaration on the Rights of Indigenous Peoples (UNDRIP) has been a central document used by Indigenous groups to fight for environmental protections, land rights, and cultural sovereignty. UNDRIP builds upon existing human rights standards, particularizing them to the specific realities of Indigenous peoples. Australia, Canada, New Zealand, and the United States voted against the act in 2007. All later reversed their positions; however, UNDRIP is only a resolution, and in both Canada and the US, it remains unratified.

Douglas Treaties: Named after Sir James Douglas, the Hudson's Bay Company's chief factor, who negotiated fourteen treaties with Vancouver Island First Nations from 1850 to 1854. These treaties exchanged lands for clothing, blankets, small amounts of cash, hunting and fishing rights, and land occupation rights. First Nations leaders reported they were misled by Douglas on the terms and significance of the treaties.

enfranchisement: The legal process of terminating a person's Indian status and granting Canadian citizenship. Made compulsory through the Indian Act in 1876, enfranchisement has been a central part of Canada's assimilationist policies. The "compulsory enfranchisement" section of the law (section 112) was removed in 1961.

enrollment: A process through which Indigenous peoples in the US and Canada become a member of a tribe. Tribal enrollment criteria are determined by tribes and are articulated in the tribal constitutions, articles of incorporation, or ordinances of individual tribes. However, the process has a troubled history, as tribal enrollment originated as part of a strategy toward solving the American Indian "problem." Indians interfered with Western expansion and settlers saw their assimilation into Euro-American society as the solution to this problem. For the federal and state governments that introduced it, the agenda behind tribal enrollment was to manipulate enrollment, particularly through the criterion of blood quantum, or degree of Indian blood. In contrast, tribal criteria preserve the unique character and tradition of each tribe as they decide for themselves who is granted membership. Two common requirements for membership are demonstrating lineal descent from someone on the tribe's base roll (its original list of members) and showing relationship to another descendant of the base roll.

First Nations: A term used to describe Indigenous peoples in Canada and a group identity that is distinct from Inuit and Métis communities.

In the 1970s and 1980s, during heightened Indigenous activism in Canada, *First Nations* became the collective name of choice and generally replaced *Indian* in many contexts. Although *First Nations* is not defined legally (unlike the term *Indian*, which does have legal status), *First Nations* is most commonly preferred by members of the group.

genocide: A term defined by the 1948 UN Convention on the Prevention and Punishment of the Crime of Genocide as "any of the following acts committed with intent to destroy, in whole or in part, a national, ethnical, racial or religious group, as such: (a) killing members of the group, (b) causing serious bodily or mental harm to members of the group, (c) deliberately inflicting on the group conditions of life calculated to bring about its physical destruction in whole or in part; d) imposing measures intended to prevent births within the group; e) forcibly transferring children of the group to another group."

Canada's recent National Inquiry into Missing and Murdered Indigenous Women and Girls concluded that the violence that witnesses testified to constitutes a race-based genocide of Indigenous peoples, including First Nations, Inuit, and Métis, that especially targets women, girls, and 2SLGBTQQIA (two-spirit, lesbian, gay, bisexual, transgender, queer, questioning, intersex, and asexual) people. The inquiry reports: "This genocide has been empowered by colonial structures, evidenced notably by the Indian Act, the Sixties Scoop, residential schools and breaches of human and Indigenous rights, leading directly to the current increased rates of violence, death, and suicide in Indigenous populations."

Idle No More: An ongoing protest movement that "calls on all people to join in a peaceful revolution, to honor Indigenous sovereignty and to protect the land and water." The mass movement originated in Saskatchewan to protest parliamentary bills that would have compromised Indigenous sovereignty and environmental protections there, and ultimately inspired teach-ins, rallies, and protests across the continent.

Indian: A term with different meanings and forms of use throughout North America. In Canada, *Indian* refers to First Nations peoples under the Indian Act. Aside from this legal definition, the term *Indian* is generally considered offensive and outdated in Canada. In the United States, *Indian* also has legal significance and refers to the Indigenous nations, tribes, and peoples who fall under this category. Additionally, *Indian* is used colloquially within Native American communities to refer to one another and the larger Indigenous community of the United States (for example, "Indian Country"). However, it can be considered offensive when used by a non-Indian person. The best way to refer to an Indigenous person or group is to use their specific nation, tribe, or band.

The Indian Act: An act passed in 1876 by the Canadian Parliament that established the basis upon which the Canadian government would interact with First Nations bands and peoples. Specifically, the act granted sole authority and jurisdiction to the federal government over Indian reserves. This act, though amended numerous times, is still in force today.

Indian Health Service (IHS): The principal US federal health care provider for American Indians and Alaska Natives. A component of the trust responsibilities the US government must provide under historical treaty agreements, the IHS has two avenues through which it provides health care to American Indians and Alaska Natives. First, the agency operates 46 hospitals and 230 clinics for which it hires medical personnel and determines what services to provide. Second, the agency contracts with federally recognized tribes, providing funds to tribes for health care delivery to its members based upon each tribe's decisions about what services to provide.

Indigenous: A term widely used to refer to Aboriginal communities and peoples around the world. It is most commonly used in global and international contexts. It gained popular usage in the 1970s when Indigenous groups organized to have specific rights respected by the United Nations. *Indigenous* is not explicitly defined by the UN; however, through the efforts of the UN Working Group on Indigenous Populations, the term is now understood to refer to communities, peoples, and nations that have a "historical continuity with pre-invasion and pre-colonial societies that developed on their territories" and "consider themselves distinct from other sectors of the societies now prevailing on those territories."

longhouse: A long and relatively narrow dwelling; various types were built by different peoples throughout Indigenous North America. The word also refers to the cultural and religious movement founded in 1799 by the Seneca prophet Sganyodaiyo, or Handsome Lake, which combined Iroquois belief with some elements of Christianity.

Métis: A distinct Indigenous identity in Canada that is rooted in unions between Indigenous and European peoples. One of the three recognized Indigenous groups in Canada (the other two being First Nations and Inuit), Métis peoples are individuals who self-identify as Métis and are accepted by a historic Métis nation. In recent years, Métis activists have fought for more group recognition and rights.

nation: A group of Indigenous peoples who share a common language, culture, and traditional lands. Often used interchangeably with *band* in Canada and *tribe* in the US, the term *nation* is sometimes preferred because of the sovereign rights and independence that its meaning asserts.

National Congress of American Indians: The oldest and largest American Indian and Alaska Native organization, founded in 1944. It addresses a wide range of interests of tribal governments and communities.

Native: A term that refers to Indigenous peoples across the Americas. It does not refer to a specific nation, tribe, or band. In the United States, *Native* and *Native American* are commonly used terms to refer to Indigenous peoples. In Canada, *Native* is rarely used; instead, *Indigenous* is a more common term of choice. In general, when referring to an Indigenous person or group it is best to use their specific nation, tribe, or band.

potlatch: From the Chinook word *patshatl*, a ceremony central to the governmental, cultural, and spiritual traditions of many First Nations on the Northwest Coast and in areas of the interior western sub-Arctic. Its functions are to redistribute wealth; to bestow status to individuals, kin groups, and clans; and to set up hunting and fishing territories and rights.

powwow: A cultural celebration and social gathering, held by many Indigenous communities, that features singing and dancing.

pueblo: An Indigenous settlement of the southwestern US, consisting of multistoried adobe housing built by the Pueblo people.

protective custody: A form of separation imposed by prison officials to protect someone from threats that other prisoners in the general population pose for that person. In many jails and prisons, prisoners held in "PC" status are kept in the same cells and units as those in administrative or disciplinary segregation.

reservation, reserve: A place where an Indigenous group has been forcibly moved to and confined within a specific area of land. Called a *reserve* in Canada and a *reservation* in the US, this land is set apart by the respective federal governments for the use and occupation of an Indian band, First Nation, or Native American tribe. Some reserves/reservations are located on the traditional homeland of the nation, while other tribes and bands were removed and relocated to new and unfamiliar territories.

Seven Years' War: The last major war (1756–63) before the French Revolution to involve all of Europe's major powers. For the colonies, the relevant struggle was centered on the maritime conflict between Britain and its enemies, France and Spain. Britain's triumph in these naval victories enabled its North American colonial conquests at Louisbourg (1758), Quebec (1759), and Montreal (1760).

squaw: From the Algonquin word *squa* for woman, a word historically used to refer to an Indigenous woman or wife. In contemporary use it is considered a derogatory, misogynist, and racist slur.

Sun Dance: A healing ceremony primarily practiced by Indigenous people of the Plains cultures.

sweat or sweat-lodge: An enclosed hut in which steam is created by hot rocks and cold water. It is a place for gathering, healing, and ceremony. Many Indigenous groups and nations practice sweats in order to heal the body, mind, and spirit.

tribe: A term most commonly used in the United States to refer to a Native American group or community that shares a common language and culture and is recognized by the federal government. A federally recognized tribe is a sovereign nation and has a government-to-government relationship with the federal government as stated in

Article I, Section 8 of the US Constitution. Tribal governments and federal governments have a complicated relationship built on years of treaty making and breaking, and Supreme Court decisions. Most significant to tribal governments is the Marshall Trilogy, a collection of three Supreme Court cases that set the standard for tribes as "domestically dependent nations" within the United States.

Truth and Reconciliation Commission of Canada (TRC): A commission established as part of the Indian Residential Schools Settlement Agreement. The goal was to reflect on the loss, disruption, and violence that Indigenous children experienced in residential schools, and to facilitate reconciliation among students, families, and Canadian citizens. The TRC was active between 2007 and 2015, during which time it researched the legacy of residential schools, reported on the resilience of students, and sought to educate Canadians on this violent history.

two-spirit: A term referring to a person who identifies as having both a feminine and a masculine spirit. The term is used by some Indigenous people to refer to their sexual, gender, or spiritual identity.

HISTORICAL TIMELINE OF
INDIGENOUS NORTH AMERICA

This timeline draws largely upon "The Inherent Right of Self-Governance: A Timeline," by the Centre for First Nations Governance, "Key Moments in Indigenous History Timeline," created by Historica Canada, "History and Culture," by Partnership with Native Americans, and "Native American History Timeline," by the editors of History.com.[1] Footnotes are used when material is drawn from other sources or specific quotes are included.

10,000 BCE–present: Indigenous settlements and communities are present from coast to coast in North America and establish complex religious, artistic, and literary practices and economic, social, and political structures.

1492: Christopher Columbus lands on a Caribbean Island after three months of travel. Under the impression he had arrived in the East Indies, he refers to the Indigenous people he encounters there as "Indians." He orders six of these people to be seized as servants on his first day on the island.

---

1. Centre for First Nations Governance, "The Inherent Right of Self-Governance: A Timeline," www.fngovernance.org/timeline/timelinewindow; Historica Canada, "Key Moments in Indigenous History Timeline," http://education.historicacanada .ca/en/tools/495; Partnership with Native Americans, "History and Culture," www.nativepartnership.org/site/PageServer?pagename=pwna_native_history; History.com Editors, "Native American History Timeline," www.history.com /topics/native-american-history/native-american-timeline.

1493: The Doctrine of Discovery, or *Inter Caetera*, a papal bull issued by Pope Alexander VI on May 4, states that any land not inhabited by Christians is available to be discovered, claimed, and exploited by Christian rulers.

1513: Spanish explorer Juan Ponce de León makes contact with Indigenous peoples after landing on continental North America, in what is now Florida. In 1521, Ponce de León returns to Florida from the Spanish settlement of San Juan to start a colony. Months after his arrival, he is attacked by local Indigenous people and fatally wounded.

1539: Spanish explorer and conquistador Hernando de Soto arrives in Florida. He explores the region with guidance from the Native Americans who are taken captive along the way.

1598–1692: Juan de Oñate founds the colony of New Mexico and continues the process, already begun in nearby regions, of subjugating the locals: imposing taxes paid in food crops, cotton, and labor; launching an attack on their religion; and sometimes selling them into slavery. The colonizers let their cattle overgraze Pueblo land, which eventually leads to drought, erosion, and famine. In 1680, the Pueblo peoples conduct a successful revolt against the Spanish and drive them from the region. By 1692, Spanish forces reconquer the capital, Santa Fe.

1754: Native American alliances support the French from the outset of the French and Indian War, between British and French imperialists. The war is one of several struggles in the global Seven Years' War.

1763: In February, the Treaty of Paris marks Britain's triumph in the Seven Years' War against the French. The Royal Proclamation of 1763 is issued outlining how European settlers should interact with Indigenous nations. It states that land cannot be taken by individual settlers, but rather can only be ceded through nation-to-nation treaties.

- On May 7, Ottawa chief Pontiac leads Native American forces into battle against the British in Detroit. The British retaliate with an attack on Pontiac's warriors on July 31, in what becomes the Battle of Bloody Run. Pontiac and his troops successfully defend themselves from the British, but there are casualties on both sides.

1785: The Treaty of Hopewell is signed in Georgia, establishing a western boundary for American settlement. European settlers violate these boundaries and the Cherokee retaliate against them.

1787: The Northwest Ordinance, enacted by the Congress of the Confederation of the United States, establishes the Northwest Territory in the area between the Appalachian Mountains region, the Ohio River, the Great Lakes, and the Mississippi River. It effectively extinguishes Indigenous claims to this territory.

1791: After the erosion of the Treaty of Hopewell, the Cherokees' boundaries were invaded by settlers. The Treaty of Holston is signed, to "re-establish peace and friendship" and reestablish boundaries for Cherokee land, which encompassed most of what is now Kentucky and Tennessee, and parts of Alabama, Georgia, North Carolina, South Carolina, Virginia, and West Virginia.[2]

1803: The United States acquires the territory of Louisiana from the French through the Louisiana Purchase. The territory encompasses all or part of the Indigenous nations of the Sioux, Cheyenne, Crow, Pawnee, Osage, Arapaho, and Comanche, among others, bringing these nations under the control of the US government.

---

2. "Treaty of Hopewell: Treaty with the Choctaw, 1786," Choctaw Nation, www
.choctawnation.com/sites/default/files/2015/09/29/1786_Treaty_of_Hopewell
_original.pdf.

1811: US forces attack Prophetstown, a pan-Indian village founded by Shawnee warrior and chief Tecumseh and his younger brother Lalawethika. Tecumseh was the leader of a multi-tribal confederacy at the site. The community they established, at the juncture of the Tippecanoe and Wabash Rivers in what is today the state of Indiana, is destroyed.

1812: On June 18, President James Madison signs a declaration of war against Britain, launching the war between US forces and the British, French, and Native Americans over independence and expansion of territory.

1814: In the Battle of Horseshoe Bend, General (later President) Andrew Jackson, US forces, and Native American allies attack Creek Indians who oppose American expansion and encroachment on their territory. After their loss, the Creeks surrender more than twenty million acres of land.

1817–18: The First Seminole War is fought between Jackson and the Seminoles in West and South Florida, culminating in a US victory over the Spanish for control of Florida and the creation of a Seminole reservation at the center of the state.

1819: The US Congress passes the Civilization Fund Act, which encourages the education and "civilization" of Indigenous peoples. It allocates federal funds to set up boarding, or residential, schools.

1821: Spain cedes Florida to the United States.

1823: The Doctrine of Discovery is adopted into US law by the Supreme Court in the case of *Johnson v. McIntosh*. In the decision, written for a unanimous court, Chief Justice John Marshall argues that Christian European nations had assumed "ultimate dominion" over the lands of America during the Age of Discovery, and that—upon "discovery"—the Indians had lost "their rights to complete sovereignty, as independent nations," and only retained a right of "occupancy" on their lands.[3]

1830: US president Andrew Jackson signs into law the Indian Removal Act, authorizing the removal of Indigenous people from their ancestral lands via war and treaties (ultimately eighty-six treaties in all) to federal territory, or reservations, west of the Mississippi.

1836: The last of the Creek Native Americans leave their land for Oklahoma as part of the process of Indian removal. Approximately 3,500 of the 15,000 Creeks who embark on the voyage do not survive.

1838: The Trail of Tears, or forced relocation of the Cherokee Nation from Georgia and Alabama to what would become northeastern Oklahoma, takes place. President Martin Van Buren enlists General Winfield Scott and seven thousand troops to implement the process by holding the Cherokee at gunpoint and marching them twelve hundred miles. Approximately eight thousand individuals, half of the Cherokee Nation, perish in the march.

1835–42: In the Second Seminole War, the US government attempts to defeat the Seminole Nation and remove it from Florida to Indian Territory established by the Indian Removal Act of 1830. After eight years of skirmishes, guerilla warfare, and disease, the Seminole Nation is significantly depleted.

1844: The New Brunswick Act for the Management and Disposal of Indian Reserves is passed by the province, allowing for the sale and lease of land reserved for Indigenous peoples.

---

3. US Supreme Court, *Johnson & Graham's Lessee v. McIntosh*, 21 U.S. 543 (1823), https://supreme.justia.com/cases/federal/us/21/543/.

1850–54: Sir James Douglas, the leader of the Hudson's Bay Company, negotiates fourteen treaties with Vancouver Island First Nations from 1850 to 1854. These treaties exchange lands for clothing, blankets, small amounts of cash, hunting and fishing rights, and land occupation rights. First Nations leaders report they are misled by Douglas on the terms and significance of the treaties.

1851: British colonial governments throughout North America begin keeping records and registries of Indigenous groups.

- February 27: Congress passes the Indian Appropriations Act, which establishes the Indian reservation system. Native Americans are not allowed to leave their reservations without permission.

1857: The Canadian Parliament passes the Gradual Civilization Act, which requires that male Indigenous individuals over the age of twenty-one must read and write the English or French language, undergo the Canadian education system through elementary school, and be free of debt in order to be enfranchised.

1855–58: The Third Seminole War lasts for three years. By the end of the war, most of the remaining Seminole people are relocated to Oklahoma, while a few stay behind in the Everglades.

1862: The US government passes a series of acts resulting in the seizure and reallocation of Indigenous lands. President Abraham Lincoln signs the Homestead Act of 1862 and the Morrill Land-Grant Acts, which allow homesteaders or states to purchase Indigenous lands for the establishment of land grant universities. The Pacific Railroad Acts provide private companies free access to Indigenous land so they can participate in the establishment of a transcontinental railroad.

1864: The US Army forcibly removes eight thousand Navajo individuals from their land in Arizona to Fort Sumner, New Mexico, in what becomes known as "The Long Walk." This removal follows years of the US Army's widespread destruction of Navajo land and resources.

1867: The British North America Act, also called the Constitution Act, is passed by the Parliament of the United Kingdom. Under the act, three of its colonies—Nova Scotia, New Brunswick, and Canada—are united as "one Dominion under the name of Canada." The act gives the federal government responsibility for Indigenous peoples and their lands.[4]

1868: On April 29, the Treaty of Fort Laramie is signed between the US and the Oglala, Mnicoujou, Brulé Lakota, Yanktonai Dakota, and Arapaho Nations. The treaty guarantees the Sioux peoples continual and exclusive ownership over the sacred Black Hills, as well as land and hunting rights in South Dakota, Wyoming, and Montana.

1869–70: Métis and First Nations allies defend the Red River Colony from the federal government's effort to hand over Rupert's Land, a territory comprising a third of what is now Canada and the exclusive domain of the Hudson's Bay Company, to Canada without consultation. The Métis, led by Louis Riel, establish a provisional government to manage the resistance and lead an uprising. Riel flees to the United States in the midst of the armed conflict, and white settlement continues to expand westward. The Métis draft the Métis Bill of Rights, calling for improved treatment of all residents in relation to land rights, political representation, and better education.

---

4. Government of Canada, "Constitution Act, 1867," https://laws-lois.justice.gc.ca /eng/const/.

1871–1921: The Numbered Treaties are signed by the Canadian government and Indigenous nations. These eleven treaties, still controversial and contested today, make huge areas of traditional Indigenous lands available for settler use in exchange for a system of reserves, cash payments, the use of agricultural tools, and hunting and fishing rights.

1874: After gold is discovered in the Black Hills by miners on an expedition led by General George A. Custer, the Treaty of Fort Laramie is subject to repeated violations by prospectors. Miners, protected by the US Army, move into Sioux territory, and the army is ordered to fight the Sioux.

1876: The Canadian Parliament passes the Indian Act, establishing the basis upon which the government interacts with First Nation bands and peoples. Specifically, the act grants sole authority and jurisdiction to the federal government over Indian reserves. This act, though amended numerous times, is still in force today.

1876–77: Custer and his army detachment come upon the Sioux and Cheyenne encampment at the Little Bighorn River, in what is known to many as the most famous battle of the Great Sioux War, the Battle of Little Bighorn. Lakota Sioux and Cheyenne warriors, led by Crazy Horse and Sitting Bull, defeat Custer's army there, but the United States continues to battle the Sioux in the Black Hills until 1877, when the US government confiscates the land.

1880: An amendment to the Indian Act formally disenfranchises Indigenous women, proclaiming they "cease to be an Indian in any respect" if they marry "any other than an Indian, or a non-treaty Indian."[5]

---

5. Government of Canada, "The Indian Act, 1880," www.aadnc-aandc.gc.ca/eng /1100100010272/1100100010274.

1884: The federal government of Canada bans the potlatch, a ceremony central to the governmental, cultural, and spiritual traditions of many First Nations on the Northwest Coast, under the Indian Act. For coastal First Nations in the West, potlatch is a hugely important ceremony, used to mark special occasions and distribute wealth. Indian agents and missionaries see the ceremony as counterproductive to their assimilation tactics. Other tribal ceremonies, such as the Sun Dance, would also be banned in the following years.

1885: The North-West Rebellion, a brief uprising of the Métis and their First Nations allies against the federal government in what is now Saskatchewan and Alberta, occurs. The Métis form a second provisional government in the region and draft the Revolutionary Bill of Rights. In response to their unmet demands, the Métis, under the command of Gabriel Dumont, take military action, but federal troops overcome them. Louis Riel is hanged for treason and Cree chiefs Mistahimaskwa (Big Bear) and Pitikwahanapiwiyin (Poundmaker) are imprisoned.

1887: President Grover Cleveland signs into law the Dawes Act or General Allotment Act of 1887, authorizing the president of the United States to survey, seize, and allot Indigenous lands to Indigenous individuals. The goal of this act is to convince Indigenous individuals to separate from their tribe and assimilate into US society by rewarding them with land and citizenship.

1880s–90s: Residential schools for Indigenous children in Canada rapidly expand during this period. Christian missionaries, paid by the government, are the first to operate these institutions. Children are forced to give up their Native American names, language, and culture and become victims of widespread sexual, physical, and emotional abuse.

1890: The Wounded Knee Massacre, a conflict between the US Seventh Cavalry Regiment and the Lakota peoples on the Lakota Pine Ridge Indian Reservation, results in the massacre of up to three hundred Lakota individuals and the deaths of twenty-five US soldiers.

1911: The Oliver Act, an amendment to the Indian Act of 1876, is passed by Canadian Parliament, allowing for the appropriation of reserve lands for use for public purposes—that is, railroads, municipalities, and other public services.

1914–18: Between four thousand and six thousand Indigenous people serve in the Canadian military during the First World War. Although many of them win awards and become celebrated soldiers, they are denied veterans' benefits on return. Likewise, twelve thousand Native Americans serve in the US Army during the war.

1919: Frederick Ogilvie Loft, a Mohawk man from Six Nations of the Grand River, forms the League of Indians, a campaign for improved quality of life and the protection of Indigenous rights and customs. Government harassment, police surveillance, and discord among Indigenous groups compromise its efficiency, but it forms a basis for future Indigenous political organizing.

1923: Deskaheh, a condoled chief of the Iroquois Confederacy of Canada, speaks in Geneva, Switzerland, to the League of Nations on the topic of disputes between the Confederation and Canadian government.

1924: The Indian Citizenship Act of 1924 extends citizenship—though not unilaterally or completely—to Indigenous peoples in the United States as part of an effort to assimilate these peoples into broader US society.

1927: The Canadian federal government adds Section 141 to the Indian Act in response to more extensive Indigenous political organizing and the pursuit of land claims. The amendment makes it illegal for Indians to hire or seek the counsel of lawyers. As a result, attending any political gathering risks a jail sentence, but does not entirely stop underground organizing efforts.

1928: In the US, the Institute for Government Research publishes the Meriam Report, maintaining that Indigenous peoples suffer on reservations and in boarding schools and that the federal government has failed to recognize and address key issues.

1934: The Indian Reorganization Act of 1934 is passed by the US Congress. It ends further allotment of tribal communal lands to individuals and mandates the return of surplus lands to tribes rather than settlers. The act also offers a return to self-government on a tribal basis and a restoration of tribes' rights to manage their own assets. However, since tribes are not involved in shaping the new constitutions, their implementation often results in weaker tribal governments, and many decisions remain subject to the approval of the secretary of the interior.

1939–45: Between five thousand and eight thousand Indigenous soldiers serve Canada in all the major battles and campaigns of World War II. Most are not granted the same support or compensation as other veterans following their service. Around twenty-five thousand Native Americans serve with the US Army during this time.

1940s–60s: The Indian termination policy, made up of policies and laws geared toward assimilating Indigenous peoples into the broader US society, is implemented during these decades. It results in the mass migration of Indigenous peoples off reservation land into urban centers and the loss of millions of acres of protected land.

- **1940:** The Kansas Act of 1940 passes, granting states primary or sole jurisdiction over Indigenous individuals.
- **1944:** The establishment of the National Congress of American Indians, which successfully limits the effects of the Indian termination policy, advocates on behalf of Indigenous rights and sees the rise of major Indigenous leaders.
- **1948:** The UN Convention on the Prevention and Punishment of the Crime of Genocide is formed in response to the Holocaust, defining genocide and the five acts that constitute it.

1950s and 1960s: A government assimilationist initiative called Sled Dog Slaughter, the intentional and systematic killing of thousands of sled dogs, forces the Inuit of Northern Quebec to forego their nomadic way of life and moves them off their traditional lands.

1950s–80s: The Sixties Scoop is a catch-all name for the "scooping up" of Indigenous children from their families and communities, to be placed in foster care or put up for adoption. The practice is facilitated through a group of policies enacted by Canada's provincial child welfare agencies. These children lose their names, languages, and connections to culture and ancestry.

1951: In post–World War II Canada, many citizens shocked by the war's atrocities begin to learn about the concept of human rights and understand that Indigenous Canadians are often among the country's most oppressed. This is especially problematic at the time because Canada's First Nations soldiers are simultaneously being celebrated for their contributions to the country's military efforts. This understanding coincides with Canada's signing of the UN Universal Declaration of Human Rights and leads to the revision of the Indian Act, with many of the act's more oppressive sections removed, including the ban on potlatch and other traditional ceremonies.

1953: Congress passes the Indian Termination Act, yet another new policy that US government administrators hope will assimilate Indians into the US mainstream. The policy seeks to end the special relationship between tribes and the federal government by ending recognition of tribal sovereignty and trusteeship over Indian reservations. Conversely, Indians are given all the rights and privileges of US citizenship. The tenets of termination include closing tribal rolls and liquidating and distributing tribal assets as per capita payments to current members. Between 1953 and 1964, the government will terminate the recognition of over a hundred tribes as sovereign dependent nations and remove approximately 2,500,000 acres (10,000 km^2) of trust land from protected status. The policy also terminates federal support of health care, education programs, and police and fire departments on reservations that had been guaranteed through earlier treaties.

- Public Law 83-280 is passed by the US Congress. The law authorizes a transfer of jurisdiction from the federal government to the states in Indian Country. With its enactment affected states are given criminal jurisdiction over Indians living on reservations. Indian nations are not consulted on the decision.

1956: The Indian Relocation Act of 1956 passes in the United States, encouraging Indigenous peoples to move to urban centers and away from reservations.

1960: Native people are granted the right to vote in Canada's federal elections.

1968: The Indian Civil Rights Act is signed into law by US president Lyndon B. Johnson, extending aspects of the Bill of Rights to Native American individuals and tribal governments. While the act strengthens individual rights, it encroaches on tribal sovereignty by requiring tribal governments to submit to the Bill of Rights.

1969: The Canadian federal government, under the leadership of Pierre Trudeau, releases the "Statement of the Canadian Government on Indian Policy," a proposal to end the Indian Act, terminate treaties, and essentially eliminate Indian status, with the goal of assimilating Indigenous peoples fully into Canadian society.

1973: Approximately two hundred Oglala Lakota occupy Wounded Knee, South Dakota, on the Pine Ridge Indian Reservation, the same reservation upon which the massacre of 1890 unfolded, in opposition to the allegedly corrupt tribal chairman Richard Wilson. For seventy-one days, the individuals occupy the town, until US marshals are dispatched to break up the siege. Wilson is later reelected and remained chairman of the Oglala Lakota Sioux until 1976.

- January 31: The Nisga'a people's assertion of land title is brought to the Supreme Court of Canada in the case of *Calder v. British Columbia*. The court recognizes that Aboriginal rights to land existed before European colonization and continue to exist in Canadian law, and forces the government to negotiate land claims with Indigenous peoples not recognized by treaties.

1975: The Indian Self-Determination and Education Assistance Act of 1975 grants Indigenous tribes authority over their own social and economic development, reversing much of the effort of the US government to sever treaties with tribes as part of the Indian termination policy.

1977: The Conference on Discrimination against Indigenous Populations in the Americas is held in Geneva, Switzerland. It results in the production of the "Declaration of Principles for the Defense of the Indigenous Nations and Peoples of the Western Hemisphere."

1978: The American Indian Religious Freedom Act is enacted in the US, requiring governmental agencies to eliminate any interference with Native American religious practice.

- November 8: The Indian Child Welfare Act is passed by the US Congress. The law governs jurisdiction over the removal of Native children from their families and grants tribes greater control in child custody proceedings in which children reside on the reservation or are wards of the tribe.

1980: On June 30, the Sioux win a victory in the long-standing Black Hills dispute when the Supreme Court upholds the tribe's award of $15.6 million (the 1877 market value of the land) along with 103 years' worth of interest, valued at an additional $105 million. The Lakota refuse the payment and reiterate the demand that their territory be returned to them. Ownership of the land remains the subject of a legal dispute with the US government.

1982: The Assembly of First Nations, emerging from the National Indian Brotherhood, is formed to advocate on behalf of First Nations on issues such as treaties, Indigenous rights, and land and resources.

1984: Following sustained efforts from Native communities and activists, The Child and Family Services Act introduces Part X – Native and Indian Rights, which mandates "customary care," a model of Aboriginal child welfare service.

- June 28: The Inuvialuit Claims Settlement Act passes in Canada, giving the Inuit of the western Arctic control over resources.

1985: The Indian Act is amended. Bill C-31 allows women who had lost their status through marriage to regain it. However, the bill is still seen by many as unconstitutional, as it allows those who have their status reinstated to pass it on for just one generation. Other changes in 1985 to the Indian Act grant status to the Métis and previously enfranchised peoples living off reserve land.

1988: The US Senate ratifies the UN Convention on the Prevention and Punishment of the Crime of Genocide, extending the application of the convention to US–Indigenous relations.

1990: The Oka Crisis, also called the Mohawk Resistance, occurs in response to the proposed expansion of a golf course and development of buildings on Mohawk burial grounds in Oka, Quebec. A seventy-eight-day standoff between Mohawk activists and the Canadian police and army takes place between July and September. The golf course expansion ceases; however, the land remains under the control of the Canadian government.

1991: The Royal Commission on Aboriginal Peoples is established in the wake of Canada's Oka Crisis to address issues of Aboriginal status.

1993: The Tla-o-qui-aht First Nation, along with other First Nations and environmental groups, protests clearcutting in Clayoquot Sound. More than eight hundred people are arrested during the "War in the Woods," and the protest remains one of the largest in Canadian history.

1995: Members of the Kettle and Stony Point First Nation assert their claim to land by occupying Ipperwash Provincial Park, Ontario. During the occupation, the Ontario Provincial Police kill unarmed protester Dudley George.

1996: The Royal Commission on Aboriginal Peoples releases its final report, which calls for the complete restructuring of relations between Aboriginal and non-Aboriginal Canadians.

- January 2: Gordon's Indian Residential School in Punnichy, Saskatchewan, the last federally run residential school in Canada, is shut down. Its students speak out about the sexual abuse they experienced at the hands of administrators and staff.

1998: The Indian Affairs minister, in response to the Royal Commission on Aboriginal Peoples' report of 1996, acknowledges the trauma of residential school abuses and issues approximately $350 million as part of a healing fund.

1999: After decades of Inuit political advocacy, Nunavut, "our land" in Inuktitut, becomes the newest, largest, and northernmost territory in Canada.

2000: The federal government approves the Nisga'a Treaty, which grants the Nisga'a about $196 million over a period of fifteen years and self-government and jurisdiction over natural resources in parts of northwestern British Columbia.

2007: The UN General Assembly passes the Declaration on the Rights of Indigenous Peoples. The United States and Canada are among four "no" votes on the declaration at the time.

2008: Indigenous and Northern Affairs Canada (the department now called Crown-Indigenous Relations and Northern Affairs Canada) formally acknowledges Supreme Court rulings on the "duty to consult." This obligates the Canadian government to consult and, if appropriate, accommodate Indigenous peoples when considering projects or decisions that may impact Indigenous rights or treaty rights.

2009: The US Congress passes a resolution to apologize to Indigenous peoples of America.

2007–15: The Truth and Reconciliation Commission of Canada spends six years traveling throughout Canada and hearing testimony from more than 6,500 people as a component of the Indian Residential Schools Settlement Agreement. It hosts seven national events to engage and educate the Canadian public about the history and legacy of the residential schools and to honor the experience of survivors and their families.

2012–present: The ongoing protest movement Idle No More begins in Saskatchewan. The movement "calls on all people to join in a peaceful revolution, to honor Indigenous sovereignty and to protect the land and water."[6] The mass movement protests parliamentary bills that threaten to compromise Indigenous sovereignty and environmental protections in Saskatchewan and inspires teach-ins, rallies, and protests across the continent.

2016: Individuals of the Sioux Nation, alongside Standing Rock Lakota Nation and allies in the Lakota, Nakota, and Dakota Nations, organize to oppose the Dakota Access Pipeline.

- May 10: The Canadian government signs the UN Declaration on the Rights of Indigenous Peoples.
- In response to demands for action from Indigenous families, communities, and organizations, the Canadian government launches the National Inquiry into Missing and

---

6. Idle No More, "The Vision," www.idlenomore.ca/vision.

Murdered Indigenous Women and Girls. Its mandate is to gather evidence and to investigate and report on the systemic causes of violence against Indigenous women, girls, and 2SLGBTQQIA individuals in Canada.[7]

- In *Daniels v. Canada*, the Supreme Court rules that Métis and non-status Indigenous peoples are "Indians" under section 91(24) of the Constitution Act, 1867.

2017: US president Donald Trump signs executive orders to facilitate the construction of the Keystone XL pipeline and the completion of the Dakota Access Pipeline.

2018: Sharice Davids (Ho-Chunk) and Deb Haaland (Laguna Pueblo) become the first Native American woman elected to Congress.

2019: Joy Harjo becomes the first Native American US poet laureate.

- June 3: The 1,200-page final report of Canada's National Inquiry into Missing and Murdered Indigenous Women and Girls is released and calls the crisis "genocide."
- September 6: The Canadian Human Rights Tribunal orders the Canadian federal government to compensate First Nations children who were apprehended or taken from their homes on reserve. The ruling covers all children removed from 2006 to a date yet to be determined by the tribunal. It is estimated that fifty thousand children will be affected by the decision.

2020: COVID-19 begins to spread around the world and North America. The Trump administration initially resists providing any relief to tribal nations in the $2 trillion stimulus package passed in

---

7. 2SLGBTQQIA stands for two-spirit, lesbian, gay, bisexual, transgender, queer, questioning, intersex, and asexual.

early April, and although the legislation ultimately appropriates $10 billion to tribal governments, the Treasury Department, tasked with distributing these funds, fails to disburse them.

CONTEXTUAL ESSAYS
by Rozanne Gooding Silverwood

1

THE TRAIL OF BROKEN PROMISES: US AND CANADIAN TREATIES WITH FIRST NATIONS

"The Indians Giving a Talk to Colonel Bouquet, October 1764," illustration by Benjamin West, from William Smith's *An Historical Account of the Expedition against the Ohio Indians*. Courtesy of the Library Company of Philadelphia.

Without historical context, it would be impossible to grasp the depth of loss of land and self-determination that Indigenous peoples in North America have experienced. Below is a brief summary of historic treaties between US and British colonizers and America's original occupants that can help dispel some of the whitewashed myths of treaty making. Instead of serving as documents of diplomacy that equal sovereign parties mutually agreed upon, treaties functioned as coercive tools of colonization aimed toward the displacement of North America's Indigenous peoples and the seizure of their land and resources.

Cultural differences might partially explain how the colonizers were able to use treaties to take advantage of Canada's First Nations and the American Indians of the United States. Indigenous peoples hold a very different worldview of diplomacy and property from those of US and British officials. Anglo and European governments regarded treaties as legal written documents. Intended to secure political loyalties and exchanges of lands and natural resources, treaties left room for US and British governments to reinterpret depending upon the prevailing whims of a given political moment. Furthermore, the concept of written treaties was completely foreign to early North American Indians. In an interview, Native novelist N. Scott Momaday (Kiowa) explains that in the oral-based culture of Indigenous societies, treaties represent "the giving of one's word and the accepting of someone else's word [and] were taken very seriously and thought to be sacred. When someone gave his word, it was kept."[1] The leaders of Native nations may have misunderstood the legal longevity of the colonizers' treaty agreements, but perhaps their gravest misinterpretation of the terms in treaty negotiation concerned the object that was most central to and sought after by colonizing empires—land.

---

1. N. Scott Momaday, interviewed by Suzan Shown Harjo, "The Indians Were the Spoken Word," in *Nation to Nation: Treaties between the United States and American Indian Nations*, ed. Suzan Shown Harjo (Washington, DC: Smithsonian Books, 2014), 115.

Before the arrival of British and other European colonizers, Indigenous tribes scattered throughout North America had well-established territorial boundaries. And to make the most productive use of a region's abundant resources, territorial mapping allowed for seasonal movements between summer and winter camps. Meanwhile, across the Atlantic in the mid-fifteenth century, political theorist John Locke wrote a treatise "Of Property" that laid out a bedrock principle used by colonizers to justify their land seizures in the "New World." According to Locke, land was to be "subdued" by the labor of man who "hath taken it out of the hands of nature, where it was common, and belonged equally to all her children, and hath thereby appropriated it to himself."[2] This distinctly European viewpoint of land as a commodity and the assumed right to ownership stands in direct opposition to early Indigenous peoples' collective stewardship of land and subsistence practices of gathering, hunting, fishing, and trapping for food and survival.

Raymond J. DeMallie, in his research on Plains Indian history, finds that "the concept of land ownership, separate from using the land, made no sense in Indian cultures."[3] For many Indigenous people, land is alive and sacred, and therefore cannot be owned. Leaders of Native nations would balk at treaties restricting their sacred landscapes, as when the Oglala Sioux chief Black Hawk exclaimed, "You have split the country, and I don't like it" at the Great Treaty Council at Horse Creek in 1851, also known as the Fort Laramie Treaty of 1951.[4]

America's original occupants depended upon a conception of land as shared space in order to accommodate seasonal movements crucial to a subsistence lifestyle that had supported Indigenous communities for millennia. Rather than contracts of sale, First Nations

---

2. John Locke, "Of Property," *Second Treatise of Government*, ed. C. B. Macpherson (Indianapolis: Hackett Publishing, 1980) 29, 32.

3. Raymond J. DeMallie, "The Great Treaty Council at Horse Creek," in Harjo, *Nation to Nation*, 105–7.

4. DeMallie, "The Great Treaty Council at Horse Creek," 107.

and American Indian tribes understood land treaties as agreements to share the bountiful resources of a region. And not only did treaty agents take advantage of this different conceptualization of land, "problems in translation, too often known only to those who spoke and read English," were used to obscure the true intent of land seizure and empire building.[5] Tribal representatives made their marks as signatories with the belief that they would share a specific territory and its resources. Instead, their signatures authorized the colonizing government to seize their people's land and resources and place restrictions on traditional subsistence practices, ultimately eroding the self-determination of sovereign Indigenous nations.

TREATIES OF PEACE AND FRIENDSHIP OR NEUTRALITY

In the early years of colonial occupation, the British and other European forces used treaties to engage the military aid of Indian nations. Escalating territorial disputes between competing colonizers forced the hand of North America's original inhabitants. Treaties secured the Indians' loyalties or guarantees of neutrality in these conflicts. But as colonial conflicts were settled, with victories claimed or defeats acknowledged, the treaties of peace and friendship or neutrality became irrelevant and deemed no longer necessary for colonial expansion. Once the United States claimed independence and later defeated European forces in the War of 1812, and as Great Britain established its military dominance over European empires competing for resources in the Canadian territories, their alliances with Indian nations required rethinking. Tribes once revered for their superior guerrilla warfare tactics were now treated as dependent nations.

In the Treaty of Ghent (1814), the United States officially addressed its Indian alliances. Along with the treaty's recognition of

---

5. Robert N. Clinton, "Treaties with Native Nations," in Harjo, *Nation to Nation*, 20.

Indian sovereignty, it decreed that American Indian nations would continue to enjoy "all the possession, rights and privileges" of specific territories that they held previous to the War of 1812.[6] In essence, the treaty was meant to assure that there would be no penalties imposed on the Indian nations that had sided with British or other European powers against the United States. In the Canadian territories, after Great Britain's defeat of France in the Seven Years' War, King George III issued his own response to the Indigenous population of Canada. The Royal Proclamation of 1763 gave recognition to First Nations as legal title holders of specific areas of North America, affirming Indigenous peoples' rights to occupancy and resources. Through this document the Crown proclaimed that "the several Nations or Tribes of Indians with whom We are connected, and who live under Our Protection, should not be molested or disturbed in the Possession of such Parts of Our Dominions and Territories as, not having been ceded to or purchased by Us, are reserved to them. Or any of them as their Hunting Grounds."[7]

The proclamation acknowledges First Nations' rights to specific territories and resources but also emphasizes Great Britain's assumed upper hand in its relationship with the region's Indigenous people. The Crown drafted this proclamation not so much to assure the rights of First Nations but with an eye toward the flood of settlers arriving in North American territories. This influx of British subjects in search of land required management, and the proclamation established the Crown's primary rights to the Canadian territory. Advances in colonial military technology, such as the improved accuracy and range of firearms, freed the US and Canadian governments from their need for military alliances with Indian nations. So,

---

6. "Treaty of Ghent (1814)," Our Documents, www.ourdocuments.gov/doc.php ?flash=false&doc=20&page=transcript.

7. "No. 1: The Royal Proclamation, October 7, 1763, by the King George R. A Proclamation," James Smith Cree Nation, www.jamessmithcreenation.com/downloads /ROYAL%20PROCLAMATION%201763.pdf.

with an increased appetite for land, treaty negotiations shifted from being diplomatic agreements between sovereign equals to serving as strong-arm vehicles for land acquisition.

TREATIES OF LAND TITLE DISPOSSESSION
AND TERRITORIAL SURRENDER

Between 1764 and 1862, agents representing the British crown negotiated more than thirty land surrenders of Canadian territories.[8] Unlike treaty agents in the United States who tended to negotiate with individual sovereign Indian nations, Canadian agents more often lumped chiefs and sachems from various tribes of a region into assemblies. This group approach destabilized First Nation sovereignty while providing the Crown title to wide swaths of land. The governor of Vancouver, James Douglas, namesake and primary negotiator of the Douglas Treaties, sought to guarantee the Hudson's Bay Company, a British fur trading company, access to the natural resources in Indian-controlled territories. Written from the point of view of the First Nations signatories, these treaties stated that in exchange for land title, "village sites and enclosed fields are to be kept for our own use, for the use of our children, *and for those who may follow after us* and the land shall be properly surveyed hereafter. It is understood, however, that the land itself, with these small exceptions, becomes the entire property of the white people for ever [*sic*]; it is also understood that we are at liberty to hunt over the unoccupied lands, and to carry on our fisheries as formerly."[9] Negotiated with First Nations individually, each Douglas Treaty conveyed a tribe's

---

8. "Upper Canada Land Surrenders and the William Treaties (1764–1862/1923)," Crown-Indigenous Affairs and Northern Affairs Canada, www.rcaanc-cirnac.gc.ca /eng/1370362690208/1544619449449.

9. "Teechamitsa Tribe – Country Lying between Esquimalt and Point Albert," Crown-Indigenous Affairs and Northern Affairs Canada, https://www.rcaanc-cirnac .gc.ca/eng/1100100029052/1581515763202#teech, emphasis added.

territory to the Canadian government but with allowances for First Nations' occupancy and use. Because these treaties state that the rights carry over to the future generations in perpetuity, the Douglas Treaties have been an especially potent reference for legal arguments that today's Canadian government should honor First Nations' promised hunting, fishing, and trapping rights.

RESERVATION AND REMOVAL TREATIES

At the same time as Douglas was systematically gaining land title through treaties with the First Nation peoples of Canada, the US Congress sent its own representatives out to negotiate treaties for aiding the westward expansion of the United States. Treaties of this era strategically consolidated Indian-occupied territories for state annexation. Native American history scholar Philip Deloria (Standing Rock Sioux) breaks down the empire-building tactic in its simplest terms: "If you want to cease being a territory and become a state, you have to have sixty thousand free, white male voters. . . . To do it when you've got confined territory, you have to take the Indian people who are disbursed within that territory and . . . shrink them down, compress them and put them in a single space. That space is called a reservation."[10]

Reservation treaties enabled colonial land acquisition through the geographic control and territorial confinement of Indian populations. Removal treaties functioned toward that same end, but rather than shrinking the area of occupancy, members of an Indian nation were rounded up and relocated. The Indian Removal Act, signed into law by President Andrew Jackson in 1830, sanctioned the removal of the Cherokee, Choctaw, Chickasaw, Seminole, and Creek Indian nations from their original homelands in the southeastern United States.[11] Individual treaties with specific Indian nations initiated the

---

10. Philip J. Deloria interviewed by Suzan Shown Harjo, "American Indian Land and American Empire," in Harjo, *Nation to Nation*, 13.

11. "The Indian Removal Act of 1830," in *A Century of Lawmaking for a New Nation: US Congressional Documents and Debates, 1774–1875*, Library of

series of forced removals known as the Trail of Tears. One example is the Treaty of Dancing Rabbit Creek, which compelled the Choctaw nation of Mississippi to "cede to the United States, the entire country they own and possess, east of the Mississippi River; and they agree to move beyond the Mississippi River, early as practicable." In exchange, the United States "shall cause to be conveyed to the Choctaw Nation a tract of country [in Indian Territory] West of the Mississippi River in fee simple, to them and their descendants."[12] Under Congressional command and military escort, Indian nations were ordered to pack up all of the belongings that they could transport on foot or by wagon and move to an area that the US government had determined expendable. Leaving behind established homes and farms, these Indian nations had to start all over again in a territory that tribes like the Osage and Comanche had historically claimed as their own. In a discussion of the cruel conditions of these removals, former Apache tribal judge Carey N. Vicenti explains that "the various treaties were not really negotiated in an evenhanded way. They were negotiated at the point of a bayonet."[13] And adding insult to injury, these removed Indian peoples would soon discover that their adopted homelands were just another rest stop on the long trail of broken treaty promises.

Congress American Memory Project, https://memory.loc.gov/cgi-bin/ampage?collId =llsl&fileName=004/llsl004.db&recNum=458.

12. "1830 Treaty of Dancing Rabbit Creek," Choctaw Nation, www.choctawnation .com/sites/default/files/2015/09/29/1830_Treaty_of_Dancing_Rabbit_Creek _original.pdf.

13. Cary N. Vicenti interviewed by Suzan Shown Harjo, "Removal Treaties," in Harjo, *Nation to Nation*, 85.

"Indian Land for Sale," 1911 advertisement poster published by US Department of the Interior, Library of Congress, www.loc.gov/item/2015657622/.

TREATIES OF ASSIMILATION
AND CULTURAL DISPOSSESSION

Within two generations the United States would renege on its treaty guarantees that removed Indigenous peoples would remain unmolested in their new homeland. The US Congress drafted the General Allotment Act, also known as the Dawes Act of 1887, with the intent of breaking up Indian land holdings and governments in Indian Territory and elsewhere. Legal historian Stuart Banner explains how Congress envisioned the Allotment Act as the democratic means of liberating the Indian from subsistence practices, transforming them from "savage" survivalist to a "civilized" and productive "yeoman farmer."[14] Communally held Indigenous farmlands were broken up into a grid of 160-acre plots and distributed to the male member of individual households. Not only did allotment disrupt traditional farming practices, it eroded some Native nations' governance systems, as male members of tribes replaced women as primary landholders.[15] Following the distribution of allotment parcels to Indian families, the remaining surplus freed up significant swaths of land for non-Native settlement. With so much land at stake, corruption abounded, with non-Native homesteaders snatching up the choicest tracts and resources.[16]

Similar to the US General Allotment Act were the Numbered Treaties (1871–1921), which allocated individual farmable tracts of land to First Nation families of Canada. As in the United States, the Numbered Treaties aimed to dismantle traditional subsistence lifestyles. Furthermore, the treaties outlined specific regulations, such as prohibitions against alcohol, which on the surface would appear to benefit tribal communities by preventing alcohol abuse. Unfortunately, the prohibition completely side-stepped predatory traders' culpability in distributing alcohol among Indigenous communities. And as with so many of these colonizing mandates, the fundamental harm of many mandates fed into Indian stereotypes and undermined

---

14. Stuart Banner, *How the Indians Lost Their Land: Law and Power on the Frontier* (Cambridge, MA: Harvard University Press, 2005), 257, 266.

15. Theda Perdue, *Mixed Blood Indians: Racial Construction in the Early South* (Athens: University of Georgia Press, 2003), 16.

16. David Treuer, *The Heartbeat of Wounded Knee: Native America from 1890 to the Present* (New York: Riverhead Books, 2019), 83.

First Nation systems of self-governance.[17] Noncompliance with prohibitions resulted in the withholding of guaranteed annuities of money, clothing, food, agricultural tools, ammunitions, educational support, and medical resources. Ultimately, and in a cruelly ironic twist, allotment rendered Indian communities dependent upon the state's allocation of these necessities and services for survival rather than freeing them from a subsistence lifestyle. Under the guise of "civilizing" Indian populations, US and Canadian allotment treaties best exemplify how assimilation policies further colonization and land acquisition to the detriment of Indigenous peoples.

MODERN TREATIES

This brief summary of historic treaties outlines the coercive tactics that robbed Indians of their land and the trail of broken promises that cultivated poverty and a dependency among many Indigenous communities on nation-state support. But in 1973, Canada entered the era of modern treaties, signaling something of a shift toward recognition of Aboriginal rights. Canada's modern treaties attempt to address a variety of issues, from financial and territorial settlements and collaborative resource management to protections of cultural traditions and self-governance.[18] This pivot toward assuming some responsibility for the harms of settler colonialism extended south to the United States as well. In 1970 President Richard M. Nixon criticized the Indian Termination Act of 1953 in an address to Congress. Nixon called for a sweeping reorganization of US-Indian policies with the reinstatement

---

17. Jill E. Martin, "'The Greatest Evil' Interpretations of Indian Prohibition Laws, 1832–1953," *Great Plains Quarterly* 23, no. 1 (Winter 2003): 35–53, https://digitalcommons.unl.edu/cgi/viewcontent.cgi?article=3432&context=greatplainsquarterly.

18. "Modern Treaties," Crown-Indigenous Affairs and Northern Affairs Canada, www.rcaanc-cirnac.gc.ca/eng/1100100028574/1529354437231#chp4.

of Indian nations' self-determination through federal recognition.[19]
State and federal refusals to honor Indigenous land rights in the conflicts of recent years, such as the #NoDAPL struggle at Standing Rock,
confirm that settler colonialism is very much alive and well in the
United States and Canada.[20]

First Nations people and Native Americans continue to rely upon
historic treaties to argue for land use and governance rights. But not
all members of Native nations agree on "rights-based" politics. There
are some Indigenous resurgence networks in the United States and
Canada that call for a rejection of the "colonial politics" inherent to
treaties. Native scholars like Audra Simpson (Mohawk) and Glen
Coulthard (Yellowknives Dene) make convincing arguments that the
US and Canadian nation-states, built upon colonization and stolen
land, do not have the right to dictate the terms of any occupied Indian nations' sovereignty.[21] Historic and modern treaties, while unbal-
anced and injurious, continue nonetheless to provide Native peoples

---

19. Richard M. Nixon, "Special Message on Indian Affairs," July 8, 1970, tran-
script, National Congress of American Indians. "This policy of forced termination
is wrong, in my judgment, for a number of reasons. First, the premises on which
it rests are wrong. . . . The second reason . . . is that the practical results have
been clearly harmful in the few instances in which termination actually has been
tried. . . . The third argument I would make against forced termination concerns
the effect it has had upon the overwhelming majority of tribes which still enjoy a
special relationship with the Federal government. . . . The recommendations of this
Administration represent an historic step forward in Indian policy. We are pro-
posing to break sharply with past approaches to Indian problems." www.ncai.org
/attachments/Consultation_IJaOfGZqlYSuxpPUqoSSWIaNTkEJEPXxKLzL-
caOikifwWhGOLSA_12%20Nixon%20Self%20Determination%20Policy.pdf.

20. For more on Standing Rock and the #NoDAPL movement, see appendix essay 3.

21. See Audra Simpson, *Mohawk Interruptus: Political Life across the Borders of
Settler States* (Durham, NC: Duke University Press, 2014); Glen Coulthard, *Red
Skin, White Masks: Rejecting the Colonial Politics of Recognition* (Minneapolis: Uni-
versity of Minnesota, 2014); Leanne Betasamosake Simpson, *As We Have Always
Done: Indigenous Freedom through Radical Resistance* (Minneapolis: University of
Minnesota Press, 2017).

of North America with some legal recourse for securing or regaining contested territories, resources, moneys, and rights to resources and land use. And although school curricula may skip over the trail of broken treaty promises left in the wake of settler colonialism, Native voices attest to the resilience of Indigenous nations and peoples and the collective determination to survive and resist the past and ongoing harms resulting from the colonization of North America.

2

INDIGENOUS PERSPECTIVES ON HISTORICAL TRAUMA: AN INTERVIEW WITH JOHNNA JAMES

This essay is organized around an interview with Johnna James (Chickasaw), who holds a master of science in Native American leadership and currently serves as tribal liaison to Oklahoma's thirty-eight federally recognized tribes. James provides these Oklahoma tribes with access to resources and treatment for mental health and substance use disorders specific to the unique needs of each community. James's knowledge of historical trauma is derived not only from her years of experience as a mental health adviser to Native populations and as an Indian child welfare caseworker, but is also grounded in her own family's intergenerational cycle of historical trauma.

James's words are accompanied by references to policy and research articles relevant to historical trauma as experienced by First Nations and American Indian communities and peoples. The data support the connections, drawn by James and others, between the historical trauma of Indigenous peoples and its impact on the high rates of mental health and substance use disorders, homelessness, and incarceration, and the prevalence of physical, sexual, and cultural violence suffered by Native communities. More specifically, the findings in these sources illuminate the detrimental effects that Indian residential schools, adoption, and foster care policies have had on Indigenous individuals, family systems, and communities.

ON INTERGENERATIONAL CYCLES
OF HISTORICAL TRAUMA

Johnna James: I am a citizen of the Chickasaw Nation. I am the granddaughter of Roxie Capes, and I am the great-granddaughter of Ida Anoatubby. I grew up in Anadarko, Oklahoma, where there is a large tribal population. But when I was a little bit older, I was moved away from my community. I had four grandparents who all struggled with alcoholism—every single one of them. And they were open about their recovery as well. My Chickasaw dad had mental health issues, he had substance use disorder, and he had a long-term incarceration. On top of that, he was the child of a boarding school survivor, who loved her children but maybe did not have the parenting skills necessary to show my dad a good path. I want people to know that I'm an expert on trauma and can talk about it because I know firsthand that transcending trauma is possible. I know this as a Native woman who is raising children, who received an education, who holds a job, who has a home.

The American Psychiatric Association's 2017 report on the mental health disparities affecting American Indians and Alaska Native states that "AI/AN [American Indian / Alaska Natives] have disproportionately higher rates of mental health problems than the rest of the US population. High rates of substance use disorders (SUDs), posttraumatic stress disorder (PTSD), suicide, and attachment disorders in many AI/AN communities have been directly linked to the intergenerational historical trauma forced upon them, such as forced removal off their land and government-operated boarding schools which separated AI/AN children from their parents, spiritual practices, and culture."[1]

Maria Yellow Horse Brave Heart (Hunkpapa / Oglala Lakota), whose work with her community led to the development of the therapeutic model of historical trauma that has been applied to Indigenous communities

---

1. "Mental Health Disparities: American Indians and Alaska Native," American Psychiatric Association, 2017, www.psychiatry.org/home/search-results?k=Mental -Health-Facts-for-American-Indian-Alaska-Natives.pdf.

throughout the world, defines historical trauma as "a cumulative emotion-
al and psychological wounding over the lifespan and across generations,
emanating from massive group trauma experiences. The historical trauma
response . . . often includes depression, self-destructive behavior, suicidal
thoughts and gestures, anxiety, low self-esteem, anger, and difficulty recog-
nizing and expressing emotions. It may include substance abuse, often an
attempt to avoid painful feelings through self-medication."[2]

In addition, as Dian Million (Athabascan) explains in her seminal
work Therapeutic Nations: Healing in an Age of Indigenous Human
Rights, *placing Indigenous history within the framework of trauma also*
comes with political risks. Although First Nations' use of "trauma theory"
is "an active mobilization for justice . . . to ask for justice for past wrongs
the First Nations Peoples would have to fully assume this victimhood
at the same time they [seek] political power and autonomy, spheres that
speak the very opposite languages."[3]

ON QUANTIFYING ADVERSE CHILDHOOD
EXPERIENCES OF NATIVE PEOPLES

Johnna James: My ACE score is a ten—"ACE" stands for Adverse
Childhood Experiences. And I share that because that is as high as you
can get on the ACE scale.[4] The ACE study was created in the 1990s by
the Centers for Disease Control and Prevention (CDC) and Kaiser Permanente.[5] Basically, there are ten questions you are asked about ACEs.

---

2. Maria Yellow Horse Brave Heart, "The Historical Trauma Response among Natives and Its Relationship with Substance Abuse: A Lakota Illustration," *Journal of
Psychoactive Drugs* 35, no.1 (2003): 7–13.

3. Dian Million, *Therapeutic Nations: Healing in an Age of Indigenous Human Rights*
(Tucson: University of Arizona Press, 2013), 78–81.

4. "Finding Your ACE Score," National Council of Juvenile and Family Court Judg-
es, www.ncjfcj.org/sites/default/files/Finding%20Your%20ACE%20Score.pdf.

5. "About the CDC-Kaiser ACE Study," Centers for Disease Control and Prevention,
www.cdc.gov/violenceprevention/childabuseandneglect/acestudy/about.html.

The first five address the personal, which includes physical abuse, verbal abuse, sexual abuse, physical neglect, and emotional neglect. The next five questions are related to family members: Did you have a parent who was an alcoholic? A parent who was the victim of domestic violence? A family member who was incarcerated? A family member who was diagnosed with mental illness? And were your parents divorced? What we know from that study is that for those who have an ACE score of four or more, their rate of suicidality increases. We have also learned that ACE scores are higher in Native American communities.

From 1995 to 1997, Kaiser Permanente surveyed seventeen thousand Health Maintenance Organization members from Southern California for the original CDC-Kaiser ACE Study, which found that "persons who had experienced four or more categories of childhood exposure, compared to those who had experienced none, had 4- to 12-fold increased health risks for alcoholism, drug abuse, depression, and suicide attempt."[6] *A 2010–11 research study by the US Department of Health and Human Services on the ACEs of AI/NA children 0–17 years of age found the "ACE scores of AI/AN more than double that of the Non-Hispanic White [NHW] youth control population. . . . AI/AN children were 2–3 times more likely than NHW children to have a parent who served time in jail (18% versus 6%), to have observed domestic violence (15.5% versus 6.3%), to have been a victim of violence / witnessed violence in their neighborhood (15.9% versus 6.7%), and to have lived with a substance abuser (23.6% versus 11.6%). Finally, AI/AN children were 1.5 times more likely to live in families with difficulty covering basics like food or housing (35.7% versus 22.8%), to have lived with a divorced/ separated parent (33% versus 21.4%), and to have lived with a parent who died (4.2% versus 2.5%). Due to the high rates of mortality/*

---

6. V. J. Felitti et al., "Relationship of Childhood Abuse and Household Dysfunction to Many of the Leading Causes of Death in Adults: The Adverse Childhood Experiences (ACE) Study," *American Journal of Preventative Medicine* 14, no. 4 (1998): 245–58.

morbidity among AI/ANs, including PTSD, suicide, and vehicular or
violent injuries and death in adolescents and young adults, it is essential
to find their roots in childhood to better prevent a self-perpetuating cycle
of physical and behavioral health problems."[7]

ON MENTAL HEALTH ISSUES
FACING TODAY'S NATIVE COMMUNITIES

Johnna James: When you look at rates of suicide, it's higher in
our Native populations. Suicide is the number two leading cause
of death for our Native youth. Both professionally and personally, I
feel that the high rates of suicide for Native people are tied to historical trauma. Our stories and our experiences are not validated. We're
told to get over it, or we're told to move on. Or we're told it's in the
past. And in reality, whether it's this generation or two or three generations ago, there were so many periods of historical trauma that
nobody got to stop and heal from. So we have unhealed, unresolved
grief. And because the traumas are so compounded, so complex, so
generational, people without proper resources can begin to feel so
hopeless and so helpless. Our people don't see a way out. They lose
hope. The pain becomes so great and has accumulated for so long.
And when we can't find help, our choice is to give up. Ways of giving
up include suicide and also substance use disorders, to numb the
pain. I think our people are numbing the pain of many generations.

A 2017 report by the US Department of Health and Human Services
cites "suicide as the second leading cause of death for AI/AN youth be-
tween the ages of 5 and 24 years old." It also indicates that "the ad-
justed suicide rate for AI/AN individuals between 15 and 24 years old

---

7. Mary Kay Kenney and Gopal K. Singh, "Adverse Childhood Experiences among
American Indian/Alaska Native Children: The 2011–2012 National Survey of
Children's Health," *Scientifica* (2016), Article ID 7424239, www.hindawi.com
/journals/scientifica/2016/7424239/.

was 39.7 per 100,000 compared with the US all-race rate of 9.9 per 100,000."[8] According to another set of findings released in 2017, by the American Psychiatric Association, "approximately 9% of AI/ANs ages 18 and up had co-occurring mental illness and substance use disorder in the past year—almost three times that of the general populations."[9]

ON INCARCERATION AND THE PERPETUATING CYCLE OF HISTORICAL TRAUMA

Johnna James: Incarceration rates for Native people are higher for sure. What we're chalking up to bad behaviors or bad decisions are historical trauma and its effect on our people for several generations. And one of the questions on the ACE questionnaire, one of the ten most traumatic things that they target is: Did you have a parent who was incarcerated? When you have a parent who is incarcerated, and that person has three or four or five children, you've just raised the ACE scores of those five children. So, not only have we failed at rehabilitating the incarcerated person; now their children are having adverse childhood experiences. When we incarcerate somebody, we have to look at not only what we are doing to that person but what is the result in that generational loop.

A 1999 report by the US Department of Justice compiled data showing that in the US "Native Americans are incarcerated at a rate 38% higher than the national average." Statistics reveal that "Native American men are incarcerated at four times the rate of white men; Native American

---

8. This is the age-adjusted suicide rate, i.e., the suicide rate is adjusted for the age structure of the population being studied. "Suicide Clusters within American Indian and Alaska Native Communities: A Review of the Literature and Recommendations," US Department of Health and Human Services, Substance Abuse and Mental Health Services Administration (SAMHSA), SMA17-5050, 2017, https://store.samhsa.gov/product/suicide-clusters-within-american-indian-and-alaska-native-communities.

9. "Mental Health Disparities: American Indians and Alaska Native."

women are incarcerated at six times the rate of white women."[10] *And in Canada, according to the country's Office of the Correctional Investigator, "the incarceration rate of Indigenous people is now at 26.4 per cent of the Canadian population. . . . Indigenous people are more often criminalized and imprisoned for acts that are linked to poverty, lack of educational and employment opportunities, lifestyles of substance use, mental health concerns and histories of sexual abuse, violence and trauma—in other words, colonialism."*[11] *Moreover, data gathered by Statistics Canada indicate that "aboriginal youth [of Canada] made up 46 per cent of admission to correctional services in 2016–17 while making up only 8 per cent of the youth population."*[12]

ON HOMELESSNESS AND ITS LINKS
TO HISTORICAL TRAUMA

Johnna James: Homelessness rates are high for Native populations. You look at those who have been incarcerated who are also struggling with co-occurring disorders: mental health and substance use disorders. This was my dad's story. He was pretty much chronically homeless when he wasn't in the sober living houses. The struggle to access services can be compounded to where it seems almost impossible to get on a journey of feeling useful and purposeful again. How do we address all of these bundles of problems that have accumulated, and not just in a person's lifetime?

---

10. Lawrence A. Greenfeld and Steven K. Smith, "American Indians and Crime," US Department of Justice, Office of Justice Programs, Bureau of Statistics, February 1999, NCJ 173386, https://bjs.gov/content/pub/pdf/aic.pdf.

11. Ivan Zinger, "44th Annual Report: Office of the Correctional Investigator [Canada], 2016-2017," Office of Correctional Investigator, June 28, 2017, www.oci-bec.gc.ca/cnt/rpt/pdf/annrpt/annrpt20162017-eng.pdf.

12. Kelly Geraldine Malone, "Nearly Half of Youth Incarcerated across Canada Are Indigenous: Statistics Canada," *Globe and Mail*, June 25, 2019, www.theglobeandmail.com/canada/article-nearly-half-of-youth-incarcerated-across-canada-are-indigenous/.

A 2012 panel on homelessness organized by the Substance Abuse and Mental Health Services Administration noted that although "only 1.2 percent of the national population self-identifies as AI/AN (Census Bureau, 2013), 4.0 of all sheltered homeless persons, 4.0 percent of all sheltered homeless individuals, and 4.8 percent of all sheltered homeless families self-identify as Native American or Alaska Native."[13] In Canada, a 2019 report by the Homeless Hub shared similarly troubling figures in that country, noting that "in some Canadian cities such as Yellowknife or Whitehorse, Indigenous peoples make up 90 percent of the homeless population," and further cited one study's findings that "1 in 15 Indigenous Peoples in urban centres experience homelessness compared to 1 in 128 for the general population, [meaning] that Urban Indigenous Peoples are 8 times more likely to experience homelessness."[14] The group attributes these high rates of homelessness among First Nations people to "various types of historical trauma," such as "adoption, foster care and residential schools."[15]

ON THE CRISIS OF MISSING AND MURDERED INDIGENOUS WOMEN AND GIRLS (MMIWG)

Johnna James: The murder rate for our women is ten times higher than the national average.[16] I mean, we are losing our sisters at very,

---

13. "Expert Panel on Homelessness among American Indians, Alaska Natives, and Native Hawaiians," United States Interagency Council on Homelessness, December 2012, www.usich.gov/tools-for-action/report-on-homelessness-among -american-indians-alaska-natives.

14. "About Homelessness: Supporting Communities to Prevent and End Homelessness—Indigenous Peoples," Canadian Observation on Homelessness, 2019, www. homelesshub.ca/about-homelessness/population-specific/indigenous-peoples.

15. "About Homelessness."

16. Note that most sources that provide this figure qualify that this is the reality "on some reservations"—e.g., "On some reservations, Indigenous women are murdered at more than ten times the national average." See "Ending Violence against Native Women," Indian Law Resource Center, https://indianlaw.org/issue

very high rates. When you're talking about MMIWG, most of the
stories bring up the woman's substance abuse, her criminal record,
her homelessness. You don't hear, "Oh, this woman is missing."
Instead you hear all these terrible things. Our women, they are in
hard places. They are homeless, and they are using substances, and
they may be participating in sex work. In these stories, that's what's
pointed out or alluded to, and it minimizes what's going on with our
women. Without an understanding of the ongoing circle of trauma
responses, there's not compassion, there's not empathy. And this is
why it's still ongoing.

*A May 2016 statistical report by the US National Institute of Justice
notes that "more than 4 in 5 American Indian and Alaska Native [AI/
AN] women (84.3 percent) have experienced violence in their lifetime."[17] North of the border, the "2015 Fact Sheet on the Murdered
and Missing Aboriginal Women and Girls," published by the Native
Women's Association of Canada (NWAC), states that "between 2000
and 2008, Aboriginal women and girls represented approximately 10%
of all female homicides in Canada. However, Aboriginal women make
up only 3% of the female population."[18] And while the NWAC states*

/ending-violence-against-native-women; "Protecting Native American and Alaska
Native Women from Violence: November Is Native American Heritage Month,"
US Department of Justice Archives, November 29, 2012, www.justice.gov
/archives/ovw/blog/protecting-native-american-and-alaska-native-women-violence
-november-native-american; and Glenna Stumblingbear-Riddle, "Standing
with Our Sisters: MMIWG2S," American Psychiatric Association communi-
qué, November 2018, www.apa.org/pi/oema/resources/communique/2018/11
/standing-sisters.

17. André B. Rosay, "Violence against American Indian and Alaska Native Wom-
en and Men," National Institute of Justice, June 1, 2016, https://nij.ojp.gov/topics
/articles/violence-against-american-indian-and-alaska-native-women-and-men.

18. "2015 Fact Sheet: Murdered and Missing Aboriginal Women and Girls," Native Women's Association of Canada, www.nwac.ca/wp-content/uploads/2015
/05/Fact_Sheet_Missing_and_Murdered_Aboriginal_Women_and_Girls.pdf.

that there are no existing national statistics regarding missing persons, data gathered by the Saskatchewan Association of Chiefs of Police note that "almost 59% of missing women and girls in Saskatchewan are of Aboriginal ancestry."[19] Dian Million, reacting to the alarming statistics about the crisis as well as the unresponsiveness of Canada's law enforcement and justice systems, notes that "it would appear that it is hardly a crime to rape, kill, and 'disappear' an Aboriginal woman, and perhaps even less notable if she has become 'untouchable' or homeless or has entered the sex trade."[20] Amnesty International's Stolen Sisters human rights campaign shares Million's view, and, she writes, "situates this gendered violence within a long history of colonial violence against Indigenous people stemming from the formation of the Canadian state."[21]

ON THE INDIAN RESIDENTIAL BOARDING SCHOOLS AND THE DESTRUCTION OF NATIVE FAMILY SYSTEMS

Johnna James: Boarding schools starved our kids. They didn't give them medical attention. They let them die. And there was a prohibition of our language and our religions, which had a really lasting effect. It destroyed our family systems. The biggest and longest-lasting outcome of this period is attachment disorders. Children were taken from their families and given to strangers who didn't speak their language or know their ways. Then they were sent home as they became adults. Now they are trying to get married, and they are trying to parent, and they don't know how to be parents, and they don't know how to attach because no one tucked them into bed, or gave them hugs, or told them they were special. In fact, the opposite of those things occurred in those boarding schools. They were being beaten

---

19. "2015 Fact Sheet."

20. Million, *Therapeutic Nations*, 34.

21. Million, *Therapeutic Nations*, 34–35.

and neglected and malnourished. And now we expect them to be
healthy parents?

In her research on her Lakota people's historical trauma, Maria Yellow
Horse Brave Heart categorizes boarding school traumas as including
"physical and sexual abuse, neglect, abandonment, and deprivations,"
with "descendants of boarding school survivors report[ing] severe trau-
ma both at reservation day schools and sometimes at the hands of their
boarding school survivor parents."[22] In Million's analysis of the testimo-
nies of Canadian residential-school survivors, she notes that "the harm
they suffered had centered not only on their physical abuse, but on the
manipulative management of their emotions, which made their later
articulation tortured and laborious, since they had usually never verbal-
ized them as children. . . . Later, they coped without an ability to name
or explain their complex feelings, particularly their experiences with
sexual assault. . . . The children frequently became ineffective adults
or parents because they had been removed from parenting models and
could not cope with the force of their own feelings or others'. Many drank
themselves to death."[23] With such devastating physical and psychological
wounds in mind, it should come as no surprise that in Justice Murray
Sinclair's opening address for the Truth and Reconciliation Commission
of Canada, he declared Canada's residential schooling of Aboriginal
peoples "an act of genocide."[24]

---

22. Maria Yellow Horse Brave Heart, *Wakiksuyapi: Carrying the Historical Trau-*
ma of the Lakota (New Orleans: Tulane University, School of Social Work, 2000),
254–55.

23. Million, *Therapeutic Nations*, 79.

24. Andrew Woolford, Jeff Benvenuto, and Alexander Laban Hinton, introduction
to *Colonial Genocide in Indigenous North America* (Durham, NC: Duke University
Press, 2014), 2. For more on related proclamations of genocide, see the UN's Convention on the Prevention and Punishment of the Crime of Genocide (1948), at
www.un.org/en/genocideprevention/genocide.shtml. See also the glossary.

ON ADOPTION AND FOSTER CARE AS A
CONTINUATION OF HISTORICAL TRAUMA

Johnna James: I have a background in Indian child welfare, and
I'm a huge advocate of the Indian Child Welfare Act. When you are
taken from your family, when you are taken from your environment,
and when you are taken from your culture [to be placed into adoption or foster care environments outside of the tribal community],
reconciling your identity as an adult can be very difficult. You need
to know who you are as a healthy human being to create healthy
attachments. And we aren't giving Native families appropriate treatment so that they can figure out how to be parents again. More than
a hundred years of all these periods of historical trauma, and we're
giving them ten to fifteen months to work out a plan before terminating the parents' rights to keep their families intact. So the cycle
becomes perpetual. We're not addressing the problem appropriately.
We're not digging far enough back. You can't look at a Native family
and say, "Oh, well, here's mom and dad's problem." No, you need
to look at mom and dad and grandma and grandpa, and maybe
great-grandma and great-grandpa, and what can we do to find some
healing for this entire family?

*In the late 1950s, the US government enacted the Indian Adoption Act,
legislation that legally sanctioned the removal of American Indian children from their parents and tribal communities to be adopted by white
families. The intent of the Indian Adoption Act was to assimilate the
native child.[25] It took twenty more years for the US to pass the Indian
Child Welfare Act (ICWA) after it finally recognized the validity of
studies showing this policy's harm to Indigenous children, families, and
tribal communities. Research showed that "25%–35% of all Native*

---

25. Kathy D. LaPlante, MSW, "The Indian Child Welfare Act and Fostering
Youth Cultural Identity," *Children, Youth and Families News*, American Psychological Association, December 2017, www.apa.org/pi/families/resources
/newsletter/2017/12/indian-child-welfare.

children were being removed; of these, 85% were placed outside of their families and communities—even when fit and willing relatives were available. . . . Although progress has been made as a result of ICWA, out-of-home placement still occurs more frequently for Native children than it does for the general population, [with Native families] four times more likely to have their children removed and placed in foster care than their white counterparts."[26]

ON THE PHYSIOLOGY OF HISTORICAL TRAUMA

Johnna James: Historical trauma is also transmitted through our epigenetics, our DNA. We are wired for survival. We have a built-in parasympathetic system that, when we are in danger, it fires. It sends off our fight, flight, or freeze response. Our heart rate increases, our breathing may become more labored—all of the things that our body needs to do to protect us and prepare us to fight. And we know for Native American people, because of historical trauma, our parasympathetic system is more sensitive, meaning it can be triggered easier. And when our heart starts pumping because adrenaline is trying to give us the energy we need to fight, well, obviously, we are going to end up developing heart problems, especially if our body is reacting to every little thing throughout our whole lives. And then you go into the epigenetics. Trauma is an expression on our genes. If there is something that has been tagged on our DNA because of trauma, then that stress response could be tagged onto our children's and grandchildren's DNA, as a trait. But I tell people that if trauma is in our genes, then so is surviving. And so is resilience. And so is healing.

A 2014 report by the American Academy of Pediatrics on adverse childhood experiences notes how "early adversity can affect long-term change by altering the way an individual's genetic blueprint is

---

26. "About ICWA," US Department of Interior Indian Affairs, www.nicwa.org /about-icwa/; National Indian Child Welfare Act (Canada), www.nicwa.org.

read, thus influencing the stress response. . . . When the body learns under conditions of extreme stress, epigenetic modifications in gene transcription ultimately determine the brain structure, which governs behavior. The behavior can result in interactions that reinforce or reactivate the stress response, causing additional negative modifications."[27] First Nations and American Indian Native communities have been shown to "disproportionately experience ACEs and health disparities [along with] the persistence of stress associated with discrimination and historical trauma . . . [that] may contribute to an increased vulnerability for developing psychiatric disorders."[28]

ON ADDRESSING HISTORICAL TRAUMA IN NATIVE COMMUNITIES

Johnna James: "Trauma-informed care" is starting to become a buzzword. We have to look at trauma, to see why things are happening, if we are going to address those things appropriately. So now we are able to say, "Hey, all of these things happened," and we can start doing some things to stop that cycle. But the reality is, we are three or four generations into this cycle. And because we have over five hundred tribes in the United States, when you speak about historical trauma, it's specific to every tribe and family. Not every tribe went through the same type of trauma. I do some work in developing cultural competency programs that help Native communities develop tribe-specific treatment programs, and people ask, "Well, what does that really look like?" And what it really looks like is I hand them the microphone and then sit down and listen. For the federal model

---

27. "Adverse Childhood Experiences and the Lifelong Consequences of Trauma," American Academy of Pediatrics, 2014, www.aap.org/en-us/Documents/ttb_aces_consequences.pdf.

28. Teresa N. Brockie et al., "A Framework to Examine the Role of Epigenetics in Health Disparities among Native Americans," *Nursing Research and Practice* (2013): 410395, www.ncbi.nlm.nih.gov/pmc/articles/PMC3872279/.

there's what's called "A Gathering of Native Americans"—GONA.[29] It's a three-day event that has been created as a ceremony to address historical trauma. They bring in their elders, they have these conversations, and then they go through a day of processing all of it and grieving, and they have good ceremonies at the end of the day. Then they come up with a plan, like how are we going to address this and move forward? Everywhere I travel, there are different tribal communities, and they're all doing wonderful things. Whether it be food sovereignty, reclaiming their land and growing their food, or stickball or basketball in their communities. I saw another neat event—a simple bingo night where they invited the elders and the kids. I think the key is that it's community driven, and that we're healing together generationally.

The significance of community-based approaches to historical trauma has been noted by Maria Yellow Horse Brave Heart, whose research findings show that "those carrying the historical trauma can transcend trauma through a collective survivor identity and a commitment to traditionally oriented values and healing." Coping strategies include "emphasizing traditional Lakota values, focusing on helping others and future generations. Ideas about healing incorporate awareness of and talking about the past with a focus on the commonality among the Lakota of shared trauma."[30] Million, in her account of the historic 1991 First National Conference on Residential Schools in Vancouver, British Columbia, describes the keynote address by Xats'ull Cmetem' First Nations' chief Bev Sellars (Soda Creek Band) and its emphasis on the importance of community healing. Million is careful to point out that Chief Sellars, as a fellow residential-school survivor, understood the long-term suffering of the survivors: "Twenty-one of the first men who testified to their sexual

29. "Gathering of Native Americans Fact Sheet," Substance Abuse and Mental Health Services Administration, HHS Publication No. SMA-16-4994, https://store .samhsa.gov/product/Gathering-of-Native-Americans-Fact-Sheet/SMA16-4994.

30. Yellow Horse Brave Heart, *Wakiksuyapi*, 245.

abuse [in the residential schools] subsequently committed suicide. But Bev Sellars concluded that their abuse did not have to be their destiny. They could do something now. . . . The answer was to strengthen Native family bonds and revive the traditions. To revive the people would take a sustained effort, but it was their choice as Indigenous nations. The solution to their problems would have to come from within their own communities. The church and state should be made accountable, but in the end, they, the First Nations people, would have to be responsible for one another and for any life they could have beyond bare existence. Sellars concluded, 'It's time we started living again, and not just surviving, as so many of us did for so long,' to 'begin the task of rebuilding our nations.'"[31]

---

31. Million, *Therapeutic Nations*, 79.

3
INDIGENOUS RESURGENCE

"Direct Action Principles," Oceti Sakowin Camp, Standing Rock Indian Reservation, North Dakota, October 22, 2016. Photograph by Valerie Fendt, used with permission.

That a war of extermination will continue to be waged between the two races until the Indian race becomes extinct must be expected; while we cannot anticipate this result but with painful regret, the inevitable destiny of the race is beyond the power or wisdom of man to avert.

—Governor Peter H. Burnett, California State of the State Address, delivered January 6, 1851

We can look back over the five hundred years since Columbus stumbled onto this continent and see utter devastation among our people. But as we approach the twenty-first century we are very hopeful. Despite everything, we survive.

—Wilma Mankiller, principal chief of the Cherokee Nation, speech following her reelection, August 18, 1991

Ever since Anglo and European colonizers first arrived on the continent with the goal of acquiring land for settlement, Indigenous people have responded with resurgence. From the unassuming expressions of Indigenous identity and culture that First Nations and American Indians perform on a daily basis to the potent environmental activism that commanded worldwide attention at Standing Rock, Native peoples have been affirming their presence in colonially occupied landscapes. As Patrick Wolfe, a leading scholar of settler-colonial studies explains, "Settler colonialism destroys to replace." That is, a colonizer's quest for land requires that the original inhabitants of that territory be eliminated. The consequence of that destructive drive naturally provokes what Wolfe calls "the native counter-claim."[1] Resistance to elimination, entailing the many forms of erasure and genocide enacted by settler colonialism, is the counter-claim of Indigenous peoples. That inextinguishable impulse to not only survive but to thrive is what we call resurgence.

---

1. Patrick Wolfe, "Settler Colonialism and the Elimination of the Native," *Journal of Genocide Research* 8, no. 4 (2006): 388–89.

EARLY EXPRESSIONS OF RESURGENCE

Many historians point to a moment in time—December 29, 1890, the date of the Wounded Knee Massacre—as the official end of the Indian wars. But once we consider that settler-colonizers came to stay, we can see that "invasion is a structure, not an event."[2] The massacre can be viewed as just one tragic instance in an ongoing chain of Indigenous removal for the purpose of colonial occupation. Dee Brown's seminal text *Bury My Heart at Wounded Knee* presents a narrative of the massacre that has become emblematic of Indigenous trauma and despair. Unfortunately, according to David Treuer (Ojibwe), author of *The Heartbeat of Wounded Knee: Native America from 1890 to the Present*, Brown's work has helped to undermine the reality of First Nations and American Indian peoples' resilience.[3] To shift from the prevailing fixation on Brown's version of Wounded Knee—or what Treuer calls "the same old sad story of 'the dead Indian'"—we need only look at the Lakota Nation's continued existence to find evidence of Indigenous peoples' tremendous fortitude and will to survive colonization. And a closer look at one of the factors that precipitated the massacre can help illuminate Lakota peoples' enduring spirit of resurgence. From 1889 to 1890, as word had spread about the prophecy of a Paiute holy man named Wovoka, Indigenous peoples were joining with the Lakota from all over the North American continent to participate in the Ghost Dance.

Early accounts of the era, collected by nineteenth-century ethnographer James Mooney, describe the Ghost Dance as a religious movement founded on the idea that "the whole Indian race, living and dead, will be reunited upon a regenerated earth, to live a life of aboriginal happiness forever free from death, disease, and misery." This precolonial utopia was, naturally, contingent upon the disappearance of the white colonizers responsible for bringing so much destruction

---

2. Wolfe, "Settler Colonialism," 388.

3. Treuer, *Heartbeat of Wounded Knee*, 10–11.

to the Indians' world.[4] Followers believed that their Ghost Dance ceremonies would make this dream world a reality. Indigenous peoples' practice of their religion, in defiance of the US government's prohibitions against traditional dancing, in part led Indian agents to sound the alarm that called in military forces at Wounded Knee. The military response is infamous for its heavy-handed brutality— the Seventh Cavalry massacred more than 250 Lakota, one-third of whom were women and children. Yet the Ghost Dance is often pushed to the margins of history books and misrepresented as Indigenous superstition. According to Nick Estes (Lower Brulé Sioux), an American Studies scholar and founder of the Indigenous resistance organization Red Nation, "There exists no better example of Indigenous revolutionary theory, and its purposeful distortion, than the Ghost Dance."[5] This direct action against colonial authority takes on new meaning when understood as a movement of resurgence representing Native peoples' aspirations for self-determination. After all, "if it were *just* dancing that was the threat," asks Estes, "then why did the United States deploy nearly half its army against starving, horseless, and unarmed people in order to crush it?"[6] Within this context, the Ghost Dance just might be one of the most subversive displays of Indigenous activism of the nineteenth century.

TWENTIETH-CENTURY RESURGENCE

This Indigenous resurgence continued its momentum into the twentieth century. Historian Colin Calloway notes the irony of how "boarding schools . . . gave Indians a common experience and common means of communication. . . . A new generation of Indians,

---

4. James Mooney, *The Ghost Dance Religion and the Sioux Outbreak of 1890* (Chicago: University of Chicago Press, 1965), 19.

5. Nick Estes, *Our History Is the Future: Standing Rock versus the Dakota Access Pipeline, and the Long Tradition of Indigenous Resistance* (New York: Verso, 2019), 16.

6. Estes, *Our History Is the Future*, 18.

schooled in the white men's ways, took steps toward pan-Indian unity and formed the Society of American Indians in 1911."[7] Similarly, the Indian Relocation Act of 1956 in the United States, by encouraging Indians living on or near reservations to relocate to urban areas and integrate into the American workforce, also indirectly helped to mobilize them. Although the promise of economic prosperity failed to materialize for many Native families, the relocation to urban settings did seem to increase Indigenous community building. Powwows, the seasonal gatherings of traditional dancing, singing, and storytelling, served as important venues for intertribal gatherings. Again, we see a Native counter-claim to assumed colonization at work: government policies that were intended to assimilate Indigenous peoples into non-Native culture instead provoked Indigenous peoples' celebration and affirmation of their identity and traditional cultures.[8]

These intertribal connections were also expressed through Indigenous political actions. In the late 1960s, the confrontational tactics of the American Indian Movement (AIM) helped bring attention to the issues and injustices plaguing Native communities. AIM's leadership successfully mobilized "fourteen hundred Indians from over eighty tribes" to gather in the reservation border town of Gordon, Nebraska, for an investigation into the brutal attack and murder of Raymond Yellow Thunder (Oglala) by four white men.[9] AIM demanded that the known assailants be held accountable for the crime and that US justice systems be held accountable for all crimes against Native peoples.[10] The group also worked to highlight the ineffectiveness and corruption

---

7. Colin G. Calloway, epilogue to *Our Hearts Fell to the Ground: Plains Indian Views of How the West Was Lost*, ed. Colin G. Calloway (Boston: Bedford Books of St. Martin's Press, 1996), 205.

8. Wolfe, "Settler Colonialism," 389.

9. Paul Chaat Smith and Robert Allen Warrior, *Like a Hurricane: The Indian Movement from Alcatraz to Wounded Knee* (New York: The New Press, 1996), 115.

10. Smith and Warrior, *Like a Hurricane*, 115.

that many saw playing out in some tribal governments, as in the case of their protest at Wounded Knee. Calloway calls attention to the potent irony of AIM's occupation of Wounded Knee in 1973 when, "after an escalation of tensions, Indians once again confronted the armed forces of the United States in a seventy-day siege."[11] Although AIM's militancy garnered outrage from conservative corners, its aims and activism continue to inspire today's Indigenous resurgence movements in the US, both on and off Indian reservations.

CONTEMPORARY ENVIRONMENTAL RESURGENCE

The naturalist worldviews held by many Indigenous peoples found fertile ground in the environmental movements of the 1960s. And protecting the environment from capitalism's destructive actions has become one of the most pressing agenda points of Indigenous resistance movements. The Idle No More movement, which began in 2012, was a response to Canada's proposed Bill C-45, the 457-page "'omnibus' of new laws [that] introduced drastic changes to the Indian Act, the Fisheries Act, the Canadian Environmental Assessment Act, and the Navigable Waters Act (among many others)."[12] The movement unified a group of Indigenous writers, artists, editors, curators, and allies known as the Kino-nda-niimi Collective. From the movement's inception, this collective has acknowledged its place among a "very long chain of [Indigenous] resistance," stressing that "most Indigenous peoples have never been idle in their efforts to protect what is meaningful to our communities—nor will we ever be."[13] The Idle No More movement took on issues of protecting Indigenous peoples' territories from environmental exploitation, increasing health

---

11. Calloway, epilogue to *Our Hearts Fell*, 206.

12. The Kino-nda-niimi Collective, "Idle No More: The Winter We Danced," in *The Winter We Danced: Voices from the Past, the Future, and the Idle No More Movement* (Winnipeg, MB: Arp Books, 2014), 21.

13. Kino-nda-niimi Collective, "Idle No More," 21.

and educational services for First Nation communities, and improving nation-to-nation dialogue between the Canadian government and First Nations.[14] The movement also brought significant attention to the country's crisis of murdered and missing Indigenous women and girls, equating the Canadian government's unresponsiveness to genocide, given the devastating impact on Indigenous peoples.[15]

In the fall of 2016, on the heels of Idle No More and in conjunction with Canadian First Nations' resistance to infrastructure projects like the tar sands extractions and Keystone XL pipelines, environmental activism by Indigenous nations and peoples found worldwide recognition at Standing Rock. In his account of the resistance, *Our History Is the Future: Standing Rock versus the Dakota Access Pipeline, and the Long Tradition of Indigenous Resistance*, Nick Estes explains how the Standing Rock resistance "had been established to block construction of Energy Transfer Partners' $3.8 billion Dakota Access Pipeline (DAPL), a 1,712-mile oil pipeline that cut through unceded territory of the 1868 Fort Laramie Treaty and crossed under Mni Sose (the Missouri River) immediately upstream from Standing Rock, threatening the reservation's water supply."[16] A group of Indigenous youth "brought the message of the Black Snake [the Dakota Access and all pipelines trespassing through Indigenous territory] to the world through thousand-mile relay runs," galvanizing worldwide support from Natives and non-Natives who joined the movement's rallying cry "*Mni Wiconi* (water is life)."[17] The Standing Rock resistance is notable for its specifically Indigenous approach to direct action. "Water Protectors led the movement in a disciplined way,"

---

14. Kino-nda-niimi Collective, "Idle No More," 22.

15. Dory Nason, "We Hold Our Hands Up: On Indigenous Women's Love and Resistance," in *The Winter We Danced*, 186–90; Sarah Hunt, "More Than a Poster Campaign: Redefining Colonial Violence," in *The Winter We Danced*, 190–93.

16. Estes, *Our History Is the Future*, 2.

17. Estes, *Our History Is the Future*, 15.

Estes explains, "by what Lakotas call *Wocekiye*, meaning 'honoring relations.'" To the outside world, Estes continues, "this looks like 'praying,' smoking of the Canupa, the sacred pipe, offering tobacco, ceremony, and song to human and other-than-human life."[18] And while by no means comparable to the Wounded Knee Massacre in terms of casualties, the state and federal response to this nonviolent opposition was certainly heavy-handed. The military tactics deployed against unarmed Water Protectors by private security guards and law enforcement officers included the use of twenty-four-hour drone surveillance, attack dogs, Tasers, tear gas (whose canisters served as lethal projectiles), sound cannons, and water cannons, deployed during freezing temperatures, injuring hundreds of Water Protectors.[19] Ultimately, in hopes of avoiding further injuries, David Archambault, then chairman of the Standing Rock Sioux, persuaded the protesters to return to their homes, and the camps were closed. Construction of the pipeline was completed despite federal courts declaring the building permit illegal (the Army Corps of Engineers had approved the DAPL permit without the required environmental impact study being performed), and today this pipeline transports 570,000 barrels of crude oil per day.[20]

Despite the appearance of defeat, those who participated in the direct action, like social justice activist and educator Valerie Fendt, consider the resistance to the DAPL at Standing Rock a "paradigm shift in environmental activism. . . . By drawing attention to policies that prioritize the rights and profits of corporations over the risks they pose to people, by resisting those policies in a nonviolent, prayerful manner that invites others to recognize and demonstrate

---

18. Estes, *Our History Is the Future*, 15.

19. Estes, *Our History Is the Future*, 3, 55–56.

20. "The Standing Rock Sioux Tribe's Litigation on the Dakota Access Pipeline, Updates and Frequently Asked Questions," Earthjustice, November 8, 2018, https://earthjustice.org/features/faq-standing-rock-litigation; "Dakota Access Pipeline," DAPL Pipeline Facts – Energy Transfer LP, https://daplpipelinefacts.com/.

the power of their own convictions, the Standing Rock Sioux have built a movement."[21]

CONTINUOUS ACTS OF EVERYDAY RESURGENCE

The important work of Indigenous peoples' environmental movements cannot be understated; the lives of humans, other-than-humans, and the planet depend upon it. But ordinary, daily expressions of Indigenous resurgence are also of tremendous value to Native communities and peoples. Author Leanne Betasamosake Simpson (Mississauga Nishnaabeg), a prominent voice in the Idle No More movement, points out that "when resistance is defined solely as large-scale political mobilization, we miss much of what has kept our languages, cultures and systems of governance alive. We have those things today because our Ancestors often acted within the family unit to physically survive, to pass on what they could to their children, occupy and use our lands as we always had."[22]

Fundamental to this daily expression of Indigenous resurgence is the preservation of traditional foodways such as the safeguarding of heritage seeds and the practice of farming techniques and cooking methods handed down by ancestors. Anishinaabe environmental activist Winona LaDuke (Ojibwe) led the successful fight against "the genetic engineering and corporate patenting of [her people's] food."[23] As founding director of both Honor the Earth and the White Earth Land Recovery Project, LaDuke travels internationally to speak on is-

21. Valerie Fendt, "Paradigm Shift: The Standing Rock Sioux and the Struggle of Our Time" (thesis, Columbia University, April 5, 2017; revised May 4, 2017), https://history.columbia.edu/wp-content/uploads/sites/20/2016/06/Fendt_Thesis.pdf.

22. Leanne Simpson, *Dancing on Our Turtle's Back: Stories of Nishnaabeg Re-creation, Resurgence and a New Emergence* (Winnipeg, MT: Arbeiter Ring Publishing, 2011), 15–16.

23. Winona LaDuke, "Seeds of Our Ancestors, Seeds of Life," TEDx TC, YouTube video, uploaded March 4, 2012, www.youtube.com/watch?v=pHNlel72eQc.

sues of sustainability.[24] But it is LaDuke's father's admonition, "I don't want to hear your philosophy if you can't grow corn," that effectively underlines the importance of grounding Indigenous activism in our everyday lives.

In addition to the sustainment of Indigenous foodways, language revitalization programs are strengthening Indigenous culture and identity. Boarding school prohibitions against Native children speaking their mother tongues resulted in a decline of Indigenous-language speakers. Many languages were completely lost, and as the dwindling number of elders who speak Indigenous languages age, tribes are responding with urgency to recover and preserve their ancestral languages. First Nations and American Indian nations are investing significant time and energy into documenting the oral histories of these elders, spoken in their native tongue. Among the many First Nations and American Indian tribes doing so is the Chickasaw Nation, which views its "language as a gift from the ancestors" for future generations.[25]

Because Indigenous societies are oral cultures, the preservation of the linguistic heritage includes the conservation of traditional stories and oral histories, like those compiled in this Voice of Witness collection. Native peoples' gift for storytelling has also carried forward in the resurgence of voices in today's literary arts. The distinctly Indigenous fiction, narrative nonfiction, and poetry of Native American authors like N. Scott Momaday (Kiowa), James Welch (Blackfeet and A'aninin), Leslie Marmon Silko (Laguna Pueblo), Louise Erdrich (Chippewa), Tommy Orange (Cheyenne and Arapaho), Rosanna Deerchild (Cree), Lee Maracle (Stó:Lōh Nation), and

---

24. "Meet the Team," Honor the Earth, honortheearth.org/meet_the_team; "About Our Founder," White Earth Land Recovery Project, welrp.org.

25. After partnering with Rosetta Stone to develop a language software program, the Chickasaw language learning DVDs are now available free of charge to its more than sixty thousand citizens. "Chickasaw Language Revitalization Program," The Chickasaw Nation, www.chickasaw.net/Services/Chickasaw-Language-Revitalization-Program.aspx.

Tomson Highway (Cree), to name but a few, continue to earn ac-
colades. These authors' characters disrupt notions of the exotic or
savage "otherness" of Indians by helping readers imagine the fullness
of the contemporary, lived experience of Indigenous people. Anishinaabe novelist Gerald Vizenor (Minnesota Chippewa) contends
that "many people in the world are enamored with and obsessed by
the concocted images of the Indian—the simulations of indigenous
character and cultures as essential victims."[26] This outlook prompted Vizenor to apply the term *survivance* to describe Native stories
that act as "renunciations of dominance, tragedy, and victimry."[27]
Vizenor's preference for *survivance* over *survival,* a word connoting a
more reactive position, captures the endurance and resilience of Native peoples while acknowledging the remarkable effort required for
resurgence. Jeff Corntassel (Cherokee), scholar of Indigenous political movements, characterizes this balancing act in its simplest terms:
"Whether they know it or not (or even want it), every Indigenous
person is in a daily struggle for resurgence."[28]

These everyday struggles include the challenge of withstanding
countless offensive Indian references perpetuated in literature and
pop culture. The evil Injun Joe in Mark Twain's *The Adventures of Tom
Sawyer* and the depiction of drunken and childlike Indians in John
Wayne's movies are but a few examples. American history scholar Gary
B. Nash maintains that these stereotypes indoctrinate non-Natives
with the belief that the destruction of Indigenous peoples' culture and
their loss of land and self-determination was an "inevitable historical

---

26. Gerald Vizenor, "Acts of Survivance," Survivance, http://survivance.org/acts-of
-survivance/.

27. Gerald Vizenor, *Manifest Manners: Narratives of Postindian Survivance* (Lincoln: University of Nebraska Press, 1999), vii.

28. Jeff Corntassel, "Re-envisioning Resurgence: Indigenous Pathways to Decolonization and Sustainable Self-Determination," *Decolonization: Indigeneity, Education & Society* 1, no. 1 (2012): 89.

outcome."[29] Yet Indigenous people's presence persists. From the Ghost Dancers at Wounded Knee and the Water Protectors at Standing Rock more than a century later to everyday Indians eating the foods, speaking the languages, and listening to the stories handed down to them from early ancestors, acts of Indigenous resurgence affirm the presence of Native peoples, our resilience, and our spirit of determination to not only survive but to thrive. Indigenous peoples have always known that it is our resurgence, not our disappearance, that is the inevitable historical outcome of our peoples and nations.

---

29. Gary B. Nash, "The Concept of Inevitability in the History of European-Indian Relations," *Inequality in Early America*, ed. Carla Gardina Pestana and Sharon V. Salinger (Hanover, CT: University Press of New England, 1999), 267.

TEN THINGS YOU CAN DO

1. Know whose traditional territory you live on. The map developed by Native Land Digital (native-land.ca) is a good place to start your research.

2. Learn how to do a land acknowledgment to bring awareness to Indigenous peoples' presence and to recognize our ongoing relationship with the land. For a guide on how to observe this practice, visit http://landacknowledgements.org.

3. Don't let the land acknowledgement be a token gesture. Know your history. Use the Further Reading section in this book to round out the incomplete education you likely received in school. If you are an educator, add more Native content to your syllabi.

4. Advocate for your local school boards to include Native American history in the curriculum, specifically the history of local tribes.

5. Read books by Indigenous writers like Tommy Orange, Terese Marie Mailhot, Vine Deloria Jr., Louise Erdrich, and N. Scott Momaday to learn how Native people represent themselves and their cultures, histories, and communities.

6. Visit your local Indian center. You can find them in Los Angeles, Toronto, Denver, Winnipeg, Chicago, New York City, Victoria, Minneapolis, and many more cities and towns throughout North America. Also, search #NativeTwitter to find Native users, opinions, and events.

7. Learn about how to support the work of tribes in your region.

8. Donate money or time to programs and organizations that support Native communities. For example, support the work of our narrator James Favel and the Bear Clan Patrol at www.bearclanpatrolinc.com.

9. Divest! Avoid banks, like Wells Fargo and Chase, that violate Native treaty rights by bankrolling environmentally devastating fossil fuel developments.

10. Campaign and vote for Native candidates at all levels of government—we need more representation at the local, state, and national level. Demand more of currently elected governments, too; advocate for policy and legislation that supports Native communities.

FURTHER READING

FICTION/POETRY/MEMOIR

Louise Erdrich, *Love Medicine*

Joy Harjo, *Crazy Brave: A Memoir*

Thomas King, *The Inconvenient Indian: A Curious Account of Native People in North America*

Layli Long Soldier, *Whereas*

Terese Marie Mailhot, *Heart Berries*

N. Scott Momaday, *House Made of Dawn*

Tommy Orange, *There There*

Leslie Marmon Silko, *Ceremony*

NONFICTION

Vine DeLoria, *Custer Died for Your Sins: An Indian Manifesto*

Trace A. DeMeyer and Patricia Cotter-Busbee, *Two Worlds: Lost Children of the Indian Adoption Projects*

Roxanne Dunbar-Ortiz, *An Indigenous Peoples' History of the United States*

Walter R. Echo-Hawk, *In the Light of Justice: The Rise of Human Rights in Native America and the UN Declaration on the Rights of Indigenous Peoples*

Nick Estes, *Our History Is the Future: Standing Rock versus the Dakota Access Pipeline, and the Long Tradition of Indigenous Resistance*

Suzanne Methot, *Legacy: Trauma, Story and Indigenous Healing*

Dian Million, *Therapeutic Nations: Healing in an Age of Indigenous Human Rights*

John S. Milloy, *A National Crime: The Canadian Government and the Residential School System*

Leanne Betasamosake Simpson, *As We Have Always Done: Indigenous Freedom through Radical Resistance*

Anton Treuer, *Everything You Wanted to Know about Indians but Were Afraid to Ask*

David Treuer, *The Heartbeat of Wounded Knee: Native America from 1890 to the Present*

ACKNOWLEDGMENTS

Audra Simpson, your classes at Columbia helped me to ask the right questions and gave me the critical grounding necessary to pursue and consider these narratives.

The Columbia Oral History Master of Arts community, especially Amy Starecheski and Mary Marshall Clark, thank you for your encouragement of this work during my time at OHMA. Your enthusiasm for this project at its outset made me feel confident that I was on to something worthwhile.

Rick Chavolla, this project began with you. Thank you for lending me some of the trust that so many have in you.

To my family, Miles and Julian, thank you for buoying me up throughout this process and for making this work possible. My parents, Douglas and Joanie, and my sisters Stephanie and Minoway, thank you for being my touchstones and my "home."

Rozanne Gooding Silverwood, thank you for your presence, your commitment, and the fierce attention you brought to the book's appendix essays.

The entire Voice of Witness team, thank you! Special thanks to our education curriculum advisors Miranda Edwards and Alysa Landry and curriculum specialist Suzanne Methot. And to managing editor Dao X. Tran, for your frankness, your guidance, and for asking a great deal of questions that made the book better.

Finally, to my narrators, it has been an honor and a privilege to sit with each of you. Thank you for becoming my teachers and my friends. *Meegwech.*

ABOUT THE EDITOR

Sara Sinclair is an oral historian, writer, and educator of Cree-Ojibwe and settler descent. Sara has contributed to the Columbia Center for Oral History Research's Covid-19 Oral History, Narrative and Memory Archive, Obama Presidency Oral History, and Robert Rauschenberg Oral History Project. She has conducted oral histories for the Whitney Museum of American Art, New York City Department of Environmental Protection, and the International Labor Organization, among others. Sara is coeditor of *Robert Rauschenberg: An Oral History*.

ABOUT VOICE OF WITNESS

Voice of Witness (VOW) is an award-winning nonprofit that advances human rights by amplifying the voices of people impacted by injustice. Cofounded by Dave Eggers, Mimi Lok, and Dr. Lola Vollen, we explore issues of criminal justice, migration, and displacement, and forge space for marginalized voices to be heard. Our book series depicts these issues through the edited oral histories of people most closely affected by them. Our education program connects educators, students, and members of justice movements with oral history tools for storytelling and social change.

THE VOICE OF WITNESS
BOOK SERIES

The Voice of Witness nonprofit book series amplifies the seldom-heard voices of people affected by contemporary injustice. We also work with impacted communities to create curricular and training support for educators. Using oral history as a foundation, the series depicts human rights crises in the United States and around the world. *How We Go Home: Voices from Indigenous North America* is the nineteenth book in the series. Other titles include:

SURVIVING JUSTICE
America's Wrongfully Convicted and Exonerated
Compiled and edited by Lola Vollen and Dave Eggers
Foreword by Scott Turow
"Real, raw, terrifying tales of 'justice.'" —*Star Tribune*

VOICES FROM THE STORM
The People of New Orleans on Hurricane Katrina and Its Aftermath
Compiled and edited by Chris Ying and Lola Vollen
"*Voices from the Storm* uses oral history to let those who survived the hurricane tell their (sometimes surprising) stories." —*Independent* UK

UNDERGROUND AMERICA
Narratives of Undocumented Lives
Compiled and edited by Peter Orner
Foreword by Luis Alberto Urrea
"No less than revelatory." —*Publishers Weekly*

OUT OF EXILE
Narratives from the Abducted and Displaced People of Sudan
Compiled and edited by Craig Walzer
Additional interviews and an introduction by Dave Eggers and Valentino Achak Deng
"Riveting." —*School Library Journal*

HOPE DEFERRED
Narratives of Zimbabwean Lives
Compiled and edited by Peter Orner and Annie Holmes
Foreword by Brian Chikwava

"*Hope Deferred* might be the most important publication to have come out of Zimbabwe in the last thirty years." —*Harper's Magazine*

NOWHERE TO BE HOME
Narratives from Survivors of Burma's Military Regime
Compiled and edited by Maggie Lemere and Zoë West
Foreword by Mary Robinson
"Extraordinary." —Asia Society

PATRIOT ACTS
Narratives of Post-9/11 Injustice
Compiled and edited by Alia Malek
Foreword by Karen Korematsu
"Important and timely." —Reza Aslan

INSIDE THIS PLACE, NOT OF IT
Narratives from Women's Prisons
Compiled and edited by Ayelet Waldman and Robin Levi
Foreword by Michelle Alexander
"Essential reading." —Piper Kerman

THROWING STONES AT THE MOON
Narratives from Colombians Displaced by Violence
Compiled and edited by Sibylla Brodzinsky and Max Schoening
Foreword by Íngrid Betancourt
"Both sad and inspiring." —*Publishers Weekly*

REFUGEE HOTEL
Photographed by Gabriele Stabile and edited by Juliet Linderman
"There is no other book like *Refugee Hotel* on your shelf." —*SF Weekly*

HIGH RISE STORIES
Voices from Chicago Public Housing
Compiled and edited by Audrey Petty
Foreword by Alex Kotlowitz
"Joyful, novelistic, and deeply moving." —George Saunders

INVISIBLE HANDS
Voices from the Global Economy
Compiled and edited by Corinne Goria
Foreword by Kalpona Akter
"Powerful and revealing testimony." —*Kirkus*

PALESTINE SPEAKS
Narratives of Life under Occupation
Compiled and edited by Cate Malek and Mateo Hoke
"Heartrending stories." —*New York Review of Books*

THE VOICE OF WITNESS READER
Ten Years of Amplifying Unheard Voices
Edited and with an introduction by Dave Eggers

THE POWER OF THE STORY
The Voice of Witness Teacher's Guide to Oral History
Compiled and edited by Cliff Mayotte
Foreword by William Ayers and Richard Ayers
"A rich source of provocations to engage with human dramas throughout the world." —*Rethinking Schools Magazine*

LAVIL
Life, Love, and Death in Port-Au-Prince
Edited by Peter Orner and Evan Lyon
Foreword by Edwidge Danticat
"*Lavil* is a powerful collection of testimonies, which include tales of violence, poverty, and instability but also joy, hustle, and the indomitable will to survive." —*Vice*

CHASING THE HARVEST
Migrant Workers in California Agriculture
Edited by Gabriel Thompson
"The voices are defiant and nuanced, aware of the human complexities that spill across bureaucratic categories and arbitrary borders." —*The Baffler*

SIX BY TEN
Stories from Solitary
Edited by Mateo Hoke and Taylor Pendergrass
"Deeply moving and profoundly unsettling." —Heather Ann Thompson

SAY IT FORWARD
A Guide to Social Justice Storytelling
Edited by Cliff Mayotte and Claire Kiefer
"Reminds us the process through which we document a story is as important and powerful as the story itself." —Lauren Markham

SOLITO, SOLITA

Crossing Borders with Youth Refugees from Central America

Edited by Steven Mayers and Jonathan Freedman

"Intense testimonies that leave one . . . astonished at the bravery of the human spirit." —Sandra Cisneros

ABOUT HAYMARKET BOOKS

Haymarket Books is a radical, independent, nonprofit book publisher based in Chicago.

Our mission is to publish books that contribute to struggles for social and economic justice. We strive to make our books a vibrant and organic part of social movements and the education and development of a critical, engaged, international left.

We take inspiration and courage from our namesakes, the Haymarket martyrs, who gave their lives fighting for a better world. Their 1886 struggle for the eight-hour day—which gave us May Day, the international workers' holiday—reminds workers around the world that ordinary people can organize and struggle for their own liberation. These struggles continue today across the globe—struggles against oppression, exploitation, poverty, and war.

Since our founding in 2001, Haymarket Books has published more than five hundred titles. Radically independent, we seek to drive a wedge into the risk-averse world of corporate book publishing. Our authors include Noam Chomsky, Arundhati Roy, Rebecca Solnit, Angela Y. Davis, Howard Zinn, Amy Goodman, Wallace Shawn, Mike Davis, Winona LaDuke, Ilan Pappé, Richard Wolff, Dave Zirin, Keeanga-Yamahtta Taylor, Nick Turse, Dahr Jamail, David Barsamian, Elizabeth Laird, Amira Hass, Mark Steel, Avi Lewis, Naomi Klein, and Neil Davidson. We are also the trade publishers of the acclaimed Historical Materialism Book Series and of Dispatch Books.